The Civil Wars in Chile

THE CIVIL WARS IN CHILE
(or the bourgeois revolutions that never were)

BY MAURICE ZEITLIN

PRINCETON UNIVERSITY PRESS
PRINCETON, NEW JERSEY

Published by Princeton University Press, 41 William Street,
Princeton, New Jersey 08540
In the United Kingdom: Princeton University Press, Guildford, Surrey

Library of Congress Cataloging in Publication Data will be
found on the last printed page of this book

ISBN 0-691-07665-0

Publication of this book has been aided by the Whitney Darrow Fund of
Princeton University Press

This book has been composed in Linotron Times Roman

Clothbound editions of Princeton University Press books
are printed on acid-free paper, and binding materials are
chosen for strength and durability.

Printed in the United States of America by Princeton University Press
Princeton, New Jersey

FOR
Marilyn,
Michelle,
Carla,
Erica
WITH LOVE

Contents ➤

List of Tables and Figure ➤

Preface ➤

The history of Chile is the history of three revolutions that failed. The first, a civil war in the mid-nineteenth century, was an abortive bourgeois revolution. It was fought in armed fury by young radical mining capitalists and their peasant and artisan allies against, paradoxically, not a feudal but a bourgeois regime they found oppressive. They aimed but failed to put through a "revolution in landed property" and create a democratic republic. The second revolutionary attempt was an unsuccessful "revolution from above," unwittingly begun by a dissident aristocratic president, José Manuel Balmaceda. Committed to national sovereignty and independent economic development, Balmaceda sought to put through his program despite the opposition of his own class. But he fell in a terrible civil war in 1891, with the lords of land and capital and the owners of the main foreign enterprises united against him. Now in our own time, another historical alternative—an attempt at a socialist "revolution" not by the bullet but the ballot—has been bloodily suppressed.

This work is a sociological analysis of the civil wars of 1851–1859 and 1891. Its aim is not only to lay bare the social causes and far-reaching consequences of these violent eruptions, but also to grasp their historical significance. The analysis focuses, first, on how contradictory historical circumstances affecting decisive segments of the dominant class drove them—even against their own will—into bloody conflict with each other to defend their specific interests, if not indeed their very social existence; second, it focuses on what the victory of one side and the defeat of the other meant for Chile. These nineteenth-century civil wars, these bourgeois revolutions that never were, were historically crucial in the making of the dominant class, in the shaping of its internal relations, and in the entire process of class formation. They were crucial, however, not only in the making of the dominant class but also for the very development of capitalism and democracy in Chile. With the defeat of Balmaceda in 1891, a "coalesced bourgeoisie" of landlords and capitalists consolidated their historical reign, ruling uninterruptedly until the present, when their savage suppression of still another historical challenge left democracy in Chile in ruins but capitalism intact and their class dominion once again secure.

This work, whose leading questions cut across the boundaries of history and sociology, economics and political science, is based on a reanalysis of the data contained in the available historical writings on Chile. I searched through a considerable body of primary (though not archival) sources, particularly works written by contemporary observers and leading participants in the historical events under examination. Alas, as scholars are wont to do, I also tracked down and read many other contemporary sources, including newspapers and a number of memoirs. But these sources, although adding in some small way to my sense of the times, yielded neither new information nor understanding and so were not included in the already quite extensive list of historical references cited. I also carried out the kind of analysis that, when the respondents are there for the asking, sociologists call survey research, but when it is the dead who must disclose what has hitherto been concealed about their lives, historians call collective biography. My aim was to ascertain the "class situation" of the major individual protagonists of these nineteenth-century internecine wars. I thus compiled a list of the most conspicuous leaders of the revolutionary assaults on the Montt regime in 1851 and 1859 and of the leading Congressionalist insurgents and Balmaceda partisans mentioned in the various historical works. Then I gathered and analyzed the relevant biographical and kinship data necessary to discover and delineate the extent to which they and their families were divided by contradictory interests and opposing political needs.

But, in the main, this book rests on the yeoman work of several generations of historians who themselves sought to reconstruct what happened in Chile's history. Without their most basic archival research, the present "secondary analysis" of historical data would not have been possible. I have relied heavily, in particular, on the fundamental work of Hernán Ramírez Necochea, Harold Blakemore, and Luis Vitale and on the recent revelatory dissertations and published research of such young historians as Joanne Fox Przeworski, Arnold J. Bauer, Thomas F. O'Brien, Jr., Henry W. Kirsch, and Robert B. Oppenheimer, and I owe much to the flawed but crucial insights of Marcelo Segall. Without their common work I could not have discovered the underlying social connections I sought.

My analysis here reveals that the characters, their circumstances and actions, and the historical drama in which they were the leading individual protagonists were interconnected in ways not previously suspected. It thereby also discloses the hidden—and enduring—significance of these monumental political struggles in shaping the characteristic uniqueness of Chilean social reality. In a "reprise," I also try to assess the general theoretical implications of my analysis and findings for questions of development and underdevelopment, the creative historical role of classes and the state, and the nature of the so-called "world system."

Acknowledgments ➤

I wrote this book unintentionally, thinking that I was finishing another one, *Landlords and Capitalists: The Dominant Class of Chile*, a collaborative work with Richard Earl Ratcliff. Once having revealed the inner structure of that "coalesced bourgeoisie," we then had to ask how it was formed and how it consolidated its dominion. That question, as is now obvious, led to others, compelled by the logic of historical inquiry, and culminated in the present book. I am especially grateful to Professor Ratcliff for urging me to publish this work independently and for allowing me to incorporate ideas in it that arose in the course of our common work. I learned much from the comments on portions of this work by my friends and colleagues, Richard Ashcraft, Robert Brenner, Michael Burawoy, Temma Kaplan, Robert K. Merton and Jonathan Wiener, and I am thankful for their intellectual sustenance. Research for this work was supported in part by the Ford Foundation, the Louis M. Rabinowitz Foundation, and the Academic Senate of the University of California at Los Angeles, for which I also want to express my public thanks. Judy Stepan-Norris provided indispensable computer assistance and invaluable help compiling the Index. I am grateful to the International Sociological Association for permission to use materials here from my article, "Class, State, and Capitalist Development: The Civil Wars in Chile (1851 and 1859)," in *Continuities in Structural Inquiry*, ed. Peter Blau and Robert K. Merton (Beverly Hills, Calif.: Sage, 1981). I also want to thank Cathie Brettschneider for the extraordinary care and attention she gave to copyediting the manuscript of this book; she not only caught some errors here and there but also helped me to improve the clarity of my argument at several points. Finally, the comments and suggestions on the manuscript by Sanford G. Thatcher, Assistant Director of Princeton University Press, to some of which I reluctantly paid attention, surely made this a better book.

The Civil Wars in Chile

Chapter 1 ➤ PRELUDE: CLASS, STATE, AND CAPITALIST DEVELOPMENT

The civil wars in Chile had decisive history-making consequences. They were crucial in shaping the pattern of capitalist development in Chile, the distinctiveness of its class relations, and the form taken by the Chilean state. If the development of capitalism took contrasting "classical" paths, revolutionary and democratic in England and Western Europe, reactionary and authoritarian in Prussia and Japan, Chile took neither of these paths into the twentieth century. But at two different historic moments, in the civil wars of the 1850s and of 1891, it came close to taking both. The first civil war was, as I shall show, an abortive bourgeois revolution (though its terrain was, paradoxically, neither feudal nor absolutist); the second, a generation later, was a "revolution from above" that failed.

The first of these revolutionary possibilities opened up in the wake of the early nineteenth century incipient development of capitalist production relations, spurred especially by the accumulation of capital in copper mining, grain milling, and cereal exports and by the ensuing dislocations and rapid changes in the countryside and in the burgeoning mining centers of the northern provinces. This mid-century revolutionary movement in Chile, unlike that quintessential bourgeois revolution in France, was, as we shall see, led and participated in directly by the young bourgeoisie—by leading capitalists and their representatives, allied in armed struggle with peasants and artisans, self-consciously aiming to break the dominion of large landed property and erect a democratic state.

The second revolutionary possibility appeared with the quick growth of manufacturing that took place during the War of the Pacific (1879–1883) and the burst of capital accumulation following Chile's annexation of the nitrate territories of its defeated Bolivian and Peruvian neighbors. Under the presidency of José Manuel Balmaceda (1886–

1891), Chile's own variant of a "revolution from above"—of capitalist development enforced by an authoritarian state under the aegis of a hegemonic segment of its dominant class—became a proximate historical alternative.[1] But that historical alternative was suppressed

[1] [Sources are cited in footnotes by the author's name, the year of publication, and the pages containing the quoted material or information cited. If there is more than one author of the same surname, the footnote also gives the initial of the author's first name. Spanish surnames ordinarily include both the paternal and the maternal surnames, in that order (e.g. Ramírez Necochea) and are alphabetized by the paternal surname. The list of references contains complete publication information for every source cited in the footnotes: authors are listed alphabetically, and publications for each author are listed chronologically. If an author has more than one publication in a year, the publications are listed alphabetically by title, and the year has a letter suffix to identify it (for instance, Ramírez Necochea 1960a, pp. 99–101; 1960b, pp. 11–12). Multiple sources listed in one footnote are given in the order of reference to them in the text.]

That both the reactionary and revolutionary capitalist paths of development are historically alternative "routes into the modern world" is also the focus of Barrington Moore, Jr.'s penetrating work. See Moore 1966. That work has fruitfully influenced my own thinking in the present analysis. Unlike Moore, however, who takes what he calls the "capitalist impulse" as given, I focus in this book on the causes both of the development of capitalism and of the formation of bourgeois democracy. This double-edged question has long been a critical one in historical materialist scholarship. Marx and Engels often emphasized in their own historical essays and political writings that bourgeois revolutions paved the way for both capitalism and democracy and that revolutions from above made capitalist development possible but at the expense of democracy; this has been a recurrent theme in the relevant Marxian work since. See, as an outstanding example, the famous debate in the 1950s on "the transition from feudalism to capitalism," in Dobb et al. 1954. It was, in fact, Engels who first used the concept of "revolution from above" in his analysis of the role of Otto von Bismarck's policies in establishing the *political preconditions* for rapid capitalist development in Germany as an alternative to the revolutionary incapacity and political timidity of the liberal bourgeoisie. As is well known to students of Soviet history, Lenin also argued, after the defeat of Russia's 1905 revolution, that the "Prussian road" (as he dubbed it to contrast with the "American road" of capitalist democracy) had become an imminent historical possibility in Russia. In his view, both the "American road" and the "Prussian road" were "objectively possible paths of capitalist development" for Russia: if Czarist Premier Piotr Stolypin were successful in creating a conservative class of peasant small holders by his "land reform"—the breakup of the *mir* (village commune) and the redistribution of its lands in individual parcels—while simultaneously tightening political repression, then, Lenin argued, this revolution from above would result in a "junker-bourgeois" regime in Russia. See, for instance, Engels 1973a, p. 436; 1973b, especially pp. 192–193; 1973c, especially pp. 400, 418; and Lenin 1934, especially pp. 180ff., 254; 1954, especially the Preface to the second edition, where Lenin poses the contrasting paths as historical alternatives; and 1967, II, p. 321.

Following these early theoretical leads, E. H. Norman, in a pathbreaking historical analysis (on which Moore relies heavily), interpreted the Meiji Restoration in Japan as the most transparent historical instance of the rapid erection of capitalism "from

by Balmaceda's defeat in the civil war of 1891, just as the revolutionary democratic alternative had been suppressed a generation earlier; with that unwitting revolution from above undone, the nature of Chile's unique and composite social formation was essentially determined: a capitalist democracy in which the large landed estate was pivotal.

The historic peculiarity of Chile's "bourgeois democracy"—until it was smashed by a reactionary military *coup* in the autumn of 1973—lay in the anomaly that the society it governed never became quite bourgeois itself. What explains this? How, on the one hand, was capitalist development in Chile stunted? How, on the other, did it become a relatively stable political democracy? These are the inseparable theoretical issues involved in my empirical analyses of the causes and consequences of Chile's two decisive nineteenth-century civil wars. They are also the historical questions that, taken together, constitute the mystery of the development of, as Max Weber would have said, "the characteristic uniqueness of the reality" of Chile.[2]

THE DOMINANT CLASS AND THE STATE IN HISTORICAL DEVELOPMENT

To understand the historic consequences of these civil wars and their outcomes, to discover the extent of their social reverberations,

---

above," under the patronage and control of a centralized authoritarian state: while reinforcing landlord dominance of the countryside it established large-scale industrial enterprises and enforced rapid capital accumulation at the expense of the agrarian masses. See Norman 1940. Similarly, in the debate among Marxist scholars on the "transition from feudalism to capitalism," the Japanese historian Kohachiro Takahashi also tries to explicate the historical preconditions of the "two ways" of capitalist development that Marx mentions briefly in *Capital*. Takahashi argues that the "classical bourgeois revolutions of Western Europe aimed at freeing producers from the system of 'constraints' (feudal land property and guild regulations) and making them free and independent commodity producers; in the economic process [their] differentiation (into capital and wage labor) forms the internal market for industrial capital." In contrast, in Japan and Prussia, capitalism was *"erected on a basis of fusion rather than conflict with absolutism,"* with the result, in Takahashi's view, that the *"socioeconomic conditions for the establishment of modern democracy were not present"* (Takahashi 1952, pp. 343–344, italics added). See the compilation of the original articles and more recent ones in the debate in Hilton 1976. Recent historical works using the concept of the "Prussian road" to analyze American history include Wiener 1979 and Genovese 1965, pp. 206–207; 1971, pp. 346–347. See also Wiener 1978.

[2] The phrase is from Weber 1949, p. 72 (italics in the original): "The type of social

it is necessary first to reveal their origins. They were, I shall show, bourgeois revolutions—first from below and then from above—that never were. The thesis that these insurrections were not merely civil wars but abortive bourgeois *revolutions* is *the* issue of Chile's historical development. It also implicitly places the discontinuities, ruptures, and transformations of the precapitalist social and political fabric, of class relations and state structures, by and through concrete class and intraclass struggles, at the very center of the analysis of development and "underdevelopment." This in turn requires us to take seriously as an empirical question the issue of the so-called "autonomy of the state": of the extent to which, at critical moments, the activities of the state may generate new social relationships and productive forces or inhibit their development, even against the historical interests of the dominant class itself. State policy, and therefore the matter of who holds state power and even of who staffs it directly, can be crucial if not decisive in those determinant but contingent transitions when unwonted forms of social production emerge; it can effectively determine the extent and nature of their development and consolidation.

But this does not necessarily imply, though the possibility is not denied, that the so-called state is fully independent, unconditioned by class relations. "Class power" and "state power" assuredly differ; but the problem is what the relationship between them is, not merely in an abstract model but in concrete, historically specific circumstances. To what extent the state is effectively "insulated from the impact of non-political groups and procedures," run by "state rulers" who have "fundamental conflicts of interest" with "the existing dominant class," is not and simply cannot be a so-called general theoretical question.[3] It must be an empirical question: the question of social causality, in this instance as elsewhere, is not a question of laws or of ahistorical propositions meant somehow to be universally valid (and thus vacuous), but a question of concrete causal relationships. We shall see, for instance, that contrary to what

science in which we are interested," he wrote in 1904, "is an *empirical science* of concrete *reality* (*Wirklichkeitwissenschaft*). Our aim is the understanding of the characteristic uniqueness of the reality in which we move . . . and the causes of [its] being historically *so* and not otherwise."

[3] Huntington 1968, p. 20; Skocpol 1979, p. 27.

now passes for political theory in "structuralist Marxism," a state that was bourgeois in "structure" governed a social formation that was surely not yet dominated by capitalist relations of production, and it enforced the dominion of large landed property—if it was not indeed the mere "instrument" of the ruling great landlords of the Central Valley.[4] This can be understood only by a historically specific theory of these concrete class–state relations.

It need not trouble us either that the "political crises that have launched social revolutions" have scarcely been mere "epiphenomenal reflections of societal strains or class contradictions." It may well be correct, as Theda Skocpol argues, that "the political-conflict groups that have figured in social revolutionary struggles have not merely represented social interests and forces. [What does "merely" mean? If it means "only," then "mainly" and surely "partially" are not precluded.] Rather, they have formed as interest groups within and fought ["merely"?] about the forms of state structures."[5] For this is, again, an intrinsically empirical question. The critical question is the causal relevance of political crises and class contradictions in a revolutionary situation and how they are related.[6]

In the historical literature on the civil war of 1891 in Chile, the so-called autonomy of the opposing political-conflict groups has long been a major issue (antedating the current "structuralist" vogue by many decades). In the view of most scholars who have studied it, the fratricidal split in the dominant class under President Balmaceda was not "social" but rather "political," with the divisions that led to civil war originating over questions of state principles. In this reigning interpretation, the "Congressionalists" and their opponents, that is, President Balmaceda and his adherents, constituted political-conflict groups that arose within the state itself, fighting over how it was to be structured but not differing otherwise in their social locations. In one variant of this interpretation, the crisis that launched

---

[4] See, as the condensation of "structuralist" Marxism on the state, Poulantzas 1973b. For a discussion of the "structuralist" versus "instrumentalist" conceptions of the "capitalist state" that moves beyond them, see Esping-Andersen, Friedland, and Wright 1976. Also see Hamilton's original sociological analysis of the limits of state autonomy (1982).

[5] Skocpol 1979, p. 29.

[6] Surely for Marx himself this was the critical question. See Marx 1948, 1952, 1963, and Engels 1973b, 1973c.

the civil war of 1891 was a crisis internal to the state itself, in part generated by the state's effort to appropriate resources (nitrate revenues, in particular) and devote them to social objectives contrary to the desires and objective interests of the dominant class. The civil war of 1891 was, in short, either a conflict between the dominant class and the state, or a conflict within the state itself, according to the prevailing view. My empirical analysis will reveal, however, that the men who sought to defend their nation from continuing foreign encroachment and to put Chile on the path of independent capitalist development were not—whatever others may have found elsewhere—free-floating "state rulers" or "relatively autonomous bureaucrats."[7] On the contrary, they were the consummate representatives of a distinctive bourgeois segment of the dominant class— of a productive class segment of capitalists having its own aspirations, needs, and imperatives.

Thus a critical error in those analyses that purport to find such intrastate crises within the old regimes as the "real" source of revolutionary crises may well be their conception of "the dominant class" as an undifferentiated whole. No doubt (as was true of Balmaceda) "attempts of state rulers merely to perform the state's 'own' functions may create conflicts of interest with the dominant class."[8] But the interests of that class, and its internal structure, may be anything but homogeneous, and state policies may impinge differently and have opposing effects on its various internal segments. Although it might appear to have been a conflict within the state itself, or between "state rulers" or "relatively autonomous bureaucrats" and the dominant class, that created a revolutionary situation, either from above or below, the reality could have been quite different. In fact, that crisis could well have originated in a conflict between segments of the dominant class, on whom the activities and policies of the state impinged in opposing ways, because of their different locations in the productive process as a whole (and in the accumulation and appropriation process in particular), despite their otherwise common ownership of the means of production. Such "class segments" thus have the inherent potential of developing their

[7] See, for instance, Trimberger 1977, and especially 1978, pp. 4–5, 41–45, 91–96.
[8] Skocpol 1979, p. 30.

own specific variants of "intra-class consciousness" and common action vis-à-vis each other as well as against other contending classes. Of course, the extent to which their varying "intraclass situations," as Weber might have called them, manifest themselves politically depends on the specific combination of concrete historical circumstances and structural relations (in particular, those differentiating or integrating the various class segments).[9]

[9] See Weber 1946, pp. 181–186, 301, for his discussion of the concept of "class situation." Although Weber usually focuses on the "mode of distribution" (in contrast to Marx's focus on the production and appropriation of the social product in a "mode of production" consituted by contradictory class relations), the content of his concept of "class situation" in his actual historical sociological analyses is in fact quite similar to Marx's sense of "class location" (or "class position").

In his political writings on contemporary events, Marx especially emphasizes, though he never systematically incorporates it into his theory of history, the decisive political role of what he calls "rival fractions and factions of the appropriating class" that participate in shaping the uses of "state power" in their "antagonism to the producing classes" (1952, p. 86; 1973b, p. 337). Repeatedly, Marx asks which "fractions" or "sections" of the "bourgeoisie" actually "rule and legislate through the Chambers" and which are "non-ruling." Which segments of the bourgeoisie "actually [make] the laws, [are] at the head of the administration of the state, [have] command of all the organized public authorities" and which segments are excluded from political power? For Marx, answering these questions is a prerequisite to understanding the real workings of "the state," the formal process of governing, and the actualization of the "general class interests" of the "dominant class" (viz. 1948, pp. 37–42; 1973c, pp. 13–15). A major focus of his political analyses, then, is on the relationship between the internal differentiation of the dominant class into contending segments and the exercise of political hegemony, that is, leadership or overriding influence *within that class itself*. The segment of the dominant class that is hegemonic within it and in which other segments "find their natural mainstays and commanders" is the one that represents the class interest "in its vastest outlines, [and] represents it as a whole" (1948, p. 139; 1973c, p. 78). This class segment that "dominates the bourgeoisie itself" is "the dominant bourgeois fraction" (*"der herrschenden Bourgeoisfraktion"*) (1973c, p. 13; cf. 1948, p. 40).

In what follows, I adapt Weber's term "class situation" and Marx's term "class location" to accord with the conceptual content of my term "class segments" and I refer interchangeably to their distinctive and contradictory "intraclass situations" or "intraclass locations." By my term "class segment" I wish to denote explicitly the theoretical content usually implicit in Marx's term *"Fraktion."* Although he never offers a formal definition of *"Fraktion,"* the primary conceptual content is relatively clear from his many concrete analyses. He refers, for instance, to the "economic foundations" of the various parts of the bourgeoisie, "held together by great common interests and marked off by specific conditions of production" or "different kinds of property," among whom it is necessary to protect and advance "the common class interest without giving up their mutual rivalry" (Marx 1948, pp. 100–110; 1963, pp. 27, 47; 1965, pp. 21, 42; 1973, vii, p. 59).

I prefer the new term "class segment," with my own specification of its meaning,

But to discover the relevance of intraclass contradictions in originating what appears to be a crisis within the state itself, one has to
have a theory that is causally adequate to the historically specific,
even conjunctural, contradictory interests at stake in the conflict. The
empirical analysis of concrete causal relationships and the elaboration
of a theory of the specific historical sequence involved has to *precede*
the attempt to analyze the social location or "social composition"
of the leading antagonists in these historic struggles. No general
count of social differences or associations can be adequately re-

---

because Marx uses a variety of terms interchangeably and not always consistently:
"Teil" (part), *"Abteilung"* (section or division), *"Gegenspartei"* (opposing faction
or party), *"Faktion"* (faction), and *"Fraktion"* (which itself is translated as "faction"). Marx often uses the term *"Fraktion"* not only for different parts of the same
class but also for parts of the same party, and he even refers to each of the parties
themselves as a *"Fraktion."* He also occasionally finds religious cleavages underlying
distinct class fractions (e.g. alongside the industrial, financial, and landed factions
was "the fourth faction [*Fraktion*] of the Party of Order, the Catholic"; Marx 1948,
p. 154; 1973c, VII, p. 88). Further, although he sometimes speaks of a politically
organized part of the bourgeoisie that does *not* rest on common economic foundations
as a mere "collection" (*Sammlung*) or "coterie" (*Koterie*), he usually also calls such
a group a *"Fraktion"* (Marx 1948, pp. 109–112; 1973c, VII, pp. 58–60). The fact
that translators have usually rendered the German term *"Fraktion"* as "faction" and
occasionally as "division," "section," or "part" but only rarely as "fraction" in
English has also been confusing. It accounts, in part, for the virtual absence of this
concept until recent years from English language writings on Marx or using Marxian
concepts, although the term "fraction" has recently been used often by French Marx-
ists.
    Nicos Poulantzas unfortunately perpetuates the conceptual confusion by formally
bringing two quite different meanings under the same conceptual rubric. Thus he
states that "fractions of classes . . . constitute the substratum of eventual social forces
. . . located at the level of the relations of production"—a conceptual specification
close to my own. But he also refers to "fractions dependent on the political level
alone" or "located solely at the political level" (Poulantzas 1973b, pp. 84–85; also
see 1973a). This formulation is not only conceptually confusing, but it also tends to
obscure or ignore precisely what it is that requires analysis and empirical investigation,
namely, the relationship between intraclass structural differentiation and the "political
level." That, of course, is one major focus of this book.
    In an earlier work on revolutionary politics and the Cuban working class, I also
focus on the political implications of intraclass differentiation. My remark there is
apropos of the present analysis: focusing on intraclass structure does not imply that
"*inter*class differences, or conflicting class interests, are in any way secondary to the
internal structure [of a class] . . . as the source of its politics. Quite the contrary, any
conflict between classes tends to erase or minimize the significance of *intra*class
differences and to maximize *inter*class differences" (Zeitlin 1967, pp. 8–9). My
analysis of the civil wars in Chile has not led me to alter that estimate, although I
would now emphasize, as I do in this book, that the struggles between rival class
segments (particularly those within the dominant class) can have decisive history-
making consequences, especially at transitional moments.

vealing: one must first know where to look and what to look for; counts that are not the product of a historically specific theory of the social processes at work can only "denature historical inquiry before it starts."[10]

In fact, I do count; I do closely examine the contrasting class situations of the most conspicuous protagonists and antagonists in the nineteenth-century civil wars, in these epochal dramas in Chile's historical development. But I do so as an integral part of the analysis of the sources of the conflict and of the realm of historical possibilities they embodied and the real structural choices they represented. Only by combining an analysis of the specific historical circumstances in which they acted and of their concrete interests and objectives—and what these circumstances and interests compelled as well as permitted them to do, wittingly or not—with such an analysis of their different social locations can we learn why they fought, what the defeat of one or the other side meant for Chilean history, and what those who lost might have done had they won.

Thus if history often has the retrospective appearance of inevitability, the analysis of the concrete historical circumstances in which rival segments of the dominant class in nineteenth-century Chile fought for political hegemony in their class and power in the state reveals how contingent and historically decisive the attainment of such hegemony really is. It reveals again how thoroughly social structures are themselves historical products, actively shaped—within

[10] Stinchcombe 1978, p. 6. This applies as much to the empiricism of historians (whether or not they are "cliometricians") as it does to that of sociologists. For instance, when historians and sociologists have tried to see if there were substantial differences in the "social and economic interests" of the leading Congressionalists and Balmacedistas, they missed what they were looking for because they did not know what they were looking for. They saw the similarities but missed the crucial differences in the intraclass situations of the men in the opposing camps. See chapter 4. For the same reason, the well-known quantitative analysis of the "nobility" and "bourgeoisie" on the eve of the French revolution—which concludes that they had "a continuity of investment forms that made them, economically, a single group"— is not historically enlightening. Since its author, George V. Taylor, set out merely to show that "in the relations of production they played a common role," the question of what contradictions or social fissures actually divided them is never raised nor a specific analysis of their structural locations conducted. See Taylor 1967, especially pp. 487–488, and 1964. Skocpol (1979, pp. 58, 60) accepts Taylor's conclusions without examination as evidence for her own view that the French revolutionary crisis really originated in the "conflicts of interest between the monarchy and the dominant class" rather than in any "class contradiction . . . cutting through the dominant strata."

the limits these structures impose—in real political struggle. My research thus led me to conclude that not only the class but also the *intra*class struggles that occur when capitalist production relations are still emerging in a given area or nation can decisively shape the extent and historical form of their ascendance (or decline). In particular, which segment of the dominant class itself wins political hegemony and enforces it through the use of state power is crucial in determining the pattern of capitalist development (or underdevelopment). How a specific class segment succeeds in transforming its particular interest into the general interest of its class and nation and what historic consequences this has must thus be a central question in any fruitful inquiry into the sources of the development of capitalism and the formation of the bourgeois state.

THE ORIGINS OF CAPITALIST DEMOCRACY

The historical situation in which Chile's parliamentary republic was originally forged and the vitality of its existence for over a century until its recent violent destruction reveal once again that bourgeois democracy is the fragile flower of a specific historical constellation of class relations and political struggles. The peculiarity of Chile's own "bourgeois democracy" was that it governed a society in which quasi-manorial landed estates, extracting the surplus product of the agrarian tenantry, continued to be dominant in the countryside and preponderant in agriculture, despite the overriding sway of capital and the dominance of the capital-wage labor relationship in the economy as a whole. From the revolutionary wars of the 1850s until the Left's penetration and organization of some elements of agrarian labor a century later, the supremacy of the large-estate owners in the countryside went unchallenged, especially in the Central Valley, where most of the rural population and the bulk of agricultural production were centered.

Chile experienced neither prolonged agrarian struggles in which the rural population gradually freed itself of the dominion of the large estate nor a sudden revolutionary convulsion that broke the base and destroyed the political power of the great landlords, thereby sealing politically the emergent capitalist relations and laying the basis for the democratic republic. Unlike the capitalist development of Western Europe and England, the political hegemony of the lords of the soil was not broken or transformed in Chile nor was much of the rural population ever turned into independent farmers. If these social transformations constituted the revolutionary preconditions for the emergence and durability of capitalist democracy in the West, it was nonetheless consolidated in Chile without such transformations.[11]

A century after the radical bourgeoisie's call in the 1850s for a "revolution in landed property," Chile still had one of the highest concentrations of landownership in the world. Within the large estates reigned a paternalistic system of social control, enhanced by the ever-present threat of expulsion into a landless rural population and enforced in the countryside as a whole by an apparatus of coercion, legal and extralegal, at the behest of the large-estate owners. In practice, until the middle of the twentieth century, alternative sources of information were prohibited and independent associations forbidden in rural areas. Thus the landowners controlled both the vote and the labor power of the agrarian tenants (*inquilinos*) and dependent peasants (*minfundistas*), and this was the *sine qua non* of their continuing political hegemony.[12] Such class relations surely provided an unfavorable soil for political democracy. Yet despite the unshaken dominion of the large estate, Chile was governed for over a century by one of the world's few stable parliamentary representative governments. How was this possible? An adequate answer requires a concrete historical analysis of the origins, course, and consequences of Chile's nineteenth-century civil wars—as does an understanding of the real historical reasons for the so-called "development of underdevelopment," in Andre Gunder Frank's apt phrase, in Chile.

THE DEVELOPMENT OF UNDERDEVELOPMENT

In our own day, Chile is an "underdeveloped" country, but from the middle through the end of the last century it was a nation on the move economically and developing rapidly. Chile strode the Pacific

---

[11] Cf. Moore 1966 and see note 1 to this chapter. Also for my earliest formulations of hypotheses concerning the "social determinants of political democracy in Chile," see Zeitlin 1966 and 1968.

[12] Sternberg 1962, p. 34; Zeitlin, Neuman, and Ratcliff 1976.

Coast of South America as a hegemonic power. Its fertile valleys and grain mills fed foreign flour and cereal markets, and its economy thrived on international demand for silver and copper; its largest mines and smelters, using the most advanced technology of the time and owned and developed by Chilean capitalists, veritably dominated the world copper market for much of this period. Chileans spanned their country's huge rivers with metal bridges and crossed its length and breadth with well-paved roads and some of the world's earliest railways. They lit its major cities with gas lighting, brought them potable water, and linked them by telegraph with the world. They established not only light manufacturing but also a sizable heavy industry, which produced machinery and equipment to exploit its nitrate fields and to mine and smelt its metallic ores, and they built locomotives for the nation's railways. Chile's capitalists exploited Chilean as well as foreign labor and invested directly and indirectly in raw materials production, finance, and trade in neighboring countries—two of whose nitrate territories it then successfully annexed in its own late nineteenth-century "imperialist war." Its leading banks established branches in world capitals from London to Delhi, and its commanding capitalists manipulated world market prices for copper and other raw materials from their own seats on the London exchange and Paris Bourse. They formed partnerships with, and often supplied the capital for, English bankers, traders, and manufacturers, as well as sharing with them and other foreign capitalists in the production and sale of the world's nitrates. Chile seemed indeed, as its statesmen proclaimed, to possess its own "manifest destiny" as an independent capitalist power in the Americas.[13]

Yet its leading thinkers were soon lamenting Chile's "economic inferiority."[14] By the early decades of the present century it had already come to bear much of the characteristic physiognomy of "underdevelopment," becoming in subsequent years a country remarkable only for the sharp contrast between the vibrance of its political democracy (until the autumn of 1973) and the stagnation of its economy. Why?

For "dependency theory" the starting point for the analysis of

---

[13] Details and documentation of these economic achievements are given below, in chapters 2–4. On the sense of destiny Chileans enjoyed, see Pike 1963a and 1963b.
[14] Encina's famous—and alarming—work of that title appeared originally in 1911.

Chile's underdevelopment would be its "external relations": how "national societies . . . express external relations" is the critical question.[15] This, however, is not merely the starting point but the essence—the sum and substance—of those variants of dependency theory that explain underdevelopment as the *result* of a country's place in the "metropolis-satellite" or "core-periphery" structure of the "world-economy."[16] Thus, Frank tells us, "Latin America . . . began its post-conquest life and history as an integral exploited partner in the world's capitalist development: and this is why it is underdeveloped today."[17]

Now, Chile's development undoubtedly has been bound-up with its "participation in the world capitalist system." Few countries indeed more fully exemplify the important methodological precept, as John Holloway and Sol Picciotto put it, that "not only the existence, but also the particular shape and historical development of particular nation states can be understood adequately only through an analysis of the relation between the state, and national capital and the *international* development of the contradictions of capital ac-

---

[15] Cardoso and Faletto 1973, p. 28; see also Cardoso 1977. It should be emphasized here that Paul Baran, an original thinker and the real mentor of Frank and many "dependistas," attempted (unlike Frank) when laying out his theory to specify the concrete historical circumstances and class relations involved in shaping the "morphology of backwardness" (Baran 1957). Frank rarely, except in the most general terms, mentions any real groups or classes and tends to speak of Chile as if it were itself the historical actor. Thus, for instance, on the rare occasion when he actually refers to any nineteenth-century efforts to push Chile's economic development, Frank has *Chile* itself doing it: "For a time, indeed repeatedly, Chile tried to resolve some of its capitalist contradictions with the imperialist world metropolis. All too aware of it as it was, Chile tried to escape from its satellite status. Chile embarked on attempts to achieve economic development through state-sponsored Bismarckian policies of national development long before Bismarck had thought of it" (Frank 1967, pp. 55–56). Unfortunately, this is no mere stylistic device but is of a piece with the entire "metropolis-satellite" theory, in which Frank refers consistently to Chile's "participation in the world capitalist system" without specifying who actually did the "participating" (and how). Fernando Henrique Cardoso and Enzo Faletto, in contrast, emphasize that "there is no such thing as a metaphysical relation of dependency between one nation and another, one state and another. Such relations are made concrete possibilities through the existence of a network of interests and interactions which link certain social groups to other social groups, certain social classes to other classes" (Cardoso and Faletto 1973, p. 140).

[16] Frank 1967, 1969, 1972; von Braunmuhl 1979; Wallerstein 1974a, 1974b.

[17] Frank 1967, p. 28.

cumulation."[18] This is, in fact, the analytical focus and the burden of my studies of the civil wars in Chile: to seek the causal connections between these "variables" in a concrete historical instance.

The central question, then, is *how* Chile's development and its class and class–state relations are connected with its place in the global political economy. Given the inseparability of these "internal relations" and "external relations" in Chile, it is a paradigmatic "test case" par excellence of the theory that a country's "participation in the world capitalist system *determined* not only the underlying structure of its economy and society but also its economic and social institutions, their transformation, and indeed [its] economic and social history as a whole."[19]

This sort of "world system theory," alas, turns history topsy-turvy; what exists is made eternal; today's social relations are projected back into the past as if they have always existed; and what really happened in history disappears. The theoretically critical historical questions, as will become evident from the empirical analyses that follow, are thus begged or ignored: "The domestic economic, political and social structure of Chile *always* was and still remains *determined* first and foremost," Frank asserts, "by the fact and specific nature of its participation in the world capitalist system and by the influence of the latter on all aspects of Chilean life." Underdevelopment, Immanuel Wallerstein tells us, is thus the "*result* of being involved in the world economy as a peripheral raw material producing area." Or, again, in Frank's formulation: "The colonial and class structure is the *product* of the introduction into Latin America of an ultraexploitative export economy, dependent on the metropolis, which restricted the internal market and created the economic interests of the lumpen bourgeoisie [*sic*] producers and exporters of raw materials."[20]

These formulations, unfortunately, assume what has to be demonstrated: What explains "the specific nature" of a particular country's or area's "participation in the world capitalist system"? By assuming that underdevelopment is the "product" of an "ultraex-

[18] Holloway and Picciotto 1979, p. 29, italics in original.
[19] Frank 1967, p. 33.
[20] Frank 1967, p. 29, italics added; Wallerstein 1974b, p. 392, italics added; Frank 1972, p. 14, italics added.

ploitative export economy'' or the ''result'' of ''peripheral'' raw
material production, it is no longer necessary (or even possible,
within the confines of the theory) to ask how that exploitative export
or peripheral relationship was itself *constructed historically*. The
troublesome inquiry needed to reveal the real causal relationships
does not have to be undertaken: Why did a particular export economy
become exploited by and ''dependent on the metropolis''? How was
a particular area or nation converted into a ''satellite'' and condemned
to ''peripheral'' raw material export production? Why was its internal
market restricted? What did this have to do with its participation in
the world market? Why did raw material production and export not
impel the internal accumulation of capital and spur the growth of
domestic industry?

We know, for instance, that the mid-nineteenth century in Europe
was a period of rapid growth of trade without precedent; it increased
from 1840 to 1850 alone by 70 percent, a rise whose rapidity ''was
unsurpassed in the whole of the nineteenth century.''[21] This was also
precisely a moment of unprecedented and unsurpassed ''participation
in the world economy'' by Chile, through the production of commodities (flour, cereals, copper) for exchange in the international
market. But the participation by Chile's landlords and capitalists in
the expansion of capitalism on a world scale led, for a half-century
or more, not to stagnation but to rapid internal accumulation of
capital, the growth of the productive forces, and the efflorescence
of capitalist relations of production in Chile. Why, then, did Chile's
continued ''participation in the world capitalist system'' turn from
a spur into a fetter on that nation's development? What concrete role
did its ''producers and exporters of raw materials'' play historically?
How did the internal production relations and world market situations
of various types of raw material producers and exporters, in agriculture and mining, in finance and trade, differ, and how did this
affect their contending interests? Were there none who had ''economic interests'' in—and even championed—the internal market and
domestic industry? Were they all of a piece, mere ''compradors''?
Did none of them seek economic sovereignty and independent capitalist development for their nation? If so, why? What happened to

[21] von Braunmuhl 1979, p. 207.

them? What, in short, was the specific constellation of historical circumstances, class and intraclass relations, political struggles, and state policies in Chile that determined its particular pattern of capitalist development and, as a result, "the specific nature of its participation in the world capitalist system"?

It was just such questions that had to be answered to reveal the causes of "the development of underdevelopment" in Chile. I was thus led *necessarily* to an analysis in "principled detail" (to borrow Robert K. Merton's phrase) of the origins, course, and consequences of the civil wars in Chile.[22] I want to emphasize, then, that the "theory" in this work does not appear in the "prelude" or in the "reprise" alone; any attempt to characterize this work or grasp its theory by reference only to what is said in either or both of these chapters would burlesque it. The theory of this work is contained within the detailed analysis itself, in the effort I make to provide explanations of specific historical sequences, not only during the civil wars themselves but also within their relevant historical time. On the one hand, the test of any theory of social change or historical development is its causal adequacy for the explanation of specific historical sequences and cumulative processes. On the other, the poverty of any such theory comes—and Arthur Stinchcombe puts it well—from not "paying attention to that narrative detail. . . . People do much better theory when interpreting the historical sequences than they do when they set out to do 'theory.' . . . *Social theory without attention to details is wind.*"[23]

FACT AND COUNTERFACT

If this is a central "methodological" premise of this work—that fruitful social theory is made in the detailed empirical analysis of the causes of actual historical sequences and cumulative processes— the method is double-edged. All major historical questions break down into two others, one "factual" and one "counterfactual": what happened in history, and what might have happened?

Of course, history "as it actually happened" is itself always the

---

[22] Personal communication 1979.
[23] Stinchcombe 1978, pp. 13, 17, 21, italics added.

result of an interrogation of the so-called "facts" that thereby transforms them into "evidence" for a specific narrative sequence of occurrences or contingent events. History in this sense—that is, as the "construction of a narrative account"—is always a "reconstruction," and such a "reconstruction," as E. P. Thompson rightly argues, is "a pre-requisite and premise of all historical knowledge, the ground of any objective (as distinct from theoretic) notion of causation, and the indispensable preliminary to the construction of an analytic or structured account."[24] Thus any such reconstruction of the past so as to reveal otherwise hidden connections between phenomena, any effort at causal analysis of social change or historical development, is intrinsically "counterfactual analysis."

For what distinguishes *causation* from *correlation* is precisely the implied "statement that if the cause had not occurred, then the effect would not have occurred, whereas no such counterfactual is implied by the latter."[25] To understand why something happened in history it is always necessary to ask what difference it would have made if something else preceding it had *not* happened. If a given event had been absent, what then would have happened—how would its absence have mattered? If the putative "cause" had not happened, then of course neither should its "consequence" have happened. So historians, whether they recognize it or not, must use some counterfactual reasoning as a method of reconstructing the detailed past—"what really happened" in history. "In order to penetrate to the real causal interrelationships," as Weber remarks, "*we construct unreal ones.*"[26]

The paradox, then, is that to understand the significance of what actually happened, of the actual social world that emerged, we have to assume that something we think was decisive never happened in order to discover what else was *possible*. If what happened was neither inevitable nor ineluctable but the product of a specific constellation of circumstances, events, and activities, then that constellation also bore within it other unfulfilled (or suppressed) historical possibilities. The question, then, is not only what difference it would have made if something that "really happened" had not happened,

[24] Thompson 1978, p. 29.
[25] Elster 1978, p. 175.
[26] Weber 1949, p. 186, italics in original.

but, even more important for our historical understanding, what difference it would have made if what did *not* happen *had* happened (like the bourgeois revolutions in Chile that never were). If what was, in fact, absent had been present in history, what then would have followed from it? What might have happened?

This, in turn, means asking what was *possible* in the concrete historical situation being analyzed. What were the historical alternatives available in the given material and social circumstances? What were the real options for the decisive social actors, and what difference would it have made if one rather than another set of options had been—intentionally or not—"chosen"? In this sense and to this extent, the investigation of the significance of historical events that never happened is a prerequisite, if often hidden and implicit, of all fruitful and valid historical sociological theory. "A theory that covers the actual world and only the actual world," as Jon Elster puts it precisely, "is not a theory but a description. A theory must have implications for possible worlds by specifying the set of jointly realizable values of the relevant variables."[27] In this work, then, method and theory are inseparable in a quite precise sense. Its twin premises are the necessity both of historical specificity and of the recognition of the relatively contingent historicity of all social structures (and of their constituent class and class–state relations in particular), which means constantly asking, as the analysis proceeds, not only what happened but also "what could have happened to the *real* past"?[28]

---

[27] Elster 1978, p. 7.

[28] Elster 1978, p. 218, italics in original. I think that this characterizes the actual analytical method of Marx and Engels, as well as that of both Lenin and his methodologically self-conscious contemporary Max Weber. Weber was perhaps the first to try to explicate this method (not too successfully), referring to it as the "category of objective possibility." See Weber 1949, pp. 176–188. Also see note 1 to this chapter. Counterfactual reasoning and analysis, as I understand it, thus have little in common with "cliometrical" conceptions of counterfactual analysis (as made famous, for instance, by the work of Robert Fogel and Stanley Engerman). Such cliometricians seem to think that all counterfactual assumptions (so long as they are amenable to quantification and econometric modeling) are equally legitimate, or that all things are possible so long as they are conceivable. Thus they allow the practice of fabricating make-believe worlds circumscribed by no specific theory of what actually happened in the *real* past. On this question of the assertability of counterfactual statements and the problem of the legitimacy of counterfactual assumptions, see Elster 1978, especially chapter 6.

Chapter 2 ➤ THE ABORTIVE
BOURGEOIS REVOLUTION

Mid-nineteenth-century Chile was a period of swift metamorphoses in class and intraclass relations, of social ferment, and of sharp political conflict. The decade of the 1850s in particular opened and closed in armed insurrection and civil war—the violent expression of the continuing political struggles against the state under the presidency of Manuel Montt (1851–1859). What were their social causes and historical meaning? Of what significance were these bloody clashes for Chile's development? Were they, as writers of various theoretical perspectives agree, merely "squabbles" within an otherwise harmoniously integrated dominant class?[1] Or was the civil war of the 1850s a reflection of social contradictions whose political resolution was of decisive importance in shaping Chile's subsequent pattern of development? These are the questions at issue here, but the answers provided in this chapter are meant to be tentative; any "definitive" answers will have to await the work of others, especially of historians, for the published archival research on this period—and in particular on the events of the 1850s, on which my own analysis must rely—is both spotty and sparse. What I try to do here, at least, is to sketch the historical sociological problem as I see it and suggest an interpretation that might guide and be "tested" by future historical research.

In Chile's "small, stable and geographically compact society" of the early to mid-nineteenth century, there probably was considerable "overlap and intermingling of economic interests" in the higher levels of the class structure.[2] But this does not mean that such intermingling also resulted in "the peaceful realization of the bourgeois revolution in the colonial epoch," as Alberto Edwards Vives as-

---

[1] Bauer 1975, p. 45. Monteón's summation of the meaning of the 1850s' struggles is that "those unhappy with despotic government resorted to civil war," but lost (1982, p. 15).

[2] Bauer 1975, pp. 45–46.

sumes, "because our upper social class was simultaneously aristocracy and bourgeoisie at the moment of independence."[3] Similarly, Anibal Pinto Santa Cruz, although rejecting Edwards Vives' notion that the bourgeois revolution had already taken place through a gradual process of social symbiosis, agrees that when economic development during the first half of the nineteenth century "added other groups, outstanding among whom were the mineowners and commercial and financial sectors, to the landowning class, which had hitherto dominated the country without counterweight . . . there were differences and frictions but *no profound contradictions* among them."[4] Echoing these and other Chilean historians, James Petras also argues: "The eighteenth-century Chilean bourgeoisie merged with the original landholders and set a precedent for the absorption of significant sectors of the nineteenth-century bourgeoisie. At the top, class distinctions blended; thus there was *no sharp conflict* between the emerging capitalist groups and the old landholders."[5]

Contrary to these authors, however, my analysis will reveal that these mid-nineteenth-century armed struggles originated in emergent contradictions between land and capital as Chilean capitalism developed. Moreover, the defeat of the insurrectionaries in 1851 and again, and decisively, in 1859 amounted, I argue, to an abortive bourgeois revolution, with its own peculiar twists and profound impact on the development of capitalism and democracy in Chile. But this does not imply, I wish to emphasize at once, that the 1850s were, in Julio César Jobet's formulation, a "moment of transition between two economies: the feudal and the capitalist" or that it involved the rebellion of "a new social class, the capitalist bourgeoisie, against the reigning feudal regime."[6] Rather, the paradox and the conundrum of Chile's abortive bourgeois revolution is that its protagonists sought to abolish not a feudal but a bourgeois state,

[3] Edwards Vives 1945, p. 25.
[4] Pinto Santa Cruz 1959, pp. 38–40, italics added.
[5] Petras 1969, p. 93; italics added. Thomas F. O'Brien also repeatedly stresses the supposed harmony of interests within the so-called "elite" and asserts that "domestic divisions over trade policies, and struggles to control land and rural labor were almost unknown in Chile." He specifically claims that "as intermarriage and the purchase of estates drew them into the oligarchy, mineowners had little reason to challenge such aspects of the traditional order as an inadequate industrial base or labor-intensive agriculture. . . . Even as merchants and miners joined the elite, it remained united in its basic socioeconomic interests" (1982, pp. 24, 44, 126).
[6] Jobet 1955, p. 40.

governing a society in which large landed property and productive capital were in uneasy "balance," in which the former was neither feudal nor "fully" capitalist, and the latter was still in the throes of its incipient development. The landed and capitalist antagonists in this mid-century civil war represented not separate classes but distinctive segments of the dominant class itself, torn apart by contradictory interests and political requirements, rooted in their historically specific locations in developing productive relations.[7]

LAND AND CAPITAL IN MID-NINETEENTH-CENTURY CHILE

The emergence and development of capitalist relations of production in Chile was based, in the first place, on the accumulation of capital in mining. The discovery and exploitation of rich silver and copper veins in the 1830s and 1840s was followed quickly by a midcentury breakthrough in coal production and copper smelting and a rapid increase in agricultural and livestock production, which was itself spurred by the burgeoning "home market," especially the coastal trade in provisions for the mining areas, as well as by the opening-up of major new export markets for cereals and flour in Australia, California (the Gold Rush), and later England and Europe. Chile became the world's leading copper producer in the 1850s, accounting for roughly a third of global production in the next few decades; briefly during the same period, it all but monopolized Pacific grain markets, as agricultural export prices rose to a level never reached before or since in its history.[8] Thus the large landed estates, already long engaged in "commercial agriculture," though under a loosely seignorial form of exploitation, began to undergo an accelerated transformation of their tenure relations, under the impact of the new and sustained domestic and foreign demand for their products, the rapid inflation in land values, and the landowners' efforts to heighten their land monopoly and increase their control of agrarian labor.[9]

Chile's mineowners had begun to exploit the coal veins of the south near Concepción in the 1840s, but the main breakthrough in

---

[7] See chapter 1, note 9, on the concept of "class segment."
[8] Przeworski 1978, p. 1; Oppenheimer 1976, p. 28; Bauer 1975, p. 64.
[9] Góngora 1960, pp. 113–117; Kay 1977, pp. 106–113.

coal mining came with the colossal investments of Matías Cousiño, perhaps the embodiment par excellence of the development of Chilean capitalism at mid-century, who also owned major copper mines in the barren wastes of Atacama and rich silver mines in the hills of Chañarcillo. Utilizing English steam-driven machinery, Scottish technicians, and Chilean labor, Cousiño successfully tapped the submerged oceanic coal deposits at Lota in 1852, and within a few years coal production there and in the neighboring mines at Coronel was competing effectively against imported British coal, which had dominated the Chilean market until then. Chile's existing copper smelters and foundries, hitherto dependent on British coal imports, now had a major domestic supply of coal available. In addition, as one device to displace the British, Cousiño built a copper smelter at Lota that had the highest capacity in South America and consumed, on the average, a third of Lota's entire coal output. (Between 1858 and 1860, Valparaiso, Coquimbo, Huasco, and Colcura received 112,000 English tons and 129,000 Chilean tons of coal.)[10] Lota now had a population of 5,000, and visitors from England or Wales could easily believe they had been transported back to a corner of their own blackened countryside. Other extensive copper smelters were soon operating at Huasco, Copiapó, and Caldera. In 1858, José Tomás Urmeneta, discoverer and owner of the fabulous copper veins at Tamaya, took over the British-owned smelter in Guayacan just south of the city of Coquimbo and transformed it into the second largest on the continent, exceeded in capacity only by the one at Lota. Another smelter, imported whole from Germany, was soon at work in Tongoy.[11] Chilean copper ores, hitherto exported almost entirely *"en bruto"* (as raw ores) and refined abroad—mainly at Swansea, Wales—were now being transformed into ingots (*ejes*) and bars in Chilean smelters and foundries.

Coal production and copper mining and smelting were directly and indirectly linked to Chile's other emergent industries: major cement plants, brick and tile works, glass and bottle factories, brass foundries, machine shops, boiler works for the copper distilling apparatus, and workshops for copper utensils and equipment. The railroads in Chile's Central Valley and in the northern mining provinces,

[10] Encina 1949, p. 493.
[11] Bunster 1965, pp. 129–136, 142–143; Rippy and Pfeiffer 1948, p. 297; Centner 1942, p. 78.

fueled by domestic as well as imported coal, were mainly financed and built by Chilean capital. In addition, there were growing carriage and cartmaking works, sugar refineries, paper mills, breweries, and mechanized factories producing woolen textiles, rope and twine, boots and shoes, soap and candles, tackle, and ship's rigging and cordage. Many such factories were soon exporting their products to the United States.[12] In 1857, oceangoing steamships, some fired by Chilean coal, joined Chile's 200-vessel merchant fleet, which had consisted until then of sailing ships.

Chileans established major banks, their capital also originating mainly in the financing of copper mining and trade, and in cereal exporting. The Bank of Edwards (which a century later was one of the world's oldest banks) opened in 1846 and by the 1850s had branches throughout the country and ramified overseas, in Buenos Aires, London, Paris, Boston, and Vienna. Meanwhile ships of the house of Edwards carried silver and copper to the remote markets of India and China as well as of France and England (at Birkenhead, "Dock Edwards" was exclusively reserved for Edwards shipments).[13] Insurance companies and brokerage firms competing with the English houses were also founded during the 1850s, and the first stock exchange was opened in 1840, in the commercial center and seaport city of Valparaiso. Chilean statutes governing the formation of "joint stock companies" (*"sociedades anónimas"*) were enacted into law in 1854, signaling the beginning of the ascent of the corporation as a decisive organizational form of capital accumulation, in particular in banking, insurance, mining, and especially railroad construction. (Not, however, until the later nitrate boom in the 1870s did the corporate form and the stock exchange become central features of "the credit system" and of large-scale investment in Chile.)[14]

AGRARIAN CLASS RELATIONS

During the previous century, while juridical encumbrances on the direct producers in agriculture were progressively eliminated (and slavery and the *encomienda* abolished), the process of land en-

---

[12] Rippy and Pfeiffer 1948, pp. 297, 301–303.
[13] Bunster 1965, pp. 147ff.
[14] Escobar Cerda 1959.

croachment and concentration had gradually resulted in the domination of the countryside by the large estate. Increasingly, the great Central Valley landowners were able to convert various "free" forms of settlement on the land—such as rental agreements, sharecropping, and independent ownership of small parcels of land—into explicit labor-service tenancies; they also were able to incorporate the immediate producers directly into a manorial system of production as inquilinos, thereby assuring their estates of sufficient labor to produce for the expanding export markets. The various tenancy relations between the landowners and inquilinos were distinguished mainly by the size of the land allotment and the number of animals the inquilinos were allowed to graze on the landowner's demesne in return for supplying their family's labor, as well as additional hired labor, to the estate. Typically, they were allotted a small garden plot and dwelling, plus a rotating plot incorporated into the demesne itself, in exchange for their obligatory year-round surplus labor. During the early nineteenth century, when the Central Valley estates typically produced only small marketable surpluses, the inquilinos were rather more "tenants" (paying rent in money or kind) than "laborers."[15]

But with the efflorescence of mining and then the opening-up of new export markets at mid-century, what had been a protracted if uneven and fluctuating historical process of subordination of the immediate agricultural producer to the dominion of the large estate was now suddenly accelerated as the landowners sought to put more land into cultivation and expand production to meet the demand of these new domestic and foreign markets.[16] Not only new "markets," however, but also specifically capitalist forms of production were at the root of these structural changes in agrarian forms of production and class relations. Especially from the very beginning of the 1850s, there was a dramatic rise in migration from the countryside toward the cities and mining districts, as the supply of day-labor for the large estates was increasingly drawn off to be employed there and in the construction of the rapidly expanding infrastructure of roads,

[15] Bauer 1975, p. 15; Góngora 1960, especially pp. 113–117; Kay 1977, pp. 106–113.

[16] In fact, according to Oppenheimer 1976, p. 33, the volume of annual shipments of flour to the northern mining provinces was four to five times the exports to Great Britain, Chile's major foreign market at mid-century.

irrigation works and canals, bridges, and—mainly—railways, and in the new smelting works, foundries, and growing manufacturing establishments. The railroads were the primary employers of wage-labor on a large scale. South America's first major railway was built in Chile in the spring and summer of 1851 to unite the port of Caldera and the Atacama desert mining center of Copiapó; it was followed, from early in 1852 on, by the construction of the Santiago-Valparaiso Railroad through the rugged coastal mountain range and, from 1855 on, the Railroad of the South running from Talca up to Santiago. Some 10,000 workers a year were involved in these railroad projects.[17]

The peak of the "floating" rural population was reached in the 1850s. At this time high profits were to be had by expanded agricultural production; competition for the new markets in foodstuffs, grain, and flour was intense, and the demand for agricultural labor was rising. The rapid population movement from the countryside now made "labor scarcity" and pressures for higher wages a pressing problem for the large landlords.[18] They responded by laying new labor-service burdens on their existing inquilinos and recruiting new ones, to whom they granted smaller land allotments and reduced perquisites (meals, grazing rights, housing) for the same labor-service obligations now demanded of the older inquilinos. They also lengthened the working day, cut the number of Holy Days during the year, and increased and extended their direct control of the immediate labor process (by imposing a more complex managerial hierarchy and employing far more supervisory and surveillance personnel, i.e. the "*empleados*"). In short, in response to the emergence of capitalist production relations elsewhere in the country, the large landowners tried radically to reinforce and consolidate seignorial relations of domination and intensify exploitation of the agrarian tenantry.

How the landowners were able to impose successfully new exploitative burdens on the tenantry is by no means clear from the available published works. A combination of "extra-economic coercion" and a monopoly of the land and equipment as well as of financing appears to have been crucial in their success. Chile's Cen-

---

[17] Bauer 1975, p. 152; Oppenheimer 1976, pp. 78–79, 213.
[18] Sepulveda 1959, p. 44.

tral Valley had little unclaimed land or public domain out of which
new farms might be established. Although at this time the south
central area of agricultural settlement was gradually extended southward, despite fierce Araucanian Indian opposition, it is doubtful that
many new settlers came from tenant or small-holder families (immigrants from Europe seem to have predominated), and the land
monopoly of the Central Valley landlords was relatively absolute.
Landless, and with little or no other means of production (draught
animals, seed, equipment) in their possession, the inquilinos—old
and new—had no recourse for survival but to accept the tenancy
conditions imposed on them, unless they were prepared to resist and
revolt. Some did, especially independent small holders, as we shall
see. But the inquilinos had at best verbal agreements on the conditions
of their tenancy, and land was not available for settlement elsewhere,
even for the hardiest. Local judicial powers and even military authority (over army troops garrisoned in the area or of the regional
civic guard) were also held by the landowners themselves (aside from
the weight of the landowner-dominated centralized state apparatus).
These relationships provided fairly secure guarantees of rural "social
peace" and tenant acquiescence to the landlords' impositions.[19]

Buttressing and reinforcing this combination of land monopoly
and explicit coercion in this historically specific exploitative process
was a rural "credit system" that was also controlled by the landowners; they were virtually the only source of loans (against crops,
animals, or land) for the small holder, sharecropper, and tenant
laborer. This "economic nexus" extended the large estate's direct
control of surrounding independent cultivators, subordinated the tenantry even more fully to its dominion, and compelled them, as neither
surveillance nor supervision could, to expend themselves in production for the landlord.[20] Unlike the "usurer's capital" that weighed
heavily on landlord and peasant alike in Medieval Europe and ruined

---

[19] Bauer 1975, pp. 50–53, 145–168; Borde and Góngora 1956; Sepulveda 1959,
pp. 127–129; Kay 1977, pp. 106–113. Benjamín Vicuña Mackenna aptly called this
"agglomeration of powers in the hands of the estate-owners," as he wrote in 1856,
"a triple form of oppression of the inquilinos." The *hacendado* is simultaneously
"*patrón*, proprietor and landlord, commandant of the militia and . . . subdelegate of
the district" appointed by the central government (Vicuña Mackenna 1856, p. 68).
[20] Segall 1953, pp. 96–97; Bauer 1975, pp. 96–101; Gay 1865, I, pp. 116–117.

them both, as Marx observed, the asymmetry of debt merely strengthened the existing agrarian relations in Chile.

These production relations were, then, in no meaningful historical sense "feudal": rather than the survival of an alleged feudal past, they were the distinctive historical product of Chile's developing capitalism from the early nineteenth century on. These might correctly be described as "seignorial" relations of domination because of the labor service obligations placed on the tenants; but they were under no legal or customary compulsion to remain on the estate nor did they enjoy common claims to the use or usufruct of estate lands, except at the suffrance of the landowners themselves. What the inquilinos surrendered of their actual product or labor in "rent" was not coercively extorted from them as independent petty producers, for they had neither the land nor other means of production to produce and reproduce their own subsistence; they depended on the estate for both. This was thus a specific historical form of seignorial commodity production, neither feudal nor yet capitalist, in which the "estate" was simultaneously a "firm," competing for profits against others; its resident inquilinos were both labor service tenants and "free laborers."

Yet alongside this system of seignorial commodity production in the countryside, there already had emerged, especially in the granary works and flour mills, specifically capitalist relations of production. Employing large numbers of wage workers, as well as technicians (many foreign) and mechanics, the flour mills constructed in Chile at mid-century were "technologically equal to any mills in the world at the time." Most large estates probably retained traditional methods of production, and mechanization was still quite limited, although comparable apparently to European cereal-producing countries of the time, which had "large and stable rural labor systems," like Germany and France.[21] But some landowners, the so-called "*agricultores progresistas*," introduced mechanical threshers, reapers, and other farm machinery, fine cattle, new seed lines, and so forth.[22]

What is distinctive and significant about this process of "modernization of agriculture," however, is that limited though it was, it

[21] Bauer 1975, pp. 66, 105.
[22] Hernández 1966, p. 14; Correa Vergara 1938.

was largely the work of the new mining magnates: in Francisco Antonio Encina's words, "they bought lands to form great estates in the central valley, irrigated them . . . acquired modern machinery and implanted new types of cultivation."[23] It was apparently here, above all, that the rapid coalescence of land and capital took place in its most direct form; here, landed property became agrarian capital, and landlord and capitalist were one. It was precisely this segment of the dominant class that consummately personified the development of Chilean capitalism (mineowner and banker, railroad magnate and manufacturer, shipper and trader, *hacendado* and miller were most frequently not only close associates, or drawn from the same family, but the very same individuals: Ossa, Edwards, Vicuña Mackenna, Matta, Goyenechea, Cousiño, Urmeneta, Gallo, Subercaseaux). It was precisely this newly emergent class segment that was not only "dynamic and innovative" but also politically democratic, combative, and even revolutionary. It was this capitalist segment, above all, that constituted the bearer of radical democratic ideas in mid-nineteenth-century Chile and that fought, even in armed struggle, for class hegemony and political power.

CLASS AND STATE

Successive insurrections in 1851 and 1859 divided the dominant class from within. But in contrast to the future, even bloodier, conflict under Balmaceda as the century drew to a close, this civil war also drew important elements of other classes—artisans, small holders, and miners—into its revolutionary orbit. It thus threatened, but failed, to become a full-fledged bourgeois revolution. The intraclass conflicts that erupted in civil war were partial and contingent reflections of the rivalry between large landed property and productive capital. They were *partial* because other critical elements undoubtedly entered the causal process and set the revolutionary struggles in motion. First, certain "regionalist aspirations" were involved, although these

[23] Encina 1955, as quoted in Pinto Santa Cruz 1959, p. 58; Frías Valenzuela 1965, pp. 435–436, also notes that "the resurgence of agriculture under Bulnes [Montt's predecessor as President] was partly the work of the rich mineowners, who acquired lands in the central region and constructed great irrigation works."

too were rooted in determinate historical circumstances and specific intraclass relations. In 1851, the southern *penquista* elements of the landed proprietors (Penco, precursor of Concepción, was long the military outpost of the Araucanian frontier) joined with the northern Coquimbo mining bourgeoisie in the armed struggle against the state. Second, the political lines of division within the class were not only between "land" and "capital"; rather, in 1859, the "ultramontane" elements of the landed class were, paradoxically, cut off from their main trunk by their alliance with the Church, and they united themselves reluctantly in revolutionary conspiracy with the liberal and radical democrats.

Third, the events in Chile occurred in a "social duration" composed of "multiple and contradictory forms of time," to use Pierre Vilar's insightful formulation.[24] That is, these struggles emerged not only at a specifically Chilean historical moment but also within the European temporality of the 1848 revolutions: "the common uprising with its illusions, its poetry, its visionary content and its phrases" directly inspired many of the main protagonists of the abortive revolution of the 1850s.[25] These intraclass struggles were also *contingent*, to the extent that it was the unique combination of these elements—regional consciousness, Church–state conflict, and the example and force of European bourgeois revolutionary ideology—that "overdetermined" the entire process and perhaps made it possible. Without this specific constellation of interrelated elements, the interests and aspirations of mining capital might not have taken on revolutionary social content or led to armed struggle for state power.

What was the nature of the state against which bourgeois radicals and liberals declaimed and organized? In its origins and nature it was the product of the mixed temporalities, Chilean and European, in which it was fashioned: its inception, of course, was in the early nineteenth-century wars of independence that displaced Spanish do-

[24] Vilar 1973, p. 91.
[25] Marx's words for Alphonse Lamartine, the French poet, historian, and moderate republican who headed the provisional government of the February revolution of 1848 (1973a, p. 210). Lamartine's works "fascinated Chile's youth" of the 1850s, among them José Victorino Lastarría, Francisco Bilbao, Benjamín Vicuña Mackenna, and Santiago Arcos, the major "theoreticians" of the radical democratic movement of these years. Lamartine's *Girondins* appeared in Chile in 1850, *Los Constituyentes* in early 1859 (Edwards Vives 1932, p. 239).

minion. This meant that, at the outset, the traders, artisans, and mineowners (and notably few "revolutionary aristocrats") who constituted the main ramparts of the newly independent state, just as they had of the independence movement itself, were to strive to erect it as an antiroyalist and republican structure, heir on the one hand to the political, legal and juridical models present in the bourgeois and post-Napoleonic era and on the other to its architects' own exigent needs: unification of the country under a central administration without reimposition of the political hegemony of the large landed proprietors on which the royalist colonial state had rested. There were, however, no amalgams of property and sovereignty, no specifically feudal jurisdictions and boundaries, no warring principalities and petty states, no autonomous powers of urban corporations, such as formed the prehistory of bourgeois society in Europe, and whose destruction or unification was necessary to establish the new post-colonial state in Chile. On the contrary, to this extent Spanish royalism itself had prepared the ground for the bourgeois state. This does not mean of course that, in practice, intendant, magistrate, and landowner jurisdictions did not coincide (as they did and were to continue to do) but that, in principle and in law, the writ of the state was neither confined nor impeded by precapitalist political forms.

In this sense, then, the political options of the new revolutionary "statesmen" were relatively open. There surely were disparate social relations underlying the contrasting "constitutional" theories that guided their efforts to fashion new state forms, and the northern mining provinces in particular fought for a federalist state. But social "interests" and political consciousness were variably coincident precisely because the struggles in Chile were fought not only in a Chilean but also in an international bourgeois historical context in which that consciousness was also shaped. Therefore, in one form or another, it was a *republican* state that each early postindependence constitution (1812, 1823, 1828) framed. Nonetheless, the unavoidable question at issue throughout the political struggles of the first decades of independence, as successive regimes rewrote their state principles, was "merely" whether the state was to be not only republican but democratic as well. "The unification of capital and the principal political powers in the hands of the richest proprietors," declared Francisco Ramón Vicuña Larraín, himself a copper-mine owner and the main author of the short-lived 1828 federalist and parliamentary constitution, "is the germ of all revolutions."[26]

With the overthrow of that constitutional regime a year later, what emerged was, as its first president aptly named it, an "autocratic republic," whose juridical and political principles were embodied in the 1833 constitution. With scarce modification, this was the form of state at mid-century.

The executive of the state, not parliament, was vested with the main attributes of sovereignty: the chief of state, not parliament, decided the budget, fixed the salaries of all public officials, appointed and promoted military officers, and named the members of the supreme court. Neither the chief of state nor his council of state was subject to parliamentary censure or prerogative and could, in fact, veto parliament's legislation. The intendants, governors, and prefects who ran the provincial, local, and municipal administration were the appointees, agents, and direct representatives of the executive, as were trial judges and justices of district courts. Senators and deputies to the bicameral legislature, or "congress," were elected by limited suffrage (men, propertied, literate, 25 years old and over); candidates for the senate, though not the chamber of deputies, were nominated by the president and his ministers and had to be approved before standing for election by the appointed provincial and municipal officials of the state. (Nor was there any legal incompatibility between holding both executive and legislative office.)

Chile's mid-nineteenth-century state was, in short, a highly centralized, unitary, and hierarchical political apparatus, yet it was also a state in which were inscribed the legal and juridical principles of the inviolability of private property and equality before the law, of freedom of movement and travel (i.e. of a free labor market), of freedom of contract and trade, and freedom of press and assembly. No legal or customary prohibitions excluded any social category of individuals from trade, landownership, or industry, nor did they bind the immediate producer to the land. Indeed, the 1833 constitution even stated rhetorically that not only was equality before the law assured but also "in Chile, there is no privileged class."[27]

---

[26] Donoso 1925, p. 12. Ramón Vicuña was the father of Pedro Félix Vicuña Aguirre, whom we encounter below as a leading 1850s revolutionary.

[27] The 1833 constitution is excerpted in Valencia Avaria 1951, I, p. 161. For details

A civil code (enacted in 1855), constituting a systematic codification of the national jurisprudence, provided the "calculable adjudication and administration" in the state necessary to secure contracts, ensure property ownership, and standardize taxation and fiscal obligations (i.e. it was a bourgeois "rational legal order" with neither patrimonial, monarchical, nor feudal encumbrances).[28] Thus it was surely not a "feudal conservative state," as has been widely assumed.[29] Rather, it was a hierarchical and authoritarian form of capitalist state, in a social formation in which the large landed estate was simultaneously a decisive fount of surplus and base of power and capitalist productive relations were still emergent. It is "no accident," then, in comparative terms, that it shared so much with another capitalist state of the time, though of a different destiny: the Prussian *Rechtsstaat*.[30]

The mid-nineteenth-century struggles between landowners and capitalists thus took place on the terrain of a political and legal order

---

on the democratization of the state structure, see Galdames 1941, chapters 10–12; Gil 1966, pp. 43–47; Edwards Vives 1932, pp. 140–141. The entailment of estates (*el mayorazgo*) was abolished in law in 1852, but in practice, in the previous decade, entailing estates had dwindled considerably. Until the 1852 legislation, however, entailed property could not legally be "alienated, divided, exchanged, traded, mortgaged," or let for long-term rental, except under special circumstances (Bauer 1975, p. 21). Land had, in fact, already become a commodity in the past decade or more; with the founding of the Land Bank (*Caja de Credito Hipotecario*) in 1855, not only were the last aristocratic barriers to a free market in land superseded but also the institutional means were constituted for the immediate transformation of land into capital. See Borde and Góngora 1956, pp. 126–129. In return for a mortgage on their property, borrowers received letters of credit in standard denominations ($1,000, $500, $200, and $100), with fixed rates of interest, which they then sold on the open market; the actual "loan" thus amounted to the receipts from the sale of these letters of credit. Banks, insurance companies, and many other corporations (including foreign institutions) included such letters of credit in their portfolios (Bauer 1975, p. 90). Thus it became possible, by such trade in paper representing loans on the land, to calculate roughly the yield on "agricultural" investment as compared with other investments in industry, mining, and trade. In this sense, the "average rate of profit" apparently had already come to govern investment (or disinvestment) in agriculture. The *Caja* proved to be, as had the land banks of the Prussian Junkers, a successful method for rapidly centralizing agrarian capital. See Barros Borgoño 1912.

[28] See Weber 1961, p. 208; Neumann 1957, pp. 166–168.

[29] See, for instance, the formulations not only of socialist historians, e.g. Jobet 1955, p. 47 and Ramírez Necochea 1956, pp. 40, 61, but also of liberals and conservatives, e.g. Gil 1962, p. 13 and Galdames 1941, p. 16. Encina, in his study of the "Portalian state" (1964), does not make this error.

[30] See Neumann 1957, p. 169; Engels 1973c, p. 426.

that was itself bourgeois in "structure" but that ensured the hegemony of large landed property in both class and state. To lay hold of it and use it in their own interest was an abstract possibility for the mineowners and their allies: to turn its hierarchic, centralized apparatus against the large landed proprietors and use it to enforce their demands. Abstract it was and is because in the real historical circumstances and in the concrete conditions of the Chilean state's formation, it stood as the incarnate representative not merely of an antiquated past but of the subordination of capitalist to landlord. What emerged, then, as the supreme political demand of the liberal and radical activists of the class was a federalist, decentralized, and parliamentary democratic state. They called for the limitation of executive powers (and for the legal "incompatibility" of executive and legislative office); enlargement of manhood suffrage; direct popular election of the senate as well as the chamber of deputies; provincial and local autonomy; and popular election of intendants, prefects, governors, and judges. In short, they demanded not merely the amendment but the *abolition* of the 1833 constitution and with it the authoritarian state structure it represented.[31] After collaborating with their ultramontane allies (the so-called "Fusion") in unsuccessful parliamentary efforts to make the constitution "reformable," they then moved directly toward revolutionary political objectives. Not within the existing state but against it, in a "constituent assembly" of the people, would the new constitution be written and the old discarded. They demanded the abdication of the president and his council of state, as weil as the dissolution of congress, of the tribunals, and of the state's regional officialdom; and they called for the convening of the revolutionary constituent assembly.[32]

That the political hegemony of the landed proprietors rested on their social dominion in the countryside and on their enhanced control of the agrarian tenantry was also clear to the young bourgeoisie's most advanced political "theoreticians." The prevailing historical

---

[31] Edwards Vives 1932, pp. 387–388; Jobet 1955, p. 40; Donoso 1925, p. 94.

[32] Edwards Vives 1932, pp. 243-246. The young Benjamín Vicuña Mackenna wrote: "We do not want armed revolution; that is the dictatorship of the crowd. We want the Constituent Assembly, which means peace, truth, justice and, above all, the sovereignty of the people, the sanction of its august right" (Vicuña Mackenna 1858, no. 1, pp. 6–7); also see Donoso 1925, p. 94.

imagery of Chile is that, as Petras writes, the Chilean bourgeoisie was "never forced into combat with the traditional landholders [and] never had reason to champion the cause of the large rural population."[33] But, in fact, the oppressed rural poor did have their champions in the bourgeoisie, who fought on their behalf not only in words but in armed insurrection. They understood that "so long as *inquilinaje* endures in the *haciendas* . . . so long as that omnipotent influence of the *patrón* over subaltern officials persists . . . no [political] reform will be solidly established." These are the words of Santiago Arcos, banker's son and principal organizer, with Francisco Bilbao, of the Society of Equality, which brought artisans and bourgeois intellectuals together in Santiago and played a pivotal role in the 1851 revolt.

It was necessary, as Benjamín Vicuña Mackenna wrote in 1856, not only to "rescue our rural classes from abject servitude" through "intelligent and Christian reform" but also to abolish an agrarian society divided into "two rival classes, almost two races, that are becoming increasingly antagonistic," as Isidoro Errázuriz, one of the signers of the constituent assembly's Manifesto of December 1858, would put it.[34] Only through an "energetic, swift and forceful revolution that cuts out the roots of all these evils" and puts an end to "poverty as the normal state . . . of that class the aristocracy calls the 'ragged ones' [*rotos*], of the plebe in the cities and the day laborers, tenants and servants in the countryside," Arcos wrote in 1852, could "a stable government [be established] that guarantees social peace, and security for the laborer, the artisan, the miner, the merchant and the capitalist."[35]

Thus precisely at a historical moment when the transformation of

---

[33] Petras 1969, p. 93.

[34] Vicuña Mackenna 1856; Segall 1953, pp. 266–268. In 1854, while "absent from his country for political reasons" in exile in England, Vicuña Mackenna published a short essay on England's and Western Europe's agrarian systems and the conditions of their "rural classes" from which he drew lessons for Chile: he advocated "the redemption of the rural classes from their hunger" by providing livable rural wages and distributing "all public lands among the honorable poor, in return for a moderate rent to support the local parish and school, etc." (1854, pp. 126, 136–137). Two years later, he was calling for the "just breakup of the triple form of oppression of the inquilinos": the concentration of landownership and civil and military authority in the same hands (1856, p. 68; see note 19).

[35] Amunategui Solar 1946, p. 84.

small holders and renters into a subordinate agrarian tenantry was being consummated and the landholders of central Chile were coming to regard *inquilinaje* as their own "peculiar institution," these unwonted forms of social domination were to be tested, in a struggle for state power, by an emergent and aspiring capitalist segment of the dominant class itself at the head of armed artisans and mounted peasant detachments.

The ideas of their revolutionary movement were both the expression of an epoch in which profoundly new social relations were appearing in town and country and the direct articulation of the meaning imputed to them by its participants and bearers. At their root, in particular, were the historically specific intraclass situations of large landed property and mining capital, whose contradictory interests became more sharply defined as the state, under the hegemony of the Central Valley landowners and their commercial allies, postponed the mining bourgeoisie's aspirations.

Among the major developers of the south-central flour-milling zone, as was mentioned earlier, were the mining magnates themselves. In fact, this zone revolved around the cities of Talca and Concepción, which had "good riverine access to the sea" and from which flowed much of the grain and flour shipped up the coast to the distant mining towns of the north. Thus when the mineowners and millowners were not actually identical, they were closely integrated by trade; the mining north relied heavily on the near south's grain supply and provided it with a major market. Apparently, the southern wheat farmers and millowners and the northern mineowners were also "united by their indebtedness" both to the merchants of Valparaiso, many of them British, and to the Central Valley landowners, on whom they depended for loans and credits. Aside from imposing "usurious" interest rates, these lenders demanded liens on the land and on the output of the mines as collateral. Thus at midcentury, Charles Pregger Román argues, "the Central Valley alliance of merchants and landowners" was draining off a considerable share of the profits from these two distant productive regions in the north and south. An effort to establish a state bank to provide loans and credit at regulated interest rates, advocated by banker Antonio Arcos (father of the young radical Santiago Arcos) and by mineowner and newspaperman Pedro Félix Vicuña Aguirre, was defeated on the very eve of the 1851 revolt.[36]

Aside from this unmediated contradiction between them, the taxation and fiscal policies of the state also appropriated a sizable portion of the mining bourgeoisie's surplus but used it on behalf of projects in the interest of the Central Valley landowners and merchants. In 1851, on the eve of the first armed insurrection, public revenues came almost exclusively from taxes on mining and its exports: less than 3 percent came from the *catastro*, or land tax; the rest came from mining.[37] In this and subsequent decades, even after the abolition of the *catastro* and the enactment of taxes on agrarian income rather than landholdings in 1860, not only were taxes on the large landowners infinitesimal while their burden rested almost entirely on the mineowners, but also the "landowners enjoyed an ever decreasing tax burden."[38] Thus in his convocation of a Constituent Assembly in Concepción in 1851 to "return sovereignty to the nation," Vicuña Aguirre, whom Encina aptly calls "the author of the revolution of 1851," made this the movement's rallying cry: "The ties that bind the provinces to a tyrannical government are dissolved. It has sacrificed the interests of the entire Republic to the selfish interests of a small corrupt faction. The time has come to end the waste of the national revenues . . . Coquimbo, in the north, and Concepción, in the south, have a right to an equitable share of the public funds by which the tyranny preserves itself in the central provinces."[39] New taxes on copper exports had just been imposed before the civil war began: in August 1851, the Montt government raised them from 1.5 percent to 4 percent, and in October 1852, as the war was being "fought with fury unprecedented" in the republic's history, the Santiago regime raised the taxes even further, to 5 percent on the value of silver and copper exports, on both ingots and bars.[40]

On December 30, 1858, on the eve of the 1859 revolt, *El Curicano*, published in the near south city of Curicó, editorialized as follows:

---

[36] Pregger Román 1979, pp. 204–205, 215–218; see Vicuña Aguirre 1845, 1858, and 1862.
[37] Calculated from figures given in Segall 1953, p. 43.
[38] Bauer 1975, p. 118.
[39] Encina 1949, pp. 55, 52.
[40] Galdames 1941, p. 290.

"The Constituent Assembly [embodies] the aspirations and desires of the provinces . . . to govern themselves, to elect their own judges and intendants, to serve the interests of their own localities . . . to be represented in accordance with the taxes they pay rather than have to beg from the general Government. . . . The capital [of Santiago] absorbs all the revenues, receives all the improvements, concentrates all the advantages while the provinces are abandoned . . . to misery and backwardness. Once we were exploited by the Spanish Court . . . now by the court of Santiago. The general government does not invest a tenth of the revenues in our Department that we contribute annually to the national treasury."[41] One of the first acts of the revolutionary regime of Pedro León Gallo in Coquimbo, on January 11, 1859, was to cut in half the taxes on the ingots and bars exported abroad (despite the need to finance its own rebel army).[42] In fact, contrary to the imagery in much of the historiography of this period, Chile's mines and the necessary infrastructure for their profitable exploitation were "developed in spite of a state policy," as Enrique Bunster correctly remarks, "that increased the costs of production with immeasurable taxes."[43]

The Montt government is typically portrayed by scholars as the sponsor, as Andre Gunder Frank puts it, of proto "Bismarckian national development policies" parallel to those carried out a generation later on an even more massive scale by President José Manuel Balmaceda. Thus Encina writes that the Montt government, "by means of active and focused state action, constructed roads, railroads, bridges and telegraphs; spurred navigation; and stimulated enterprises that tapped our dormant riches." Similarly, Pinto Santa Cruz extols "the audacity and vision of Montt in the use of the resources and administrative capacity of the State in the development of the railroads." It was, he remarks, "a titanic effort."[44]

How titanic an effort it was on the part of the Montt government itself, however, is the question. Recent research on the construction of the railroads during this period suggests, as will my own analysis

[41] Vitale 1971, III, p. 252.
[42] P. Figueroa 1895, p. 318.
[43] Bunster 1965, p. 137.
[44] Frank 1967, pp. 56ff.; Encina 1949, p. 178; Pinto Santa Cruz 1959, p. 22. Cf., however, Kinsbruner 1973, pp. 96–98; and Barros Borgoño 1933.

of the mineowners' demands, that this is doubtful. First, as Luis Vitale observes, the first railway line in the country, which was built in Norte Chico from the mines near Copiapó to the smelters and port at Caldera, was financed entirely by the mineowners themselves.[45] Of the dozen stockowners who formed a "joint stock company" to build the Copiapó line, 11 were in the mining industry, and the twelfth was William Wheelwright, the famous American railroad builder.[46] Robert Oppenheimer, who examined the stockownership of a dozen northern railroad companies, found that the same was also true of their financing. The Montt government granted charters to build these railways, and the mining capitalists themselves financed their construction.

Second, the Montt government provided "direct financial aid . . . only [to] the Central Valley lines" and, despite the repeated requests of the mineowners, provided no state assistance in building the lines in the north. Indeed, when the 1857 depression jeopardized completion of the railroads, the Montt government bailed out the depression-endangered stockholders of the Santiago-Valparaiso line by purchasing their stock at its 1852 par price, which was 50 percent above its current market price. This railroad, of course, was vital to the Central Valley landowners and the commercial community in Valparaiso because it moved agricultural produce to Valparaiso for the export and coastal trade. But, at the very same moment, the government denied the request of the northern Copiapó line, which was in similar financial straits, for a loan. In response to the executive branch's "pocket veto" of the loan request, representatives of the Gallo mining family—the Copiapó line's largest stockowner—proposed legislation to congress for such a government loan, but it was tabled.[47]

Third, even the Central Valley railway going north from Santiago to Valparaiso, and the south central line connecting Talca with Santiago, were founded and largely financed privately by the major copper-, silver-, and coal-mine owners. The Cousiño family, with major coal mines and copper smelters in the southern Concepción-

[45] Vitale 1971, III, p. 250.
[46] el Mercurio, September 27, 1849, p. 3; as cited in Oppenheimer 1977, note 3.
[47] Oppenheimer 1976, pp. 151–159; Tornero 1861, p. 125.

Lota district, was the single largest founding stockowner in the San-tiago-Valparaiso Railway Company and the Gallo Goyenechea min-ing family was second largest. The same two families were among the southern Talca-Santiago line's major original stockholders: Eme-terio Goyenechea ranked first, followed by Matías Cousiño, José Tomás Urmeneta, and merchant-banker Domingo Matte. But, unlike the northern mining railways, the vast majority of the Santiago-Valparaiso Railway's 166 stockholders were Central Valley land-owners; 84 percent owned land within the Railway's "area of at-traction," according to Oppenheimer. Similarly, most of the original investors in the Talca-Santiago line were landowners in the south-central flour-milling zone: of the Railway of the South's 121 original stockholders, 46 percent were landowners in the provinces from Talca southward, and another 31 percent were in the two northern adjoining provinces, Curicó and San Fernando, which were well to the south of the traditional agricultural heartland of the Central Val-ley. It was from the grain mills of this south-central zone—in par-ticular, from Talca to Concepción—that most of Chile's flour came.[48]

Thus the Montt regime did invest in the construction of Chile's railways but only in the Central Valley and south-central zones, and then only after their construction was initiated by private investors who were preeminently the leading mineowners of the day (and who were also among the major proprietors of the advanced new flour mills of the south-central zone). But there was no public investment by the Montt government in railroads built in the Norte Chico mining provinces, which in fact provided most of the state's tax revenues. The same pattern, moreover, was apparently repeated in other state infrastructure investments: the construction of irrigation canals, roads, and bridges in the Central Valley, although often carried out by private capital, was also financed heavily by the state. But the south-central milling zone and especially the northern copper- and silver-mining zone were neglected—abandoned, as the mineowners' spokesmen lamented, to "private initiative" while the government spent "millions south of Aconcagua" (i.e. in the provinces of the Central Valley).[49]

---

[48] The stockowner regional percentages were calculated from information given in Oppenheimer 1976, appendices II and III; Oppenheimer 1976, p. 51.
[49] Vitale 1971, III, p. 250; Przeworski 1974, p. 10.

The contradictory interests of the large landed proprietors and emergent capitalists evidently had a specifically regional expression: mining and agrarian capital, on the one hand, seignorial landed property, on the other, apparently had relatively separate geographical areas in which they were preponderant. The result was to render the differential impact of state policies on these contending segments of the class all the more transparent. Their contradictory interests thus tended to deepen the social cleavages between them and to lead to sharp political conflict. It was precisely in the emergent capitalist areas of the country that democratic ideas and revolutionary conspiracies flowered in the 1850s and where the centers of armed struggle against the state were located. What distinguished them, however, was not merely that they expressed contradictory interests but also, and perhaps above all, that they contained, especially in the northern mining towns, quite divergent "societies within a society" with qualitatively different class relations at their core.

Piecing together scattered (and scant) data in various sources suggests that in the area from Talca to Concepción, small holders, independent millers and farmers, and large mechanized flour mills employing wage workers, rather than the large estates of the Central Valley based on a subordinate agrarian tenantry, were relatively dominant. Of the 145 largest estates in the country in 1854, for example, only four were located below Curicó, and it was in this zone that several of the fiercest battles in both the 1851 and 1859 revolts were fought—and were often even led—by the same men.[50]

The main leaders of the armed struggle in the south-central area were not "revolutionary aristocrats," as Encina refers to them, but large flour-mill owners and mining capitalists.[51] Outstanding among them, for example, were two men: Juan Antonio Pando and Juan Alemparte Lastra. Pando was the proprietor of a network of mills along the coast and inland (as well as in the Central Valley), including one of the world's largest mechanized flour mills at Loncomilla. He was, Encina says "the real leader of the revolution between Talca and Concepción" in 1859.[52] After an unsuccessful attempt to organize a revolutionary regime in Talca, based on artisans and laborers

[50] Encina 1949, p. 51; Bauer 1975, p. 176. See Table 2.1.
[51] Encina 1949, p. 316.
[52] Encina 1949, p. 307.

from the *"barrios bajos"* or "lower districts" in October 1859, Pando organized and led mounted guerrilla troops (*"montoneros"*) of small holders, *"huasos,"* laborers (including coal miners), and artisans, numbering over 500 men, who fought the army throughout the zone in the first two months of 1859.[53] Alemparte Lastra was the owner of coal mines near Concepción, coastal and frontier wheat mills, a string of merchant houses, and a fleet of sailing ships in the coastal trade. Under his guerrilla command were between 600 and 800 men (a third of whom were armed only with staves and other handmade weapons) and a couple of cannons. They took Talcahuano, hooked up with other guerrillas in Puchacay, and headed on to take Concepción, the main city of the south, where they were narrowly defeated in a decisive battle with the civic guard. Had they won here, they could have joined the rebel miners' army in the north, led by Pedro León Gallo, thus changing the course of the war.[54]

Another agricultural zone in which there were organized uprisings, both in 1851 and in 1859, was in and around San Felipe in the Valley of Putaendo (to the northeast of Valparaiso). Long known as "an obstinate center of liberal agitation," as Edwards Vives puts it, here, too, armed artisans and peasants fought against the regular troops. This area, lying in a nook to the north of the Central Valley, was also quite distinctive within this heartland of the manorial estate. Dairy products, fruits and vegetables, and wine were produced for Santiago's and Valparaiso's markets, not by a labor service tenantry on the large estate but, according to Arnold J. Bauer, by independent "yeoman farmers," among whom there was a relatively "equitable distribution of land." Roughly half the land of San Felipe was held in medium and small holdings (6–200 hectares) compared with just over a tenth in that category in nearby Caupolicán, the latter being a veritable "paradigm for central Chile."[55] Thus this prosperous yeomanry—now confronted by the competitive expansion of the manorial estate, urged on by the large flour-mill owners and mine-owners, and possessed of the opportunity and capacity for self-organization—fought back in armed insurrection against the state itself.

The city of San Felipe was a principal center of artisan production,

---

[53] Edwards Vives 1932, pp. 257, 285.
[54] V. Figueroa 1925–1931, I, pp. 343–344; Edwards Vives 1932, pp. 278–279.
[55] Bauer 1975, pp. 126–127; Bauer and Johnson 1977, pp. 85–86, 90.

and in 1851, the Society of Equality (in the only place where it had a base outside Santiago) led a "popular mutiny" that deposed the intendant and established a "Committee of Neighbors" to govern this provincial capital until they were defeated by the Los Andes and Putaendo civic guards. Again, in 1859, artisans and laborers "indoctrinated by the Society of Equality since 1851" and led by bourgeois "youth imbued with the doctrines" of the constituent assembly, took over the local garrison of the civic guard, "requisitioned money and fiscal specie" from the Los Andes treasury, installed their own intendant, recruited troops in the neighboring countryside, and went on to take Putaendo. After five days of "obstinate and bloody resistance," the combined troops of the Los Andes civic guard and a regular army division of the line defeated the insurrectionaries on February 18, 1859.[56]

The inquilinos, unlike their yeoman and small holder countrymen, engaged in no known insurgency. They were subject to the close supervision and immediate discipline of the estate's managerial staff, on the one hand, and insulated from the fluctuation and insecurities of the market, on the other. In comparison with these independent commodity producers, the inquilinos had little opportunity or motive to revolt. What, however, transformed yeomen and independent cultivators from, as Marx once called their counterparts in France, a "sack of potatoes" with no unifying connections among them into a rebellious and insurgent force? These peasants were relatively scattered on their own plots, and they possessed no autonomous village community to provide them with a base for organization. The countryside of Chile, under the dominion of the large estate, spawned no independent or self-governing peasant villages. As we stressed earlier, local civil and military officials and landlords were all but identical.

But the fact that the revolts were based precisely where market towns and such cities as Concepción and Talca and their artisan and laborer populations or the newly established flour mills rather than the old estates were located suggests an answer: The millers and small proprietors both faced the competitive expansion of the landed estates and were indebted to them; that the landlord was thus their common antagonist was relatively clear, especially as they met with

[56] Edwards Vives 1932, pp. 65, 28–82.

each other in the local markets and nearby towns, where they could share their immediate grievances and at the same time be agitated by the artisans, whose vocal demands for political rights they now heard. Add to this the urging and support of a revolutionary segment of the dominant class itself, which could assist and even arm them against local authorities, and we can see that these small holders and yeoman farmers had both the opportunity to recognize and the capacity to act on their common interests and their shared antagonism toward the landlords.

The epicenter of the revolutionary movement in 1859, however, was in the northern mining provinces of Atacama and Coquimbo, a relatively compact and remote region of the country where the class relations unique to early capitalism were decisive in the entire production process. On this basis, and because of the region's "geo-economic" reputation as silver and copper miner to the world, there was erected a distinctive "frontier" society of free men with a strong democratic strain. Here the class barriers between "master" and "man," *patrón* and *peón*, landlord and tenant, were foreign to the new men of rough vigor, hard work, and boundless ambition, "drawn from all social classes" and indeed from many nations, who had come there in recent years. A visitor to Copiapó, capital city of Atacama in 1846, remarked that it was a "cosmopolitan town . . . where men from England, France, Chile, Germany, Italy, and all the neighboring republics converged. . . . Copiapó had nothing in common with Chile but the political constitution, which it did not always observe, and its laws, which it broke more than a few times."[57] In a sense, what happened in the years preceding the outbreak of the armed struggles against the state was the emergence of a veritable situation of—to use Lenin's phrase—"dual power," but one that above all split the dominant class itself along deep internal fissures and spatial divisions, long before the civil war itself erupted. The Norte Chico had probably become not only an enclave of bourgeois civilization but also a second center of political sovereignty, upheld in practice by the mineowning families whose writ was all but local law.[58]

---

[57] Edwards Vives 1932, p. 258; Pérez Rosales 1886, p. 191.

[58] Charles Tilly, explicitly borrowing from Lenin (by way of Trotsky), argues that in general it is precisely the emergence of what he calls centers of "multiple sovereignty" that is the essence of a revolutionary situation. Originating first in a struggle

Although some of the silver and copper mines were highly mechanized and worked by over a hundred miners, most apparently were small establishments typically employing fewer than a dozen men.[59] Production relations in the mines and foundries were based not only on wage workers but also on a variety of mixed forms of production involving (as it still did in England during the same period) intermediary contracting and subcontracting relations between capital and labor. It was, apparently, the *pirquineros*—quasi-independent commodity producers—who typified the northern miners. Usually the owners of their own equipment, they worked either independently or in association with others, as "equal producers with the same right in the final product"; or, if a *pirquinero* was the legal owner of the claim, he might, while working alongside the men, retain a special share of the product and the right to hire and fire new workers and exert his authority in the labor process. This was, as Vicuña Mackenna called it, the "Californian" method of production. Still other *pirquineros* were dependent on merchant capitalists or incipient bankers, the so-called *habilitadores*, who supplied them with equipment and foodstuffs as an advance against a share of production. Often these miners became, in the course of such transactions, transformed into wage workers in all but name. The immediate employer of many miners was often another miner, who was at once boss, technician, and fellow worker, and in turn employee of the mineowner.[60]

Outside of mining but thoroughly integrated with it were the small production units that abounded in the region, some being workshops employing several craftsmen and artisans under the direction of the shopowner himself or a contractor of the capitalist. Still others were simply one-man artisan shops, where proprietor and worker were one, all producing or repairing the array of tools, supplies, equipment, and machinery involved in mining, smelting, and transporting the ores.[61] Here was the objective basis for a sense of identity between

---

among contending factions within the governing class itself, a situation of multiple sovereignty in turn opens the way for popular movements against the state (1975).

[59] Oppenheimer 1976, p. 233; see Vayssiere 1973, p. 14.

[60] Dobb 1947, pp. 259–272; Segall 1953, pp. 25, 62, 67–68.

[61] Edwards Vives 1932, p. 289. I use such phrases as "many," "some," and "often" to emphasize that existing historical works have little detailed data on production relations in the mines in mid-nineteenth-century Chile.

workman and capitalist, small mineowner and large—conditioned also by the quick change of fortune that mining made possible.[62] In such a world was nourished the bourgeois individualist, Andrew Ure's "self-willed and intractable workman," whom capital was later destined to subordinate and transform into its mere appendage, as it had largely done already in the coal mines at Lota and Coronel in the south of the country.[63] For now, however, the mutuality of interest between worker and capitalist; artisan, craftsman, and shop-owner; and miner and mineowner, and the clarity with which the fate of all of them depended on the same industry, whose fluctuations and fortunes determined their own, was more sharply defined than the inherent class contradictions that were soon to divide them.

It was in this virtual enclave of bourgeois civilization that mining capital came to be the bearer and personification of radical democratic consciousness—and even of utopian socialist ideology—in mid-nineteenth-century Chile. Throughout the 1850s, the intelligentsia who led the struggle for democratization of the state apparently were mainly mineowners or their scions. But because they *were* an intelligentsia, the ideas they held, the doctrines they debated, and the principles they espoused had a relative automony of their own. Their commitments and passions were no less real—and had no less a social impact—for being explicable. They were poets, dramatists, historians, philosophers, translators, journalists, and novelists, as well as political agitators and organizers, and finally revolutionaries. They moved in a milieu in which ideas counted and conscious choice became necessary between the rationalist, humanist, and democratic currents of that revolutionary bourgeois epoch in Europe and the

[62] I stress their mutual interests here, but of course there were also contradictions and antagonisms between small mineowners and large ones. Aside from the competition between them, the proprietors of small mines were often compelled to sell their raw ores to the major mining companies for processing because few had their own smelters; they thereby had a portion of their profits appropriated from them by large capital. See Przeworski 1974.

[63] Ure 1835, p. 20. Little is known about, and I have neglected, the unskilled day laborers (*jornaleros* and *changos*) in the mines. Many worked as other miners' "beasts of burden," carrying enormous loads of rock on their backs up through "a succession of galleries," scarcely able to breathe in the subterranean air, of whom "Jotabeche" (a major mid-century literary figure and himself a Copiapó mineowner) exclaimed: they "appeared as if they belonged to a race more accursed than humanity" (as cited in Fernández Canque 1973, p. 82).

clerical and reactionary justifications of inequality and authoritarian rule. Though mining capital clearly left its indelible stamp on their intellectual circles, some men who were attached to the Reform Club or Society of Equality, the Union Club or Caupolicán Society, were neither capitalist nor artisan but the sons of supreme landed families—including several who were to appear later at the helm of state, still clearly influenced by the ideological currents and political conflicts of their youth.

WHO WERE THE LEADING INSURRECTIONARIES?

It should be emphasized that not only did developing capital determine the direction of the radical democratic movement by the underlying social relations it was bringing into being, but its most active and conspicuous leaders and participants were also personally members of the bourgeoisie. Certainly, we must be wary as Paul Baran observes, of attaching decisive importance "to the class background of *individuals* participating in revolutionary events. Too many random factors influencing the decisions and behavior of individual members of different classes are at work for a close relation to be found between the *class content* of a historical movement," as Baran rightly remarks, "and the *class origin* of possibly even significant numbers of its participants and leaders." In particular, this observation would seem to apply to bourgeois revolutions, as Baran argues: "Traditionally . . . [the bourgeoisie] . . . as *individuals* have nowhere taken active part in *revolutionary politics*. Indeed, it is probably one of the outstanding characteristics of the capitalist class and is closely related to its economic and ideological habitat that it customarily operates on the political stage—particularly in times of upheaval—through retainers, agents, and allies, rather than directly through its own members."[64]

But whatever the general validity of this proposition, it is not borne out in mid-nineteenth-century Chilean experience, as I have emphasized. On the contrary, the young bourgeoisie of Chile did *not*, in Baran's words, substitute "their money for their persons in

[64] Baran 1957, p. 153, italics in original.

the struggle for freedom,'' as their counterparts may have done elsewhere.[65] Rather, they personally fought and bled, and suffered imprisonment or deportation, in the insurrectionary struggles of the 1850s—perhaps precisely because of their specific "economic and ideological habitat" in mid-nineteenth-century Chile. Indeed, the roll call of the liberal and radical democratic agitators, organizers, and insurrectionaries of the 1850s reads almost like a "Who's Who" of the Chilean mining bourgeoisie at the time.

To delineate the class and intraclass situations of the most conspicuous leaders of the revolutionary struggles against the Montt regime, I gathered and analyzed biographical and kinship data on all such persons whose names appeared in any of the major historical works covering that period and also added several names discovered in the course of the biographical research itself. Altogether, these came to 44 men. I found no biographical data on 5 of them; of the 39 men on whom I found relevant class data, 4 were artisans and 1 a small holder, whereas the 34 others were from prominent families of the dominant class itself. The names of this sample of 44 leading insurrectionaries are listed, with their individual class situations and other relevant biographical data, in Table 2.1.[66]

In both insurrections, 1851 and 1859, the modal revolutionary activist was himself a mineowner or from a mineowning family; overall, we find that two out of three of the leading insurrectionaries of the 1850s belonged to the mining bourgeoisie. When those who were identified as the actual leaders of armed revolutionary bands are distinguished from other activists, we find that the mineowners also predominated among the armed fighters in both insurrections,

---

[65] Baran 1957, p. 153.

[66] The names of the liberal and radical democratic activists (agitators, organizers, and insurrectionaries) in Table 2.1 were drawn from Edwards Vives 1932; Encina 1949; P. Figueroa 1895; Galdames 1941; and Vitale 1971. Many important 1850s activists do not appear in these works on the period. My investigation of the biographies of the leading Balmacedistas of a generation later reveals that although many of them were active also in the 1850s struggles, these works do not mention them or describe their activities. See Tables 4.1 and 4.6. Aside from the relevant biographical data I obtained from these works, the major biographical sources I consulted were V. Figueroa 1925–1931, and, secondarily, P. Figueroa 1888, 1887–1901, 1889, and 1900. Manuel Moreno, a Chilean graduate student in sociology at the University of California at Los Angeles, assisted me in this biographical research and in that reported in Tables 4.1–4.5 in chapter 4.

Table 2.1. Leading Insurrectionaries of the 1850s: Their Individual Class Situation and Insurrectionary Activity

Insurrectionaries	Mineowner[a]	Flour-Mill Owner	Industrialist	Banker	Merchant	Landowner	State Official[b]	Intellectual[c]	Artisan	Small Holder	No Data	Leader of 1851 Insurrection	Leader of 1859 Insurrection	Leader of Armed Band
Juan Alemparte Lastra	X	X			X			X				X	X	X
José Antonio Alemparte	X	X				X						X	X	X
Juan Nicolas Álvarez	X											X		
Antonio Arce	X	X				X							X	X
Santiago Arcos Arlegui				X								X		
Justo Arteaga Cuevas	X						X	X				X	X	X
Bernardino Barahona					X							X	X	X
Francisco Bilbao								X				X		
Anselmo Carabantes	X		X										X	
José Miguel Carrera Fontecilla	X											X	X	X
Olegario Carvallo											X			
José María de la Cruz							X					X	X	X
Isidoro Errázuriz Errázuriz								X					X	

Federico Errázuriz Zañartu				x		x	x
José Dolores Fernandois					x	x	x
Angel Custodio Gallo Goyenechea	x					x	
Juan Guillermo Gallo Goyenechea	x					x	x
Pedro León Gallo Goyenechea	x		x			x	x
Tomás Gallo Goyenechea	x					x	
Abdón Garín				x		x	x
José Victorino Lastarría	x		x		x	x	x
Pedro Letelier					x		x
Eusebio Lillo Robles	x	x	x		x	x	x
Felipe Santiago Matta	x					x	x
Guillermo Matta	x					x	
Manuel Antonio Matta	x		x			x	
Horacio Monteola			x				
Nicolas Munizaga	x				x	x	x
Pablo Muñoz			x			x	x
Rosario Ortíz				x		x	x
Juan Antonio Pando Urízar	x x				x	x	x

Table 2.1 (*cont.*)

Insurrectionaries	Mineowner[a]	Flour-Mill Owner	Industrialist	Banker	Merchant	Landowner	State Official[b]	Intellectual[c]	Artisan	Small Holder	No Data	Leader of 1851 Insurrection	Leader of 1859 Insurrection	Leader of Armed Band
José Dolores Passi	X						X						X	
Bernardino Pradel											X		X	X
Domingo Santa María								X				X	X	X
José Sierra									X				X	X
Vicente Subercaseaux Mercado	X		X		X	X								
Pedro Ugarte							X					X	X	X
Ramón Antonio Vallejos										X			X	X
Pedro Félix Vicuña Aguirre	X							X				X	X	X
Benjamín Vicuña Mackenna	X							X				X	X	X
Benjamín Videla Pinochet			X									X	X	X
Pedro Pablo Zapata									X			X		X
José Antonio Zavala	X												X	
Bruno Zavala Fredes	X												X	X

[a] Justo Arteaga and Antonio Arce had unspecified mining connections but were definitely identified as mineowners. Anselmo Carabantes was the owner of a foundry in Copiapó that manufactured mining equipment.

[b] Justo Arteaga and José María de la Cruz were high military officers. José Dolores Passi and Pedro Ugarte were judges. Members of congress are not indicated.

[c] Journalists, novelists, essayists, poets, and so forth.

and overwhelmingly so in 1859; for the 1850s as a whole, two out of three leaders of guerrilla bands, and the same proportion of other activists, belonged to the mining bourgeoisie. What is also striking is the finding that journalists, essayists, novelists, poets, and other intellectuals were conspicuous among the leading insurrectionaries in both 1851 and 1859; overall, one in three of them were identifiably "intellectuals," and they even made up a somewhat higher proportion of the leading guerrilla combatants than they did among the other activists. (See Table 2.2.)

A sizable contingent of large landowners also appeared among the leading insurrectionaries in both 1851 and 1859; indeed, among the 1850s combat leaders, one in four were identifiably large landowners. (See Table 2.2.) But when their intraclass situation is probed more deeply, this apparently anomalous presence of landed aristocrats fighting alongside the mining bourgeoisie against their own state is explained.

If the leading insurrectionaries who were from the mining bourgeoisie, or who were south-central flour-mill owners, are sorted out, these seemingly "revolutionary aristocrats" all but disappear: it turns out that, in fact, 4 of the 7 insurrectionary landowners were also from the mining bourgeoisie; the fifth landowner was a (non-mineowning) flour-mill owner, which leaves a proportion of landowners outside this bourgeois segment amounting only to 6 percent of the 34 leading insurrectionaries of the 1850s. Of additional interest, moreover, is the finding that most of the revolutionary intellectuals represented in our sample were also drawn from mineowning families; of the 11 such intellectuals among the leading insurrectionaries, 8 were themselves from the mining bourgeoisie. (See Table 2.3.)

Now, if the mineowners, grain-mill owners, and industrialists are understood as the personification of "productive capital" at this historic moment, then 71 percent of the leading insurrectionaries were drawn from that specific capitalist segment of the dominant class. In short, this was an abortive bourgeois revolution led and participated in directly by the bourgeoisie itself. Their epitome was Pedro León Gallo, 27-year-old scion of the silver- and copper-mining family of Copiapó, poet and translator of Victor Hugo's verses, founder of the Constituent Club where "artisans learned not only their civic obligations," as Edwards Vives puts it, "but also their

Table 2.2. Percentage of Leading Insurrectionaries of the 1850s in Specified Intraclass Situations, by Year of Insurrection and Combat Role (Separately Sorted)[a]

Year of Insurrection and Combat Role	Mine-owners[b]	Flour-Mill Owners	Indus-trialists	Bankers	Mer-chants	Land-owners	State Officials	Intel-lectuals	(N)
1851									
Leaders of armed bands	57	21	14	7	14	21	21	43	(14)
Other activists	33	0	0	17	0	17	0	50	(6)
All insurrectionaries	50	15	10	10	10	20	15	45	(20)[c]
1859									
Leaders of armed bands	71	23	12	0	6	29	12	35	(17)
Other activists	80	0	20	0	10	10	10	30	(10)
All insurrectionaries	74	15	15	0	7	22	11	33	(27)[c]
1850s total									
Leaders of armed bands	65	20	10	5	10	25	15	35	(20)
Other activists	64	0	14	7	7	14	7	29	(14)
All insurrectionaries	65	12	12	6	9	21	12	32	(34)[c]

Note. N = number of insurrectionaries in each category.

[a] Each individual is separately sorted on each category, so an individual can appear, depending on his attributes, in more than one intraclass category.

[b] Three individuals who had unspecified mining connections or who were involved in the mining industry but were not identified as actual mineowners or their kin are included here. See Table 2.1, note a.

[c] Four artisans and a small holder and another five insurrectionaries about whom no biographical data were found are not included in this table. See Table 2.1.

Table 2.3. Percentage of Leading Insurrectionaries of the 1850s in Specified Intraclass Situations, by Year of Insurrection and Combat Role (Cumulatively Sorted)[a]

Year of Insurrection and Combat Role	Mine-owners[b]	Flour-Mill Owners	Indus-trialists	Bankers	Mer-chants	Land-owners	State Officials	Intel-lectuals	(N)
1851									
Leaders of armed bands	57	7	7	0	7	0	14	7	(14)
Other activists	33	0	0	17	0	17	0	33	(6)
All insurrectionaries	50	5	5	5	5	5	10	15	(20)[c]
1859									
Leaders of armed bands	71	6	6	0	0	6	6	6	(17)
Other activists	80	0	0	0	0	0	10	10	(10)
All insurrectionaries	74	4	4	0	0	4	7	7	(27)[c]
1850s total									
Leaders of armed bands	65	5	5	0	5	5	10	5	(20)
Other activists	64	0	0	7	0	7	7	14	(14)
All insurrectionaries	65	3	3	3	3	6	9	9	(34)[c]

Note. N = number of insurrectionaries in each category.

[a] In this table, the intraclass categories are ordered by their analytical priority and individuals are cumulatively sorted so that first, all of the mineowners (and individuals with other mining connections) are separated; second, the remaining individuals are sorted to separate the flour-mill owners; third, the remaining individuals are sorted to separate the industrialists, and so on.

[b] Three individuals who had unspecified mining connections or who were involved in the mining industry but were not identified as actual mineowners or their kin are included here. See Table 2.1, note a.

[c] Four artisans and a small holder and another five insurrectionaries about whom no biographical data were found are not included in this table. See Table 2.1.

revolutionary methods and even military exercises." Gallo commanded and organized the insurrectionary army based in the nothern provinces, which "represented the most accentuated radical aspirations" in the civil war itself.[67]

In the workshops and foundries of Copiapó and Caldera, the insurrectionary miners and artisans manufactured and repaired their own rifles and bullets and even cast several cannons and projectiles. Their disciplined revolutionary army—numbering some 2,000 men and organized into infantry, cavalry, and artillery regiments—took the offensive against the regular army. They transformed the north into a "liberated zone" whose revolutionary regime imposed taxes, administered justice, and even minted its own "revolutionary pesos." After four months of battle during which the rebels threatened to carry the insurrection into the heart of Chile, they were decisively defeated on April 29, 1859, at Cerro Grande.

In a nation of less than a million and a half citizens, the civil war of 1859 took 5,000 lives. There were, as *el Mercurio's* editor Santos Tornero reported at the time, "few families in the country that did not have someone who was killed or wounded, thrown into preventive detention, imprisoned, or persecuted" during the four long months of armed insurrection against the state. After the defeat of the rebels, the regime deported 2,000 persons and meted out death sentences *in absentia* to hundreds of alleged conspirators and revolutionaries whose names were publicly posted on wanted lists throughout the country. None of the leading bourgeois revolutionaries was executed, but most of them were imprisoned or deported, or they escaped into exile. Countless artisans, miners, and peasants, however—"obscure and nameless men," as Tornero wrote—were executed in Talca, Concepción, San Felipe, Valparaiso, Santiago, Copiapó, and La Serena. "Execution is the price the people pay, because they have no voice and their sacrifice leaves no trace."[68]

The Meaning of the Civil War

Is it true that the sacrifice of these men left no trace? What were the historic consequences of these mid-nineteenth-century insurrec-

[67] Edwards Vives 1932, pp. 262–265.
[68] Amunategui Solar 1946, p. 122; Tornero 1861, pp. 190–194, 304–306.

tionary struggles, for whom artisans and peasants provided the mass base and the mining bourgeoisie the resolute leadership? In that question inheres one crucial answer. Above all, because the Chilean bourgeoisie was not even allowed to trade its right to rule for the right to make money and thus to subordinate itself and society to retrograde and repressive political forms, the 1850s civil war was to have enduring significance as a momentous contribution to the advancement and consolidation of civil liberties and political rights in Chile. The very clashes between emergent capital and the hegemonic agrarian elements reinforced the political divisions within the dominant class and provided the basis for the eventual formation of a bourgeois democratic state. Despite their defeat in armed confrontation, and precisely because the mining capitalists and their allies twice demonstrated their readiness and capacity for insurrection on behalf of their democratic aspirations, they were soon to enter the lists as organized political parties and to invigorate a hitherto docile and dependent congress with their continuing struggles to make the state democratic. They thereby laid the basis for the relatively durable and vital constitutional democracy that was gradually to replace the authoritarian and hierarchical state against which their struggles were aimed at mid-century.

The immediate result of the 1859 insurrection's defeat was, as we have seen, severe repression. It was followed immediately by the juridical expansion of the executive powers of the state, prohibition of assembly, closure of the press, and virtual abolition of legal limits to arbitrary arrest, search and seizure, preventive detention, and so forth, codified in the so-called "law of civic responsibility." The suffrage was also even further restricted by new and increased property and income qualifications for the vote.[69] But in the course of the next decade, the struggle for democratization was renewed, as many erstwhile revolutionaries, who were granted amnesty by the new president in 1861, returned to active intervention in the political arena. In 1863, several won seats in the chamber of deputies. In 1865, the "law of civil responsiblity" was abolished. In 1866, Pedro León Gallo, former commander of the revolutionary army of the north, ran for the presidency, though unsuccessfully, and in subsequent years several *Constituyentes*, including Gallo and Vicuña

[69] Amunategui Solar 1946, pp. 149–157.

Mackenna, were elected to the senate. The latter also ran for the presidency, and lost, in 1875, as the "people's candidate," with the radical slogan: "justice and liberty, bread and progress."[70] In fact in 1870, when one of the original democratic partisans of the 1850s, Federico Errázuriz Zañartu, was elected president, it was paradoxically as the *conservative* candidate; he was opposed by a coalition of liberal and radical democrats behind the candidacy of José Tomás Urmeneta, whose electoral support came almost exclusively from the northern mining and south-central milling provinces.[71]

The political rise of the democrats was undergirded by a renewed burst of capital accumulation during the early 1870s, based mainly in the exploitation of new silver mines near Caracoles and nitrate plants in the Peruvian territory of Antofogasta. This and the following decade were also, in the judgment of economic historians, "among the most progressive that Chilean industry has ever known": a host of new manufacturing industries were established to supply the growing internal market, many using steam-driven machinery.[72] Concomitant with this accelerated growth of mining and manufacturing capital, and led by the political generation formed in the 1850s, there was a relatively rapid transformation of the state structure and the increased expansion of civil liberties and political freedoms.

Successively, during the 1870s, the presidency was restricted to one five-year term of office; the freedoms of press, of assembly, and of association were guaranteed; a system of proportional representation in congressional elections was instituted; the executive authority of the state was increasingly hedged in, its extraordinary powers all but abolished; the chamber of deputies and senate gained a majority of the seats in the council of state, hitherto a docile instrument of the presidency, and measures were enacted to assure the responsibility of the president's ministers to parliament; intendants, governors, and other public officials were prohibited from simultaneously holding legislative office; senators were now elected directly by the provinces; administration of provincial elections and

---

[70] Orrego Vicuña 1939, p. 32.

[71] Amunategui Solar 1946, pp. 178–179. Errázuriz Zañartu, scion of the landed aristocracy, had been deported for his participation in the 1851 "insurrectionary agitations" (Galdames 1941, pp. 314–315).

[72] Rippy and Pfeiffer 1948, p. 300.

candidate approval was taken from the intendant and lodged in a local board of "major taxpayers"; other prerogatives of intendants and governors (and thereby of the executive of the state) were abolished; and finally the suffrage was extended to all *men* without property or income qualifications. In short, the old centralized authoritarian state went through a "gradual" but rapid political metamorphosis into one possessing the most basic features of bourgeois democracy.

But if it is unquestionably true that the insurrectionary *struggles* of the 1850s had these lasting effects in the impetus they gave and the bases they laid for political democracy, the defeat of the insurrection also mattered profoundly: it restricted Chile's chances for relatively independent capitalist development. It set in motion the decline of productive capital in the Chilean social formation and what may be termed its increasingly "subordinate coalescence" within the dominant class.[73] This, of course, cannot be "empirically demonstrated." But the specific historical circumstances in which Chile's abortive revolution occurred indicate how crucial its real triumph might have been.

These mid-century insurrections, as we have seen, reflected and embodied emergent capitalist relations of production, and the subsequent modifications in the structure of the state in the 1870s were also conditioned by continuing economic growth. These were years, however, in which the vulnerability of Chilean export capitalism also became increasingly evident. British commercial capital had long since established itself securely in the international brokerage and trade of Chile's mineral and grain exports, much of which went directly to English ports; and during the 1870s, and especially after Chile wrested the nitrate territories of Tarapacá and Antofogasta from Peru and Bolivia in the War of the Pacific, English capital took increasing hold of nitrate production itself, erecting its own plants and constructing its own railroads to carry these products to the sea for export to far-flung international markets; and it was now heavily involved in Chile's own coastal trade for the mining areas of the north.

Simultaneously, the penetration of capitalism in the countryside meant, as has been emphasized, the accelerated incorporation of

[73] See Zeitlin and Ratcliff forthcoming.

relatively independent renters and small holders into a labor-service tenantry. Thus the paradox and problem of Chilean historical development is that the so-called "commercialization of agriculture" reinforced the social dominion of the large landowners in the countryside precisely at a historical moment when the development of capitalism was also creating, in the mineowners, a rich, restive, and thoroughly bourgeois adversary for social supremacy and state power. Put differently, capitalist development led simultaneously to the landowners' successful imposition of new forms of social domination, in the guise of "precapitalist" and "archaic" seignorial relations, and to the mining bourgeoisie's struggle for the expansion of civil liberties and political freedom and the construction of a democratic state. Chilean history took, as Lenin might have said, the "Prussian road" in the countryside and the "American road" politically.[74] What might have happened if the insurrectionaries of 1859 had won and the armed artisans, miners, and peasants, led by radical bourgeois democrats, had actually taken state power? What difference would it have made for Chile's economic development if its bourgeois revolution had not been aborted?

The prevailing image of the Montt regime, as was noted earlier, is that it represented, in Frank's words, one of Chile's "two major attempts at national development" under state aegis, second only to Balmaceda's heroic efforts some three decades later. In Frank's interpretation, for instance, the insurrection against Montt was really a revolt against Montt's attempt at national development; the revolt was led, so he says, by "definite interest groups" in Chile, which were created by the "metropolis-satellite structure of the world capitalist system. . . . [They] found themselves drawn to support, above and beyond any other policy, one that served to render Chile a still more dependent satellite of the world capitalist metropolis. It is not surprising, therefore, to find these groups taking advantage of the weakness of the government caused by the 1857 world depression to revolt against President Montt and his national development policies."[75] Frank is here following Claudio Véliz and Pinto Santa Cruz (though they do not share his theory of the "world capitalist sys-

[74] Lenin 1934, pp. 180ff., 254ff.
[75] Frank 1967, p. 73.

tem''). In their view, as Pinto Santa Cruz says, the revolt came from "the advanced liberal and democratic political and intellectual elements of the time who were irreconcilably opposed to Montt's . . . initiatives to capitalize, via the state, the exceptional revenues from mining."[76] Véliz, too, argues that the insurrections against Montt stemmed "largely from the opposition to [his] strong centralist attitude toward state intervention in the economy; the opposition came from the liberal—and, *of course, free trade*—nuclei close to the export of minerals and agricultural products in the north and south of the country . . . situated in Copiapó and Concepción."[77]

What these authors fail entirely to recognize, however, is that it was precisely, as we have seen, the Montt government's use of public revenues coming almost completely from mining to construct infrastructure for the Central Valley while neglecting the mining provinces themselves that provoked the mining bourgeoisie's wrath. It was by no means merely Montt's so-called "strong statist attitude" or "state intervention" and public capital investment in the economy that was crucial in fomenting their revolt but how, and on behalf of whom, this state intervention and investment were carried out.

Nor, as these scholars also assume, was there a sort of timeless and intrinsic community of interest among the so-called "exporters of primary commodities" (agricultural and mineral) and "importers," all of whom, as Véliz asserts, "were almost *by definition* [*sic*] ardent supporters of laissez-faire liberalism, because, unless they completely misunderstood their own immediate interest, they had no option but to oppose any tax or restriction on the free movement of goods across international frontiers."[78] It was, further, "for this reason [that] foreign investors and the leaders of the Chilean economic tripod [mining exporters of the north, agricultural exporters of the south, and the large import houses of Santiago and Valparaiso] spoke the same language: *their interests coincided and no conflict among them was possible. . . .* The epitome of the Chilean was he who abhorred any attempt to protect incipient national industry."[79]

What these interpretations—none based on systematic historical

---

[76] Pinto Santa Cruz 1959, p. 22.
[77] Véliz 1963, p. 242, italics added.
[78] Véliz 1980, p. 183, italics added; also see Véliz 1963, pp. 237ff.
[79] Véliz 1963, p. 241, italics added.

research—ignore are the specific historical circumstances in which the so-called export-import "tripod" stood in mid-nineteenth-century Chile. For, in reality, the leading copper-mine owners were hostile to the Montt regime not only because it served the immediate interests of the Central Valley landowners at their own expense but also because it failed to assist and protect them in their intensive competition with British capitalists. In particular, and contrary to the assumption of these writers, the mineowners and their spokesmen urged the government repeatedly, and without success, to stimulate the growth of the copper smelting and refining industry, and of domestic manufacturing, through protectionist legislation and selective taxation, subsidies, and direct state investment.

From the late 1840s on, it will be recalled, major Chilean copper and coal magnates and south-central flour-mill owners were competing with increasing effectiveness against British mining and agricultural interests both at home and abroad. Chile's coal—exploited efficiently by Matías Cousiño, Juan Alemparte, and others—was displacing British imported coal from its dominant position in Chile's market, and Chile's advanced copper smelting plants, some purchased from German and American manufacturers, were competing effectively with the Welsh smelters in Swansea, which had hitherto monopolized the processing of the raw ores shipped there, often in British bottoms, from Chilean mines. Chilean flour-milling firms—especially those owned by Cousiño, Alemparte, and Juan Antonio Pando (the latter two, leaders of the 1851 and 1859 agrarian revolts in the south)—were displacing British-owned mills and merchant houses as the leading flour producers for export markets and for the coastal trade with the northern mining provinces.[80]

British capitalists responded by imploring the assistance of Her Majesty's Government against their tough new Chilean competitors. As early as 1846, for instance, a decade before the most advanced smelting plants were installed in Chile, the British embassy reported home that recently opened Chilean foundries and smelters would be "a great detriment" to British smelting and shipping interests. The next year, 39 commercial and mining firms in Great Britain solicited

[80] Vitale 1971, iii, p. 310. The Millowners Association (Asociación de Molineros), organized by Matías Cousiño, was a "gigantic export trust, [which] dominated the wheat and flour market of California during the gold fever" (Bunster 1965, p. 130).

their government's defense of their interests, and of their own infant smelting industry, against the new Chilean smelting industry. It was, they said, prejudicial both to the return shipping trade of minerals transported to Swansea, Liverpool, and other British copper smelting and milling centers, and to the latter, which largely depended on their processing of Chilean ores. Chile's copper smelting plants, the British businessmen declared, were now producing, "instead of raw copper ores [to be shipped to Great Britain for processing], large quantities of ingots and bars for sale to Europe to supply copper and brass manufacturers there, to the detriment of British smelting and manufacturing interests."[81] Similarly, in 1859, at the behest of coal-mine owners in England, the British embassy urged that Chile's special taxes on imported coal be rescinded, since they would have "disastrous results for all British interests." A few years later Britain's coal industry, as the British consul reported home in 1862, dumped coal exports in Chile's northern mining districts at a loss in an attempt to stymie Chile's own coal production, but it had only momentary success.[82]

Simultaneously, Chilean copper capitalists recognized that their growing smelting industry needed the state's "discreet protection" to thrive in competition with the British. "It is well known," Atacama mining capital's newspaper *El Copiapino* proclaimed on October 8, 1857, "that three or four English houses control the market in copper and create a rise and fall [in prices and demand] whenever they want." A decade later, precisely the same theme was still being enunciated: *El Ferrocarril*, whose editor was the son of a leading 1850s revolutionary, editorialized that "Chile owes the riches that have raised it above other former Spanish colonies . . . to its copper mines, which have supplied the world with more than half of its consumption. . . . But this product of our industry is subject to a monopoly that reduces our own profits by transportation fees, commissions and other charges invented by the English smelters. . . . Is this bearable in a country that has the means to free itself from this abhorrent monopoly? . . . The monopoly of the English foundries makes them not only the arbiters of the price of our copper but

---

[81] I have retranslated these passages from the Spanish translation of the original English documents given in Ramírez Necochea 1960b, p. 65.

[82] Ramírez Necochea 1960b, p. 87; Centner 1942, p. 78.

allows them to limit the growth of our mining and to subject the real wealth of our society to the interests of foreign speculators. Is it bearable that a country which has all the means to smelt the ores and to refine them into their purest form for shipment to India, China, Europe, and throughout the world, be fettered by a foreign monopoly?''[83]

Of the state policies proposed to deal with this situation, one was widely discussed among copper capitalists: a proposal to establish a state bank to provide the necessary loans and credits for Chilean mining investment independent of the English houses, and to reduce their already heavy role in the credit system as a whole (which included the issuance of bills of exchange, promissory notes, and currency). One of the leading advocates of a state bank, and of political measures to protect Chilean manufacturing from British competition, was copper-mine owner and newspaperman Pedro Félix Vicuña Aguirre, whom we met earlier as ''the author of the revolution of 1851,'' and again as a leading participant (with his son Benjamín Vicuña Mackenna) in the 1859 insurrection.[84] ''Chile's calling,'' he wrote, ''was to be, not merely agricultural but industrial.''[85] This political line, continued by his editorial successors at el Mercurio throughout the 1860s, and by El Ferrocarril, was that Chilean ''products cannot compete with European imports'' without protection, and laws were needed to limit the now unfettered importation of ''foreign manufactured products.''[86] In particular, Vicuña Aguirre wanted taxes abolished on the production and export of copper bars but retained on the export of ingots and crude ores so as to encourage the domestic smelting and refining industry. He urged that the government also pay a ''premium for the production of refined copper like that sold by the Swansea plants. . . . [The state must] protect

---

[83] Ramírez Necochea 1960b, p. 87; Vitale 1971, III, pp. 309–310. El Ferrocarril's editor during these years was Justo Arteaga Alemparte, the son of Justo Arteaga Cuevas, and also the nephew (apparently), through his mother, of Juan Alemparte Lastra (V. Figueroa 1925–1931, I, p. 624).

[84] Encina 1949, p. 55.

[85] As quoted from an undated article in el Mercurio in 1861, in Jobet 1955, p. 49. Vicuña Aguirre's first public call for the creation of a state bank appeared in a series of articles in el Mercurio in 1845; his major work on the subject appered in 1862. See Vicuña Aguirre 1845, 1862.

[86] As quoted in Ramírez Necochea 1960b, p. 89. Vicuña Aguirre was el Mercurio's first editor and a regular contributor afterwards.

the smelting industry and coal mines," he wrote in 1861, "and the railroads run by the government must facilitate the transport of these voluminous products at the lowest cost." Most important, as a means of "going into combat with the smelting and refining monopoly of . . . England . . . and arresting the competition of foreign commerce in our country," he urged Chile's leading copper capitalists to erect "a large-scale smelting plant" and thereby carry out "a great mining revolution in Chile . . . with the government . . . lending this undertaking its available funds at low interest to counterbalance the capital of the English smelter owners, who then would try in vain to lower [the price] of our copper. This would render the greatest and most necessary of services to the nation."[87]

This mixture of nationalism with the advocacy of state capital investment in and protection of Chilean manufacturing was articulated in repeated editorials in *el Mercurio*—whose owner, Santos Tornero, had been a leading partisan and spokesman of the 1859 insurrection—calling for Chile's industrialization: "In no epoch more than the present one," *el Mercurio* declared barely a year after the revolution's defeat, "has there been such a necessity to stimulate the development of our industries by means of decisive protection, for to them is linked the destiny of the nation. And if we do not make use of every resource we have [to spur industrialization], the impotence of our people will be followed by ruin."

A half-decade later, this national capitalist credo was summed up in another ringing editorial: "Chile can be industrial, since it has the capital, the labor and activity, but it lacks the will and desire. Foreign capital is heavily involved in the importation of manufactured products [and] . . . is and always will be disposed to put any and every obstacle in the way of the establishment of industry in our country. . . . Protectionism must be the mother's milk of every nascent craft or industry, the soul that really animates it positively. Without protectionism, every incipient advance is exposed to the furious and

---

[87] As quoted from Vicuña Aguirre's June 26, 1861 article in *el Mercurio*, in Vicuña Mackenna 1883, pp. 516–518; the article was part of a series "on the crisis and the opinions of Courcelle Seneuil," the French political economist and free trade advocate advising the Montt government and its successor, of whose free trade theory Vicuña Aguirre was Chile's "most vigorous opponent," according to Jobet 1955, p. 44.

coordinated assaults of foreign imports, as embodied in 'free trade.' "[88] These entreaties for state assistance to domestic industry, and to the smelting industry in particular, were never answered, except in rebuff, by the Montt regime and its successors.

Thus the question now has to be asked: would a regime established in Chile by a successful mid-nineteenth-century revolution under the aegis of the mining bourgeoisie have possessed a heightened nationalist animus and imposed state policies that could have both resisted the further penetration of British capital and provided the necessary impetus for industrialization? There is no need to endow their consciousness with unwarranted retrospective coherence to see that it might have made an enormous difference for the development of capitalism in Chile if the revolutionaries had taken state power in 1859. For, as we have seen, it was precisely some of the leading activists and partisans of the revolutionary movement who had the clearest understanding of how decisive was Chilean capital's historic choice. Certainly, as Perry Anderson has rightly emphasized, "no class in history immediately comprehends the logic of its own historical situation, in epochs of transition: a long period of disorientation and confusion may be necessary for it to learn the necessary rules of its own sovereignty."[89] With hegemony in their class and power in the state, the men who had such a comprehension, albeit inchoate, might well have learned what had to be done and imposed the state policies necessary to assure the sovereignty of national capital in Chile.[90] What can scarcely be doubted is that had the revolutionaries taken power, the state's hitherto almost complete neglect of the mining areas would have changed fundamentally; it would have built the necessary infrastructure there and provided other subsidies to develop the mining, smelting, and refining industries.

---

[88] *el Mercurio*, July 27, 1860; May 4, 1865; as quoted in Ramírez Necochea 1969, p. 200 and 1960b, p. 90.

[89] Anderson 1974, p. 55.

[90] The liberals and radicals were not entirely of one mind on state protection of industry; for instance, Manuel Antonio Matta, one of the leading 1850s young radicals, was later a prominent exponent of free trade. How deep the doctrinal divisions were among the mineowners, especially among the leading insurrectionaries themselves, is unknown, and archival research will have to ferret this out. But the evidence I have assembled in this chapter is sufficient to indicate that the assumption that they were "almost by definition" advocates of free trade is false.

Closely bound up with such a possibility was the potential inherent in the armed struggles in the countryside. It is not clear to what extent the agitation and organization of the peasants by their social "superiors" provided the main impetus to their participation in the insurrectionary movement or were, in fact, impelled by the momentum of their own class needs and grievances. But surely the latter were crucial, for it was precisely in the areas where a relatively independent segment of the peasantry, not yet subjected directly to the manorial regime, still existed that the armed *montoneras* arose. There were also armed guerrilla bands consisting of artisans, laborers, and small holders who acted independently under their own leaders. One such *montonera*, for instance, was led by "the proprietor of a small parcel near Talca," Ramón Antonio Vallejos. The insurrectionary band occupied Talca, armed new recruits from the "popular classes" with weapons that it seized in the police station and civic guard headquarters, and briefly imposed its rule in the city and surrounding area. According to Encina, Vallejos "made his harsh dictatorship felt by the arrogant Talquina aristocracy. . . . He imposed war levies on commerce and on the large estates and appropriated what was necessary to organize his army."[91] The Montt government's newspaper in Concepción, *El Correo del Sur*, reported on February 19, 1859, that "the citizens of one of the most important cities of the Republic [Talca] are submitted to the absolute power of *a simple mill worker.*" The uprising in Talca also set off spontaneous revolts elsewhere, almost, according to Edwards Vives, as though it constituted a "prearranged signal, and the countryside between Cachapoal and Itata began to be covered by groups of guerrilla fighters, most of them," he asserts, "simple hordes of marauders whose exploits were limited to sacking estates, without concern for the political coloring of their proprietors."[92]

Thus whatever the relative independence of the peasant insurrection, the bourgeoisie certainly found willing allies in the rural population. The rapid growth in the size of the floating population seeking work in the mines and in the construction of the railways, canals, irrigation works, and roads, combined with the simultaneous increase

[91] Encina 1949, p. 316.
[92] Edwards Vives 1932, p. 274.

in the landlords' impositions on the peasants, the encroachments on their customary prerogatives, and the large estates' incorporation within their domains of lands previously loosely attached to them, must have given rural resistance and revolt its own independent agrarian wellsprings. What seems certain, however, is that there *was* an insurrectionary alliance of artisans, laborers, "yeoman farmers," small holders, and mineowners that seized towns and cities and several large estates and in turn sparked other uprisings; many "representatives" of the bourgeoisie, who had the conscious aim of taking state power, actively led and participated in these armed struggles.

Specifically agrarian demands, as we know, were also articulated by the leading bourgeois revolutionaries—enough, in fact, to provoke *El Correo del Sur* to declaim, on April 19, 1859, against the *huasos* (rural workers) who were ready to "deliver themselves to socialism and communism."[93] Indeed, they had scarcely been defeated at Cerro Grande when the revolution's partisans again called for the splitting up of the large estates: On September 12, 1860, *el Mercurio* editorialized: "Our agriculture is stagnant; ancient and backward methods, slow and uneconomical, are still being used, which result in considerable loss of soil and time. . . . The origin of this evil is found principally in the maldistribution of property."

A few months later, an editorial in *el Mercurio* again declared: "We consider the division or break-up of agrarian property necessary because this would favor creditors and debtors as well as permit small capitalists to become proprietors; it would also increase production as the result of the closer and more detailed attention that can be given to a small farm. At the same time, this measure would result in a peaceful revolution in landed property." "The more divided landed property is," still another editorial declared, "the easier it is to establish equality, and equality is the constitutive principle of democracy . . . of a republic which is the government of everyone. . . . The republic exists only in name; in fact, in practice it is dominated by the aristocratic idea with even more force than in absolute monarchies. . . . *Inquilinaje*, the concentration of landed property in a few hands—under such a regime it is completely impossible for

[93] Vitale 1971, p. 282.

the republic to exist in reality and for the democratic principle to have force."[94]

These advanced political leaders and spokesmen of the Chilean bourgeoisie thus intuitively grasped the decisive place of a "revolution in landed property" in the development of capitalism and as a precondition for political democracy. It was necessary, first, to ensure both rising labor productivity in agriculture, to feed the growing working class in the mines and cities, and the continued growth of an internal market for domestic production of agricultural equipment and consumer goods, thus ending the heavy dependence on raw material exports. It was also necessary to transform a servile rural population into genuine citizens, enjoying real political rights in a democratic republic.

What social forces might have been tapped, what real impetus there might have been to the break-up of the large estates and the transformation of small cultivators into independent farmers and agrarian capitalists, if the revolutionaries had gained state power in the 1850s—in short, what the real historical potential was for a so-called "bourgeois democratic agrarian revolution" in mid-nineteenth-century Chile—is the tantalizing and unanswerable question posed by the defeat of the revolutionary bourgeoisie in these dimly remembered struggles. Instead, the old agrarian relations were reinforced and the internal market for manufacturing restricted, which in turn heightened the speculative and unproductive nature of Chilean capital through preponderant investment in landed property, in trade, and in financing the export of raw materials. Simultaneously, and in the absence of protectionist state policies, British imports competed directly and with increasing success against domestic products for even that small market, thereby also strenghtening these self-same tendencies and paving the way for Chile's subsequent "underdevelopment."

Thus the 1850s civil war was a crucial turning point. The defeat of the revolutionary bourgeoisie, I suggest, amounted to the virtual suppression of an alternative and independent path of capitalist development for Chile—a realm of objective historical possibilities

[94] *el Mercurio*, September 12, 1860; May 29, 1861; May 30, 1861; as quoted in Ramírez Necochea 1956, pp. 48, 93–94.

unfulfilled because of the failure of the bourgeois revolution. The inhibition of capitalist development in Chile—that is, its so-called "underdevelopment"—was essentially determined by the specific mid-nineteenth-century process of class formation and of class and intraclass struggle analyzed here. The eventual subordination of productive capital to both landed property and merchant and foreign capital was the long-term result of the mining bourgeoisie's failure to gain hegemony within the dominant class at this critical historical moment, when the developing capitalist relations of production and the protection of nascent industry required the effective use of state power to buttress and consolidate them. Instead, the political dominion of the great Central Valley landowners and their allies in the commercial community was secured. Under their aegis, the state facilitated the penetration and eventual ascendancy of foreign capital in nitrates and copper. This was to occur, however, only after another momentous civil war a generation later, provoked by a final unsuccessful attempt from within the dominant class itself to use state power to enforce Chile's independent capitalist development.

Chapter 3 ➤ "CHILE FOR THE CHILIANS"[1]

The civil war that erupted during the presidency of José Manuel Balmaceda in 1891 pitted elements of Chile's dominant class against each other in a violent conflagration whose origins and consequences are still being debated nearly a century later.

Balmaceda sought to prevent the consolidation of a British monopoly in Chilean nitrate production, and his administration heavily reinvested the state's new largesse in revenues from taxes on nitrate exports so as to propel the country's modernization and industrialization. His government was overthrown in a terrible civil war. But what was the connection between these two "simple historical facts"? This is the central question. Was there any inner connection, any intrinsic social relationship, between Balmaceda's national development program and the origins of the civil war? For most historians, the answer is an unhesitating no. Some argue, however, that the civil war was the open and violent expression of antagonistic social forces, and this is also my view. But, as we shall see, I differ sharply with these historians about who fought whom over what and with what consequences. I disagree, that is, as to the nature and significance of the social forces involved.

As the American envoy to Chile correctly observed at the time, the civil war was "not an attempt by the people to overturn the government or a movement in which the masses [were] . . . greatly interested, but rather a struggle for supremacy between two elements of the oligarchy."[2] Precisely for this reason, because the antagonists were drawn from Balmaceda's own class, the *sociological* answers to the basic historical questions—why was Balmaceda's government overthrown? by whom? who remained loyal to him? and with what

---

[1] This was the phrase resounding throughout public life during the Balmaceda epoch. See Russell 1890, p. 253, whose chapter 19 has the subtitle: "Chile for the Chilians." (The old spelling of "Chilians" is in the original.)

[2] Pregger Román 1979, p. 230.

consequences?—have remained obscure. The critical sociological
question is *what* "the struggle for supremacy" was about and *who*,
in social terms, were the "two elements of the oligarchy" who fought
each other so violently? What, in short, explains the split within the
dominant class and the sides taken in the civil war by its main
constituencies and leading actors? If this question remains unan-
swered, so must the historical significance of Balmaceda's defeat
remain hidden.

The consensus of authorities on the Balmaceda epoch, whatever
their otherwise differing political commitments or theoretical perspectives, is that the civil war originated as a conflict between the
dominant class and a relatively autonomous state. For Alberto Edwards Vives, for example, the war was a clash between Chile's own
"aristocratic Fronde," represented by parliament, on one side, and
the "executive power," embodying Chile's putative "absolutism"
and "monarchical tradition," on the other. The "oligarchic circles"
of the aristocracy, with their ingrained "feudal habits of domination," refused to submit to the increasingly independent executive
of the modern state, represented by Balmaceda.[3] Francisco Antonio
Encina, the dean of Chile's conservative historians, also emphasizes
that the causes of the civil war were "political and sentimental" and
concludes that it was "not a conflict of interests." Similarly, Harold
Blakemore, an English historian who is surely one of the closest and
finest students of the Balmaceda period, echoes these interpretations.
Balmaceda, he writes, was attacked by a "homogeneous class, proud
of its political self-consciousness." The embattled president's adherents and antagonists were not divided by contradictory "social
and economic" interests. Rather, the "principal determinants of
[their] conduct," in Blakemore's view, were "personal and political
allegiances within the governing class."[4]

The same implicit explanation—despite their explicit emphasis on
the material interests at stake—is offered by a number of radical
critics and dependency theorists of Chile's underdevelopment, for
whom Balmaceda represents a nationalist state challenged and overthrown by "comprador capitalists" in league with "imperialism."

---

[3] Edwards Vives 1945, pp. 173–179.
[4] Encina 1952, I, p. 396; Blakemore 1965, pp. 394, 418.

Thus, for instance, Andrew Gunder Frank finds that Balmaceda was brought down by the "combined interests" of the "satellite oligarchy" hurt by Balmaceda's nationalist state policies. "The metropolis-satellite structure of world capitalism," in Frank's view, unified the diverse "interest groups" of Chile's "oligarchy" and forged an "ever ready imperialist and domestic alliance of commercial, financial, mining, and agricultural interests." Attacked by Balmaceda, "it was not long in mobilizing its forces against" his goverment. Balmaceda was thus overthrown by "the combined interests and actions of landowners, mineowners, merchants, and industrialists," all of whom "championed their own exploitation," opposed his program, and fought his policies because they had been "effectively incorporated into [the world capitalist] system."[5] As to who the *Balmacedistas* were and what internal social forces they embodied or represented, Frank, like Edwards, Encina, and Blakemore, is silent—as he must be if, as he says, the whole of this satellite's unified "oligarchy" opposed Balmaceda. Similarly, Luis Vitale, one of Chile's leading Socialist historians, argues that "the fundamental cause of the civil war of 1891 was the nationalist program of Balmaceda's government, which generated a crisis in [Chile's] relations with the English metropolis." Balmaceda was overthrown by a combination of "English imperialism and . . . its junior partner, the Creole Bourgeoisie." A few scattered nationalist elements of the population supported him, but the "functionary bureaucracy" of the state and "the Army provided Balmaceda with his principle base of support in the civil war."[6]

Finally, although they do not, unlike Vitale and Frank, focus on "imperialism," Ximena Vergara and Luis Barros also see the civil war as a struggle between "a relatively homogeneous oligarchy, in terms of its location in production" and a relatively autonomous state executive. Also writing in a Marxist idiom, they argue that the conflict arose because the state sought to invest "the surplus value generated by the nitrate enclave, with relative autonomy from the control of the oligarchy." Thus, they conclude, "the contradictions of the epoch were fundamentally *ideological*."[7]

---

[5] Frank 1967, pp. 82, 94–95.
[6] Vitale 1975, p. 229.
[7] Vergara and Barros 1972, pp. 73–74, 86–89, italics added. Two books appeared

In opposition to these theories, I shall show that the civil war split the dominant class along deep structural fissures within it. Balmaceda's nationalist policies were undoubtedly crucial in sparking the struggle. But it arose, not primarily as a struggle between class and state (nor between "imperialism" and "nationalism") but between

---

after the manuscript of this book had gone to press that examine the relationships among Chile's nitrate economy, the civil war of 1891, and the country's "frustrated economic development." The authors of both books offer interpretations that seem to be a melange of the ideas of Frank, Vitale, and Vergara and Barros (though not citing their works for support). Michael Monteón observes. unlike Frank, that "each side contained progressive and traditional elements," but like Frank he also assumes, without close analysis, that what he calls "the native elite turned against" Balmaceda in its entirety. "The explanation of the President's conduct in 1889," he writes, "is the conflict that developed between his desire to carry out rapid economic development while preserving executive authority and the British producers' intention of increasing their margin of profit." Although he remarks that Balmaceda's policies "antagonized both the British and powerful domestic interests," the latter are never specified, except as "merchants, bankers, industrialists, and hacendados [who] refused to support any attack on the British" because the economy's "chief stimulus was the nitrate trade." Monteón, in company with all other authorities (except Segall), is also silent on who the Balmacedistas were and what they represented. Ultimately, he shares the view of Vergara and Barros that the issue was ideological and that the opposing sides simply "had a different conception of how state power should subsidize a capitalist economy." See Monteón 1982, especially pp. 25–26, 30–32.

Thomas F. O'Brien (on whose valuable dissertation research I have relied heavily in this book) also argues (much like Frank) that what he calls Chile's "elite readily accepted foreign control of the [nitrate] industry" because Chile's "absorption into the world market" and "dependency relationship . . . confined interaction between the capitalist center and the peripheral unit to essentially market exchanges [and] ensured [the elite's] continuity [and] . . . cohesion." Thus, for O'Brien, the civil war of 1891 represented (much as for Vergara and Barros) "an adjustment in state structures essential to the continued development of Chile's new relationship to the capitalist center [because] the state served as the oligarchy's key link to the nitrate industry and was the most vital force in the domestic economy. This new role of the government rapidly . . . splintered [the elite] into innumerable factions vying for a share of state resources and . . . [as] partisans of competing European nitrate producers. In the civil war of 1891 these forces converged on and destroyed the Chilean presidential system, the one institution that threatened to disrupt this process." Or again: "The elite could never countenance . . . enhancement of presidential power now that the state had become such an important economic power base." Alas, O'Brien is so convinced of the "elite's unity and cohesion" and of its "diverse but compatible economic interests" that, despite his talk about its "factionalization," it is never clear in his book who in this "elite" is fighting with whom over what. See O'Brien 1982, pp. 150, 149, 124, 143, and passim. In addition, this assumption that the so-called peripheral elite of Chile possessed internal structural unity also compels O'Brien to fail to see the real significance of one of his own valuable empirical discoveries about the contradictory interests and structural fissures actually rending the dominant class. I discuss this below in Chapter 4, note 42.

relatively discrete segments of the bourgeoisie itself, each possessing its own distinctive economic base and specific intraclass situation. They were split by contradictory interests that brought them into contention over the use of state power on their behalf. The Balmacedistas were, as I shall show in the next chapter, the incarnation of an especially powerful segment of the capitalist class consisting of the owners of the copper, silver, and coal mines who were now beset by economic crisis and seeking state assistance as their salvation. Their defeat, the failure of the mining bourgeoisie to secure political hegemony in their class and power in the state, was thus decisive in shaping Chile's historically specific path of capitalist development.

BALMACEDA: THE MAN AND THE MOMENT

No more than the Meiji leaders and Otto von Bismarck, Balmaceda's Japanese and Prussian contemporaries, was he a doctrinaire social theorist "catapulted into the arena of political responsibility."[8] Scion of one of the nation's most aristocratic families, Balmaceda came to the presidency as the culmination of a long and distinguished public career. His ancestral roots were deep in the "highest Castilian-Basque aristocracy," which had long reigned in Chile, reaching back, on his mother's side, to the "original Andalusian *conquistadores*" themselves. His father was a major landowner and a prominent senator, who, as an exemplary representative of Chile's so-called "progressive agrarians," had written *The Landowner's Manual*. A virtual codification of the methods of patriarchal domination, it spelled out in almost Taylorian detail and for 26 categories of workers "the simple obligations of our ignorant and modest rustic employees."[9]

Before reaching the presidency, Balmaceda had served in the chamber of deputies, in the senate, and in several ministerial posts, most recently as interior minister for his immediate predecessor, President Domingo Santa María. Long an "eloquent and illustrious defender" of the secularization and democratization of the state, as Arturo Alessandri puts it, Balmaceda had been opposed for the presidency

[8] Moore 1966, p. 246.
[9] Encina 1952, I, p. 9.

only by a minority of clerical conservatives to his right and "advanced liberals" to his left, whose Radical candidate, José Francisco Vergara, was a leading industrialist and mineowner.[10]

Even though he was a liberal and secularist by conviction, Balmaceda was of seignorial ancestry and aristocratic bearing, and was personally a major landowner. He was also a seminary graduate who had had a youthful predilection for the priesthood. So nothing in his social origins or active public life suggested any visible "distances of class" from his social peers. On the contrary, as the venerable conservative historian Encina notes, Balmaceda "not only belonged to the governing aristocracy, but assumed office in the most complete harmony with it."[11] Yet during the years of his presidency, Balmaceda was to find himself fighting, as Friedrich Engels said of Bismarck, to "carry out the will of the bourgeoisie against its will."[12] What explains this? What social forces did Balmaceda's attempt to use the immense powers of the state to enforce Chile's independent capitalist development conjure up against him and why? What were the enduring historical consequences of his defeat?

Balmaceda became president of a country that—with its victory in the War of the Pacific (1879–1883) against Peru and Bolivia—now enjoyed "undoubted hegemony in South America, except for Brazil," a country whose power some European leaders even considered a potential "counterpoise to the United States in the Pacific."[13] It possessed, in the words of the newspaper of South America's British mercantile community, "all the elements of national greatness."[14] The war, Chile's first and only "imperialist war" of territorial annexation, strengthened a sense of Chilean national identity and reinforced its dominant class's already quasi-racist sense of national uniqueness and superiority in Latin America—expressed by Balmaceda, as interior minister in the midst of the war, in his call to the nations of the world to recognize Chile's "civilizing mission" in Bolivia and Peru.

The War of the Pacific had been a sort of partial historical surrogate

[10] Alessandri 1950, pp. 24–25.
[11] Encina 1952, I, p. 38.
[12] Engels 1973c, p. 398.
[13] Burr 1955, p. 56; Kiernan 1955, p. 21.
[14] *The South American Journal*, April 24, 1884, quoted in Blakemore 1974, p. 70.

for the earlier abortive bourgeois revolution: the war geometrically increased state demand and secured legislative protection for domestic manufacturing; with the annexion of the contested territories, it also led to the subsequent rapid displacement from the countryside and proletarianization of large numbers of men and women flowing into the nitrate fields, though leaving intact the basic agrarian relations of production. The number of manufacturing establishments multiplied, including ones engaged in large-scale industrial production of metallic and mechanical products, and the amount of labor absorbed in industry "increased significantly, and output was qualitatively distinct from the preceding decades."[15]

In order to equip Chile's huge expeditionary forces (numbering some 60,000 in a population of 2.5 million) and prosecute the war over its five years' duration, the state centralized credit and provided subsidies and a high and growing volume of demand for the products of domestic industry, especially armaments, explosives, wagons, and even steel-clad warships. It also imposed new and high protective tariffs, in part for fiscal reasons and in part to assure the secure flow of equipment and supplies from national factories.[16] The result was the extraordinary expansion of manufacturing. Encina claims, but provides no substantiating data, that in such lines as "clothing, boots and shoes, leather goods, explosives, chemicals and pharmaceuticals, barrels, knapsacks, ship-engine boilers, etc.," production rose "as much as one hundred times." Foundries and metal fabricating plants—many already producing mining, railroad, and other heavy equipment since the mid-century mining and agricultural boom, and others established during the war—were under constant pressure to expand production; as one index of this expansion, iron imports rose during the war from 3,400 to 8,500 metric tons. At the end of the war, the estimate is that of 3,561 factories, shops, and mills surveyed in Chile, some 2,100 were mechanized factories.[17]

Consonant with this rapid growth of both light manufacturing and a heavy equipment industry was a renewed consciousness among leading businessmen of the need for state assistance and protection

---

[15] Kirsch 1977, p. 21.
[16] Galdames 1941, pp. 330–333; Segall 1953, pp. 162ff.; Álvarez 1936, p. 146; Muñoz 1968, p. 19.
[17] Kirsch 1977, pp. 6, 22–23; see also Pfeiffer 1952.

of domestic capital. The national manufacturers' association (*Sociedád Nacional de Fomento Fabril*) was established under state aegis and with public financing in 1883, and within a year had organized 305 manufacturing firms into a politically "cohesive nucleus" of industrial capital.[18] In its first bulletin, it proclaimed that

> Chile can and must industrialize. . . . It is the only rational objective of working people and capitalists alike. . . . Chile must industrialize because it has the resources to do so; it has the minerals of most importance in extraordinary abundance: copper, iron, coal, nitrates, and sulfur and all the chemical products that industry needs for its establishment and development; it has the animal products, leather, wool, and silk, for the manufacture of the most delicate fabrics and clothing. . . . Finally, Chile must industrialize, because this is the objective toward which its natural evolution as a democratic nation is taking it, and only by dedicating its forces to industry will Chile come to possess the stable base of social and political equilibrium enjoyed by the most advanced nations.[19]

Liberal President Domingo Santa María spoke by the war's end of the need to stimulate and protect "industrial activity and develop a group consciousness among manufacturers." He commissioned several investigations of how the state could assist the growth of manufacturing and integrate it with primary production. A year before Balmaceda's election, the Radical party, in whose ranks were many of the nation's leading copper-mine owners and manufacturers, proclaimed at its convention "that the most decided protection of national industry is a prime necessity and the only means to assure the greatness and prosperity of the Republic." Prophetically, one of the Radicals' outstanding younger leaders at the time, Malaquias Concha, and later a Balmacedista, argued that "the essential point of our doctrine is how to create a system of national economy that makes us independent of foreign countries. The protection of national industry is essential if we are to reach the level of productive power of the more advanced nations."[20]

18 Kirsch 1977, p. 43.
19 Ramírez Necochea 1969, pp. 145–146.
20 Ramírez Necochea 1956, pp. 209, 201.

Concha, of course, was pointing to the other crucial ingredient in Chile's recent historical experience. At the very moment that the pace of capital accumulation and manufacturing was intensifying, it also faced a heightened tendency toward the subversion of national by foreign capital in the nitrate industry. It was becoming substantially foreign-owned, although nitrate production had been pioneered by Chileans.

As the result of the War of the Pacific, Chile occupied Tacna and Arica and permanently annexed Tarapacá and Antofogasta, thus adding over a third to the national territory and incorporating an immense source of wealth: "the only commercially productive nitrate deposits in the world," plus large deposits of silver, copper, borax, and, on the Peruvian coast, guano.[21] The War of the Pacific had been triggered by the successive efforts of the Peruvian and Bolivian governments to gain control of the nitrate industry in their territories from the Chileans, who had developed it during the past two decades.

In 1875, in preparation for its proposed expropriation of foreign nitrate enterprises, the Peruvian government estimated that a fifth or more of total private productive capacity in nitrates in Tarapacá was held by Chileans, an eighth or so by English firms, a bit less than half that sum by Germans, and declining amounts by Italian, Spanish, Bolivian, and French capitalists, with the rest—slightly over half the total—held by Peruvians. Yet it was Chilean private capital that played the central, if not dominant, financial role in the industry, often in association with British capital.[22] Indeed, the "close connections" between "British capital established in Chile in the nitrate fields" and "Chilean financial and political interests" led some to suspect that the British had instigated the war. Thus U.S. Secretary of State James G. Blaine asserted at its outbreak that "It is a perfect mistake to speak of this as a Chilean war on Peru. It is an English war on Peru, with Chile as the instrument." If Blaine was probably wrong as far as its instigation by English capital was concerned— one historian renders the Scottish verdict of "not proven"—he was, paradoxically, right about the major indirect consequence of the War of the Pacific.[23] When it ended, English capital began to gain a prime

[21] Brown 1963, p. 230.
[22] Billinghurst 1889, p. 37.
[23] Kiernan 1955, pp. 23–26.

position in the nitrate industry, as the direct result of Chilean state policy itself—a policy, ironically, of which Balmaceda, as foreign minister and then interior minister, had been a significant author. As a leading advocate of the expeditionary war and permanent annexation of the nitrate territories, which were, he said, "principally Chilean in the industry and capital from which they profit," Balmaceda assured the major world powers that their capital would be welcomed there. Once "under the protection . . . of the efficacious order" that Chile would establish in the nitrate territories, they would again be open, Balmaceda declared, "for English, French, German, and American citizens, for citizens of all countries, to enrich themselves . . . in unlimited competition . . . [and] economic liberty."[24]

The reign of "economic liberty" that Chile established in these newly won territories led, however, to the ascendance there not of Chilean capital but of foreign capital. In this, Chilean state policy itself was decisive. During the prolonged debate in congress over the disposition of the nitrate properties, there were proposals to limit foreign participation and even "strong agitation in favor of nationalization."[25] But, instead, it was the fateful decision of the Santa María administration and congress to honor the government bonds issued in 1875 by Peru as compensation for expropriating the nitrate enterprises in Tarapacá. Santa María's nitrate policy was summed up in his glib remark: "Let the *gringos* [sic] work freely in nitrates. I'll be waiting for them at the door"—with export taxes.[26] In fact, a group of British investors had cornered these bonds at discount prices at a time when their chance of redemption seemed slim; much of the nitrate industry, especially in Tarapacá, thus fell into British hands, when the Chilean government chose to honor them and actually transfer the properties to the bondholders in 1881. On the eve of the war, British capital had controlled about 13 percent of the total private investment in nitrates; by 1884, its share rose to an estimated 34 percent, whereas the share held by German capital also rose to about a fifth of the total.[27]

[24] Silva Vargas 1974, pp. 30–31.
[25] Hardy 1948, p. 169.
[26] Alessandri 1950, p. 204.
[27] Hernández Cornejo 1930, p. 146; Segall 1953, p. 208. On the shenanigans and corruption of Chilean officials involved in the speculations of North and his associates,

Chilean capital not only was increasingly hemmed in by foreign capital but also faced highly concentrated foreign competitors. Only a few of the many competing Chilean firms were large, whereas among the British firms, a few nitrate houses—such as Gibbs, Balfour Williamson, and North—were paramount.

Balmaceda thus became president at a contradictory historical moment. Chile had the genuine possibility to industrialize rapidly, but prior state policies had already unintentionally led, in Encina's apt phrase, to the "formation in Tarapacá of a state within the state, with all its potentially dangerous consequences for Chilean sovereignty."[28] Recognizing this, and echoing many voices in his class, Balmaceda declared in his first annual message to congress, on June 1, 1887, that his administration was committed to *"the active and resolute encouragement of national industry."*[29] Balmaceda had said when he was still interior minister that "the modern state has a special mission" to promote national development.[30] Now, he told congress, the state would fulfill this special mission by spurring Chile's industrialization. His government's newly established Ministry of Industry and Public Works would heavily invest in "national reproductive works" so as to both stimulate and underwrite private manufacturing capital and construct the necessary infrastructure for sustained capitalist development. "Why," he asked rhetorically a year later (November 25, 1888),

is the paper that Chile consumes not manufactured in Chile? Why are the cotton fabrics and other textiles for general use not made here—here where the torrents of the Andes run, bringing their generative power to the cities . . . ? Why do we, we who possess impenetrable forests, buy our lumber from the jungles of another hemisphere? . . . How is it possible that in this land of iron and coal, we do not produce steel and manufacture steel products? How long will our agriculture live from primary pro-

see Hardy 1948, pp. 169ff., and Ramírez Necochea 1969, p. 24. In 1889, according to Segall 1953, p. 208, actual nitrate production was distributed as follows, by nationality of ownership: English, 39 percent; German, 18 percent; Chilean, 30 percent; others, 13 percent.

[28] Encina 1952, I, p. 386.
[29] Ramírez Necochea 1969, p. 147, italics added.
[30] Encina 1952, I, p. 36.

duction of wheat and cattle . . . ? Why are there no mineral
refineries in Chile, and why do we lack adequate facilities to
elaborate the crude ores that come from the rough country of
the northern mountains, only to be transported to the industrial
centers of Europe?[31]

Balmaceda's vision was rooted in his country's recent historical
experience. Both the level of industrialization already attained in
Chile and the monumental state investments now feasible made Balmaceda's aim to modernize his country a realistic historical possibility. But this was also a moment of heightened penetration, if not
a tendency toward monopoly, of the nitrate industry by foreign capital. Conscious as he now was of this reality, Balmaceda's first annual
message to congress enunciated the state's drive not only toward
rapid industrial growth but also toward the recovery of the nation's
wealth from foreign hands. "What has happened in Tarapacá," as
a later publication of the nitrate industry issued by Balmaceda's
finance ministry said sharply, "is one of many examples of how
foreigners can take control of a territory by means of their capital
even when they do not possess political dominion there. . . . The
tendency of the English market to constitute a syndicate, or a single
monopolistic company, in our nitrates is so marked, the preparatory
maneuvers so evident, that it would be inexcusable if we did not
take defensive measures. Today, a people can be conquered not
merely by weapons, but also by the legal absorption of their riches."[32]

On the basis of the abundant revenues now available to the state
from export taxes on the burgeoning nitrate industry in Chile's recently annexed "great northern" deserts, Balmaceda projected a state
investment over the coming decade in industry, transport, communications, and public education of over $200 million. Under his
predecessor, annual state revenues did not exceed $15 million; by
1886, when Balmaceda took office, the figure was $37 million, and,
within a year, $45 million; in 1890, public revenues were to top $58
million.[33] "We must invest the surplus of state revenues . . . in

[31] Ramírez Necochea 1969, pp. 144–145.
[32] Ministerio de Hacienda 1889, pp. 147–154; Ramírez Necochea 1969, p. 65.
[33] Encina 1952, I, p. 396; Galdames 1941, p. 342; Kinsbruner 1967, p. 111. In
1886, there were 2.09 Chilean pesos to the U.S. dollar, with the rate of exchange
improving somewhat during the next three years of the Balmaceda government, to

reproductive works,'' Balmaceda declared (March 8, 1889), ''so that at the moment when nitrates are exhausted or their importance diminished by natural discoveries or scientific progress, we will have transformed national industry and created . . . the basis for new sources of profit and positive greatness'' for the nation.[34]

During the four years of Balmaceda's presidency, until the outbreak of civil war, Chile experienced what Luis Galdames called ''a veritable orgy of material progress.'' The government made large orders and provided substantial subsidies to private capital for the construction of a spate of public works. The public railroads were extended over a thousand kilometers, and the Laja, Bio-Bio, Ñuble, Lircay, Maule, Perquelauquen and over 30 other rivers were spanned with metal bridges.[35] Chile's heavy industry competed effectively with foreign firms in the manufacture of steam locomotives and flat cars for Chile's railroads (all of the major parts of the locomotives, except the wheels, were manufactured domestically), and as early as 1887, it was already exporting these products to other South American countries. The new metal bridges erected were also manufactured in Chile.[36] Balmaceda's government laid new roads and repaired old ones; canalized the river Mapocho throughout Santiago; completed the viaduct at Malleco and huge drydock at Talcahuano; constructed wharves and opened new ports; installed gas lighting and running water in 20 cities and conducted surveys for another 30, including a proposed (but not implemented) program for widespread electricity; and extended telegraph lines throughout the country (the number of telegraph offices increased from 150 in 1886 to 182 by 1890). In Santiago alone, 10 major public buildings were constructed, including a school of medicine, a school of arts, a women's hospital, and a military academy; in the provinces, there

---

2.03 in 1887, 1.89 in 1888, and 1.88 in 1889, and then declining again in 1890 to 2.08 (Przeworski 1978, p. 300).

[34] Encina 1952, I, p. 396. Balmaceda's prescience concerning the replacement of nitrates by synthetics—which did, in fact, occur after World War I—is all the more remarkable because ''experts'' were still denying the possibility a quarter of a century later. Maitland (1914, p. 109), citing ''standard works'' on nitrates, remarks: ''The fear that Chile will lose her world's monopoly of nitrate, through that commodity being manufactured artifically, is so remote that it may be banished.''

[35] Galdames 1941, pp. 342, 343; Ramírez Necochea 1969, p. 148.

[36] Segall 1953; Ramírez Necochea 1969, p. 148; Pfeiffer 1952, pp. 139–140; Kirsch 1977, pp. 12–15, 32–33.

was a similar wave of construction of public buildings, streets, parks, prisons, and primary schools. In 1886, Chile had 1,394 public and private schools enrolling 79,000 pupils. By 1888, there were some 1,450 schools with more than 140,000 pupils, and by 1890, there were 1,097 public and 556 private schools, enrolling over 160,000.[37] In sum, Balmaceda's government built "more public works, almost all of them productive, or necessary for public education or security," than had been built in "the entire previous history" of the republic.[38] Yet, as he put through his development program, Balmaceda found himself increasingly, and finally violently, estranged from his own class.

POLITICAL POLARIZATION AND CIVIL WAR

In its first two years, Balmaceda's government encountered no more than the typical opposition that a lively congress had given his recent predecessors. The public works were denounced by some as instances of prodigality and waste, if not the corrupt misuse of public funds, and by others because they prevented decisive measures to make Chile's paper currency once again convertible to silver. His critics argued that rather than massive expenditures on public works, the government should have retired Chile's fluctuating paper currency on the basis of its increased silver reserves. They accused him of invading congressional prerogatives, substituting rule by presidential decree for parliamentary government, and intervening in the electoral process. In March 1888, his cabinet resigned over his alleged intervention in the elections to congress, bringing to an end the "grand liberal coalition" Balmaceda had forged since his assumption of office. During the next two years, constitutional issues were, in fact, to loom large in the increasingly bitter denunciations of his government's policies, and Balmaceda was to be accused repeatedly of the unprecedented expansion and arbitrary and capricious use of the executive powers of the state.

This was a period of swirling parliamentary struggles, of swift and sudden shifts in coalitions and alliances, and of internal party

[37] Galdames 1941, p. 343; Encina 1952, I, pp. 375–377; Blakemore 1974, p. 72.
[38] Nemo 1893, p. 172.

splits, as old comrades now and again found themselves on opposing sides in the sharpening political strife.[39] By the fall of 1890, as Encina puts it, the "ideological, sentimental and political movement [against Balmaceda] took on the force of a hurricane. . . . It was a movement involving 75 percent of the governing aristocracy. Balmaceda had aroused against him every party in Chile, except those few Liberals who were then in office. Any pretext was used to attack him."[40] Describing those events, the manager of Gibbs and Company, one of the major English trading and nitrate firms in Chile, wrote the home office in late October 1890: "There is no end of talking going on among Santiago politicians, some of whom say they would not be the least astonished if Balmaceda had a bullet put into him before long—but I don't believe it will come to more than talk & [sic] bravado. So long as he does nothing really unconsitutional, I fancy he will carry the day, but he will have to be extra careful"[41] As a later president, Arturo Alessandri, wrote of his own youthful experiences at the time: "The force of passion was so great, in our entire social circle, that it showed poor judgment if one even dared to greet or shake hands with Balmaceda's supporters. Old friendships were broken by political divergences. Families that were traditionally united broke off their relations and separated forever. . . . The country split into two irreconcilable bands. No one exchanged greetings or spoke a word with anyone in another band, and old and deep friendships no longer mattered."[42]

Thus in late December 1890, with less than a year left in Balmaceda's term, a congressional majority took the historically unprecedented action of declaring a sitting president unfit to remain in office. The support of the armed forces was sought on both sides, in the event that the other "violated the constitution," and congress itself set up a joint military committee in case resistance to the president became necessary. Congress closed its 1890 session without passing an appropriations bill for 1891, and refused to authorize expenditures to maintain the armed forces.

Balmaceda responded by denouncing this as itself a violation of

[39] See Blakemore 1974, p. 172.
[40] Encina 1952, ii, p. 50.
[41] Blakemore 1974, pp. 186–187.
[42] Alessandri 1950, pp. 96–98.

the constitution; he condemned congress for attempting to incite the army to disobey its higher officers and for plotting revolution, and he refused to "surrender the reins of government to those who vituperate against [the president] and denounce his acts and objectives." He declared that the previous year's appropriations bill would remain in force and that he would, if necessary, govern without congressional authorization. "The dilemma," he said, "is representative government or parliamentary government. I opt for the representative government ordained by the constitution." A joint congressional committee then declared that Balmaceda's presidency was no longer legitimate and, on January 7, 1891, launched an armed "revolution" to depose him.[43] So began "one of the strangest wars in history," with the navy supporting congress and the army remaining loyal to the president.[44]

The civil war lasted nine months, resulted in the death of over 10,000 persons in a total population of some 3,000,000 and cost more than $100 million; it ended with the defeat of the loyal armed forces in the decisive battles of Concón and Placilla.[45] Balmaceda took refuge in the Argentinian embassy and lived there secretly until the final day of his formal term of office; on that September day in 1891, after leaving behind a political testament and letters to his family, friends, and comrades, he killed himself by a gunshot wound to the head. He died convinced, as he had said in a speech to congress in the midst of the civil war, that Chile had suffered "an antidemocratic revolution instigated by a small centralized social class."[46]

The new regime decreed that all military officers who had served "the dictatorship were to be tried under military law," and it purged the armed forces thoroughly of Balmaceda's supporters. All ministers, counselors of state, members of the constituent congress (the Balmacedist parliament formed after the civil war began), municipal officials, provincial governors and intendants, members of the judiciary and even the lowest functionaries and ordinary employees of Balmaceda's government were investigated and, "if cause were found to proceed against them judicially," brought to trial. Over 4,000

[43] Encina 1952, II, pp. 57, 53ff.
[44] Blakemore 1974, p. 193.
[45] Galdames 1941, pp. 347–348.
[46] Ramírez Necochea 1969, p. 198.

military officials, functionaries, and state employees were fired, and 634 were imprisoned for political crimes in Santiago alone; elsewhere, the same process went on, but no accurate figures are available on the total numbers purged, tried, and imprisoned.

The words of a priest in the affluent pulpit of Carmen Alto, immediately after the defeat of Balmaceda's troops, epitomize the furies unleashed by the war: "Just as the angels at Lucifer's side became demons, so all those who accompanied Balmaceda were bandits."[47] The houses and estates of the most prominent Balmacedistas, most of whom fled abroad or went into hiding, were looted, sacked, and burned by rampaging but usually well-dressed mobs. (The later discovery of maps and instructions revealed that some of the pillaging and looting of the Balmacedistas' homes was planned by the Revolutionary Directorate itself.)[48] What tore Balmaceda and his class so violently apart?

The "Springs of Political Action" in the Civil War

Were Balmaceda's efforts to spur Chile's development and to stem the penetration of foreign capital at the root of the civil war? Surely, it was "a battle of political principles in which the contestants were motivated by genuine conviction," as Blakemore argues. But the question remains: Assuming the genuineness of their political convictions, were the contestants also divided by contradictory material interests? What, in Blakemore's phrase, were the "springs of political action" beneath that violent eruption? "How far," as he asks, did the "economic and social interests of [the] . . . Balmacedists [differ] from those of the Congressionalists against whom the Balmaceda government thundered during 1891?" Blakemore's answer, as I noted at the outset, is that they did not differ significantly in their "economic and social interests." The divisions were determined by "personal and political allegiances within the governing class."[49] This is also Encina's answer: "The faithful who stood by Balmaceda were not even bound to him by shared ideology, but only by personal

[47] Encina 1952, ii, pp. 310–311.
[48] Nemo 1893, pp. 107–109.
[49] Blakemore 1965, pp. 93, 394, 418.

affection and admiration."[50] The problem with these answers is that they dodge the critical sociological question as to the possible social bases of these "personal allegiances" and misunderstand the origins of the sharpening struggle within the "governing class." The fact is that long-standing personal and political ties were disrupted or broken and new ones established as Balmaceda articulated his program and fought to put it through.

By the eve of the civil war, Balmaceda had already lost the allegiance of many if not most of the men who had originally supported him for the presidency and who became ministers early in his administration. In fact, Blakemore himself observes, while failing to see that it contradicts his earlier claim, that "a marked feature of the political situation was the *complete change of loyalties* of many of Balmaceda's former friends."[51] How can the actions of the most prominent antagonists be explained by "personal affection and admiration" or "personal and political allegiances" if these loyalties changed completely as the struggle intensified? Thus the question remains: is the argument that the genesis of the civil war was sociologically indeterminate correct? Did the anti-Balmaceda "revolution of 1891," as Julio Heise González also argues, "have no social nature"?[52]

That the civil war had no profound social wellsprings does, indeed, become an attractive hypothesis after one has gone through the harrowing research experience demanded of any serious investigator who tries to make sense of that bloody conflict and to grasp what material considerations divided its warring antagonists. The years of Balmaceda's presidency witnessed "so active an evolution of the political parties," as Encina aptly observes, "that the finest intellectual sensibility can scarcely even sketch the changes in bold outline. To express them clearly and intelligibly for the reader is beyond the capacity of the pen." Analytical exhaustion or resort to an idealist explanation has thus often come from grappling with the Balmaceda epic. Encina concludes, for example, that Balmaceda's own class fought against him because of its "Castilian-Basque aristocratic antipathy for dynamic officials of vigorous personality and great cre-

[50] Encina 1952, I, p. 359.
[51] Blakemore 1974, p. 197, italics added.
[52] Heise González 1974, p. 108.

ative initiatives, as well as [because] the powerful winds of electoral liberty and parliamentarism had begun to blow."[53] Similarly a later president, Alessandri, recalling his own youthful participation in that fratricidal struggle, explained that it "originated in mistrust, prejudices, ambitions, opposing passions and interests, and in party and individual struggles, which crystallized in a formidable aspiration for liberty."[54]

Linked to the main argument concerning the sociological indeterminacy of the civil war is the proposition that the "historical issue dividing the ruling elite was whether the parliament representing it would be controlled by a strong executive or whether the power of parliament would prevail over presidential power and secure its undisputed dominance."[55] This was, then, supposedly a political struggle between a congressional majority committed to electoral liberty and parliamentary rule and a congressional minority and administration consisting of "doctrinaire traditionalists" and proponents of a "strong state." Indeed, the claim is made that it was "the most traditional section [of his class] which supported Balmaceda [and] the most progressive and democratic elements which opposed him."[56]

But the evidence contradicts these claims. Among Balmaceda's most outstanding partisans were men who had long devoted their political lives to promoting parliamentary democracy and to opposing authoritarian rule and clerical obscurantism. Several of the men who stood with Balmaceda to the end had, in fact, first appeared on the political scene a generation earlier, when, as young revolutionary democrats, they led or were active participants in the defeated bourgeois insurrections of the 1850s; they included, for instance, such leading ministers and political confidants of Balmaceda as Eusebio Lillo, José Miguel Valdés Carrera, and Claudio Vicuña Guerrero.[57]

Lillo, to whom Balmaceda confided his "last political testament" before his suicide, was known as "the poet of the [1850s] revolution." He had composed its hymns, agitated in the columns of the

---

[53] Encina 1952, I, pp. 62, 119.
[54] Alessandri 1950, p. 85.
[55] Gil 1962, p. 25.
[56] Heise González 1974, pp. 80, 122.
[57] See the discussion in Chapter 4 concerning the relative representation of veterans of the 1850s struggles among the leading Balmacedistas and Congressionalists.

radical democratic newspaper *Amigo del Pueblo*, participated in founding the Society of Equality, and continued, throughout his public life, to be faithful to these principles. Valdés Carrera, Balmaceda's minister of industry and a leading opponent of the British nitrate monopoly in Tarapacá, had fought in the same armed struggles, was exiled, and had then returned to become a prominent Liberal deputy and senator and a leading member of the Liberal party's political directorate. In fact, he led the call for an "independent liberal" convention and supported José Francisco Vergara's presidential candidacy against Balmaceda. He was known as an ardent advocate of decentralized public administration, of checks on executive authority, and of the strengthening of parliamentary prerogatives. Claudio Vicuña, another 1850s revolutionary, was also in the "vanguard of liberalism" and a leading proponent of "political democracy, laicization and freedom from Church constraints."[58] He became Balmaceda's interior minister and, during the civil war, was elected "president of Chile" by the rump constituent congress. These biographical data are inconsistent with the notion that a commitment to executive absolutism versus "electoral liberty and parliamentarism" was at the root of the conflict and surely contradict the peculiar claim made by Heise González that the Balmacedistas were "doctrinaire traditionalists" and their congressional opponents "progressives and democrats."

The contrary thesis is also false and misleading. Balmaceda's political enemies were by no means merely "selfish and unpatriotic reactionaries."[59] Some were surely reactionaries, corrupt politicians, selfish, and careless of the national interest, but others had a long record of commitment to democratic principle and national economic independence before they found themselves opposed to Balmaceda's policies. Here, for instance, were such men as Manuel Antonio Matta, Isidoro Errázuriz, and Enrique Valdés Vergara. Matta, who represented the Congressionalists abroad and joined their government after Balmaceda's defeat, had been a leading insurrectionary in the 1850s; he later founded and edited the Radical newspaper, *El Atacameño*, in 1879, and he was a noted parliamentary leader in "the

[58] V. Figueroa 1925–1931, IV–V, pp. 51–52, 965–966, 1043; Alessandri 1950, p. 30; Pike 1963b, p. 15.
[59] See Jobet 1962.

struggle for civil liberties."[60] Similarly, Isidoro Errázuriz not only had been a bourgeois radical and insurrectionist at mid-century but also was one of the country's few prominent advocates of agrarian reform. Indeed, one Marxian historian describes him as "the last anti-latifundist knight of the Chilean bourgeoisie."[61] On the eve of Balmaceda's presidency, in 1886, Errázuriz was still denouncing "the feudal bonds governing this country."[62] Yet Errázuriz was also "the orator of the revolution" against Balmaceda and a member of the congressional revolutionary committee. As minister of justice after the civil war, he also organized the purge of Balmaceda loyalists from the judiciary.[63] Enrique Valdés Vergara, another of "the most active revolutionaries against Balmaceda," had been a leading opponent, together with his brother Francisco, of foreign capital's penetration of the nitrate industry and long advocated government action to end it.[64] Although they opposed Balmaceda in the civil war, the brothers later paid homage to him for his nitrate policy; Balmaceda possessed "a clear conception of his historic responsibility," Francisco wrote years later, and had "traced the lines of national greatness" in his use of the government's nitrate revenues to promote industrial growth.[65] These men, certainly, were not mere representatives of "foreign and domestic reaction," who sought the "sacrifice of [Balmaceda's] . . . national development program," as has been claimed in some characterizations of Balmaceda's antagonists.[66] Rather, the advocacy by these men of agrarian reform, political democrati-

---

[60] V. Figueroa 1925–1931, IV–V, p. 291.
[61] Segall 1953, p. 268.
[62] Encina 1952, I, p. 48. Chilean society, Errázuriz wrote in 1879, was split into "two rival classes, almost two races, *inquilinos* and masters, that are becoming more and more antagonistic as time goes by" (Segall 1953, p. 268).
[63] V. Figueroa, 1925–1931, IV–V, pp. 70–71.
[64] Yrarrázaval Larraín 1940, II, p. 211; Pike 1963b, p. 38.
[65] V. Figueroa 1925–1931, IV–V, p. 975. In his work, *La crísis salitrera, las medidas que se proponen para remediarla* (Valdés Vergara, 1884), Francisco had warned that a foreign nitrate monopoly "would constitute an odious and insufferable tutelage over the public and private interests of Chile." Ramírez Necochea (1969, p. 66) and Jobet (1955, p. 112) also cite extensively from Valdés Vergara's writings to indicate the rising nationalism in Chile of which Balmaceda was to become a leading exponent. But neither author then asks the hard question, why such leading *nationalists* fought *against* Balmaceda. I return to this question below.
[66] Frank 1967, p. 92.

zation, and nationalist policies put them among the most advanced
political leaders of their class.

Thus the real question, missed by such characterizations of the
opposing camps as "democrats" versus "traditionalists," or "patriots" versus "reactionaries," is why leading conservatives *and*
liberals, democrats *and* reactionaries, advocates of a "strong executive" *versus* parliamentary government, secularists *and* clerical ob-
scurantists, now found themselves so strangely allied on *both* sides
of the conflict. The contestants on both sides argued their cases on
constitutional grounds; charges of arbitrary invasion of parliamentary
prerogatives were met with charges of parliamentary encroachment
on presidential authority. The same men, including Balmaceda himself, shifted sides in the argument, at one moment advocating constitutional reforms to strengthen parliament against the executive
power and, at another, arguing for more executive independence. If
the prerogatives of either branch of government now became a deadly
divisive issue, it was over the *content* of state policy, not merely the
form in which it was enacted and implemented. Old party divisions,
general political principles, and personal loyalties do not account for
the sides taken in the struggle, although at some points they entered
into it and affected it considerably. For, as the political polarization
within the dominant class sharpened, these previous lines of division
blurred and disappeared to be replaced by new and far deeper fissures,
brought on primarily by the contradictory interests of its leading
combatants, which were now at stake.

NITRATES AND BRITISH CAPITAL

Given the prominence of Balmaceda's nitrate policy in his program
for national development, a main focus of historical contention has
been what role it played in provoking the civil war. Chile's leading
conservative historians deny that Balmaceda's nitrate policy, "by
wounding and threatening private interests, influenced the opposition
against the Executive of 1890 and led to the armed revolution the
following year."[67] That policy, they claim, had "no influence on
the birth of the 1891 conflict."[68] In my view, however, the impact

[67] Yrarrázaval Larraín 1963, p. 9; see also 1940.
[68] Encina 1952, I, p. 396.

of Balmaceda's policies on the nitrate industry was crucial in nurturing and giving birth to the movement to overthrow him. But I reject the narrow thesis that "English imperialists" (particularly John T. North's nitrate group) and other foreign capitalists generated the opposition and sustained the armed insurrection against Balmaceda, and especially its vulgarization that their bribery of public officials and retention of Chile's leading attorneys determined the alignments in the conflict.

This view was held by many of Balmaceda's own comrades, several of whom wrote *post-mortems* defending their policies and attempting to explain their defeat.[69] In the midst of the civil war, members of the Balmacedist constituent congress specifically attacked North, the so-called "Nitrate King," as the main architect of the armed insurrection, in complicity with domestic bankers; the official press often said the same.[70] Balmaceda personally "died with the conviction," in Encina's words, "that he had been defeated by a miserable coalition . . . without roots in the country, and by English gold. 'There is a group backed by foreign gold [Balmaceda wrote to a friend at the outbreak of war, in January 1891], which has corrupted many people.' "[71] Balmaceda's brother Rafael specifically singled out "the heads of the [English nitrate] enterprises of Iquique . . . linked to the political movement [among] senators and deputies" as Balmaceda's main enemy; their objective, he wrote, was to force the government to acquiesce in policies "favorable to their interests."[72] The same charge was made by the *London Times* correspondent in Chile, Maurice Hervey. On May 23, 1891, in the fifth month of the civil war, he wrote: "beyond the possibility of contradiction, the instigators, the wirepullers, the financial supporters of the so-called revolution were, and are, the English or Anglo-Chilean owners of the vast nitrate deposits of Tarapacá."[73]

A number of historians adhere to this same, or a similar, interpretation; they put much emphasis on foreign intrigue and the corrupting influence of "foreign gold" as the principal source of the

---

[69] Villarino 1893, especially pp. 213–233; see also Valdés Carrera 1893; Nemo 1893.
[70] Blakemore 1974, pp. 200, 401; Heise González 1974, p. 123; Encina 1952, I, p. 164.
[71] Encina 1952, I, p. 164.
[72] Nemo 1893, p. 7.
[73] Cited in Brown 1958, p. 475. See also Hervey 1891–1892.

revolt against Balmaceda.[74] Again, the centerpiece of this interpretation is the Nitrate King. There was a "probable connection,"
Osgood Hardy concludes, "of the British nitrate industry as apoth-
eosized by North with the revolution of 1891. . . . The President's
ambition for Chilean domination of the nitrate industry ran counter
to the interests of British capital as represented by Colonel North.
It is probably that, without North's aid, the Congressionalists could
not have equipped their land forces."[75] Hernán Ramírez Necochea
also argues even more sharply that the "animators of all the opposition raised against the nitrate policy of Balmaceda were undoubtedly His Majesty the Nitrate King, Mr. John Thomas North and the
other entrepreneurs who acted in Tarapacá." In particular, the opposition to Balmaceda was orchestrated largely by lawyers and other
such "distinguished elements of Chilean political life" in the employ
of North and other foreign capitalists.[76]

Certainly there is much in favor of this interpretation, but it also
suffers, as we shall see, from factual problems and misplaced ex-
planatory emphasis. Balmaceda's efforts to break the transport monopoly of the Nitrate Railways Company in Tarapacá doubtlessly
aroused North's own hostility to Balmaceda, and such hostility was
scarcely trifling. The North Group was a complex of interwoven
financial, mining, commercial, and railway corporations. North personally was connected "at one time or another, with more than two-
thirds of the British joint-stock enterprises operating in northern
Chile." He and his associates had organized at least 17 nitrate corporations, and he was probably the principal stockowner of 12 of
them.[77]

North's enterprises in Tarapacá included the Waterworks Company, gas lighting firm, and Nitrates Provision Supply Company,

[74] See Hardy 1948; Brown 1958; Jobet 1955, 1962; Ramírez Necochea 1958, 1960a,
1960b, 1969. Ramírez Necochea remarks that "Not only the Nitrate Railways Company . . . but all the northern enterprises spent extraordinary sums to pay for attorneys
and advisers, corrupt politicians and antipatriots, and their diligent services" and lists
a number of such "politicians in the service of the nitraters [salitreros]" (Ramírez
Necochea 1969, pp. 74ff.). The same emphasis in explaining the origins of the civil
war appears in Jobet 1955, pp. 103 and 89–90; "Mr. Thomas North . . . ," he writes,
"manipulated the Congress and the opposition press."
[75] Hardy 1948, pp. 177–180.
[76] Ramírez Necochea 1969, pp. 100, 83.
[77] Rippy 1948, pp. 459, 460; Encina 1952, I, p. 387.

which had a "monopoly of the provisioning commerce of the *pampas*, from flour and coal to meat and vegetables." Nitrate exports and much of the imports for consumption in the area were carried on North's Nitrate Producers Steamship Line. The Nitrate General Investment Trust Company, which handled a large volume of the trading in nitrate shares, and the Bank of Tarapacá and London— established in 1888, the major bank in the territory and its singularly most important source of credit for nitrate producers—were also under North's control. Finally, North had become by 1889 the principal shareholder and board chairman of the Nitrate Railways Company, which had a transport monopoly in Tarapacá. The latter "discreetly served North's goals," as Encina observed, with burdensome tariffs for his competition.[78] North, it appears, was "the virtual embodiment [of] . . . the penetration of Tarapacá by British capital."[79]

The Nitrate Railways Company was vital to North's financial-industrial complex. It controlled not only the main lines linking the major ports at Iquique and Pisagua with the outlying nitrate fields and refineries but also the most important feeder lines; this allowed it both to impose high freight rates as an immediate source of profit and to weaken, if not hold in thrall, much of the competition to North's producing companies. In the spring of 1889, when North made his much-publicized visit to Chile, he was planning to use this transport monopoly to compel his competitors to join in a business syndicate or actually to merge into a single nitrate company in Tarapacá, headed by himself.[80] The company's railway monopoly (originally granted by Peru) had been canceled by the outgoing Santa María government in 1886, in which Balmaceda was interior minister, before North gained control of it; the decree had not made much of a public stir at that time. Indeed, Pedro Montt, then Balmaceda's minister of industry and public works but later a spearhead of the opposition to him, signed the decree and "stoutly defended the right and rectitude of the policy and the legality of its execution."[81] But the company's appeal through the courts, once North

[78] Encina 1952, I, p. 387; Rippy 1948, p. 460.
[79] Blakemore 1974, p. 63.
[80] Blakemore 1974, pp. 48–55, 111.
[81] Alessandri 1950, p. 205.

was heavily involved in it, became a major political issue. In early 1888, the government had referred the case to the council of state.[82] This was a major reason for North's visit to Chile; as its authorized chronicler wrote, North came "to solidify and extend interests, in respect to any increase of which President Balmaceda's programme, as reported, might be taken as adverse."[83] Throughout North's visit, the case was before the council of state, and a decision ratifying or rejecting the validity of Balmaceda's cancellation of the company's monopoly was awaited. It came on September 13, 1889, upholding Balmaceda and denying the jurisdiction of the supreme court or of any ordinary court of law in the company's appeal.[84]

To fight the revocation of the Nitrate Railways monopoly, the company had been employing a battery of attorneys and publicists and had spread around considerable cash among men in public life. Bribery and corruption played some part in the actions of not a few political figures.[85] More important, many leading members of Congress, including several of Balmaceda's most vociferous opponents, were legitimately employed as lawyers by North and other foreign nitrate interests, for whom local legal representation was a business necessity.[86] They must have found it, at the least, difficult to separate their personal interests, the nation's interests, and the company's interests.

The adverse decision of the council of state opened the way for the construction of competing lines in Tarapacá, and the Balmaceda government promptly solicited competitive bids to construct a railway linking the major nitrate fields at Agua Santa with the port of Caleta Buena, which made the threat to North's transport monopoly im-

[82] The council of state was a quasi-judicial advisory body under the constitution appointed by the president.
[83] Russell 1890, p. 81.
[84] Encina 1952, I, p. 396.
[85] A stockholders' suit after North's death led to an investigation that "revealed that North had spent over one-quarter of a million pounds sterling [at 4.8 U.S. dollars to the pound in 1890] in his effort to preserve the monopoly privilege" (Brown 1958, p. 480; Przeworski 1978, p. 300).
[86] Among them, most notably, were Julio Zegers and the MacIver brothers, Enrique and David, "lawyer politicians retained by North" (Blakemore 1974, pp. 183, 219). Enrique, a founder and leader of the Radical party, and Zegers, a leading Liberal, usually couched their opposition to Balmaceda's policies in constitutional terms in their speeches in congress.

mediate. Company attorneys then sought to exploit constitutional issues as a means of defending its monopoly and openly injected them into the already heated political situation. North's lawyers took the extraordinary action of appealing directly to the senate against the president and implicitly charged that he had violated the constitution when he canceled the company's monopoly by decree and had this upheld by his own council of state. They argued that Balmaceda's actions violated the constitutional separation of powers, by arrogating to the executive both the "discretional powers . . . conferred upon Congress" and the independent functions of the judiciary.[87] At the same time, earlier opposition to Balmaceda's development program, couched as opposition to the president's allegedly arbitrary exercise of executive powers to launch the massive government projects without congressional approval, were also joined to this contentious issue involving the Nitrate Railways Company, a linchpin of British capital.

The diplomatic intervention of the British government at North's direct behest also became an element in the political clash. "The Company," William H. Russell reported at the time, "was obliged to invoke the assistance of the home Government which, no doubt with all due regard for the dignity and susceptibilities of Chile, authorized the British representative at Santiago to place before the Chilian [sic] Government the view that it took of a matter affecting five million sterling of English capital, embarked on a legitimate and beneficial enterprise in the province of Tarapacá." No doubt also the company's case was supported before the British government by the "large London financiers" to whom the company was indebted for "an outstanding loan of two million pounds sterling."[88] The British ambassador in Chile was instructed to protest against the "infraction" of the Nitrate Railways monopoly, and this he did both in a lengthy memorandum and personal meeting with Chile's foreign minister in February 1890.

Within several months, however, more than mere diplomatic means of intervention were being exercised by the British. England's consul in Coquimbo, in Chile's north, enthusiastically encouraged the reb-

[87] Blakemore 1974, pp. 113–114.
[88] Russell 1890, pp. 225, 359.

els, and once the civil war was in progress, British naval officers stationed in Chile, as well as ships owned by private English companies, actively aided the insurrection against the Balmaceda government. "There is no doubt," the British ambassador himself reported home at the civil war's end, "our Naval Officers and the British community of Valparaiso and all along the Coast rendered material assistance to the opposition and committed many breaches of neutrality."[89] Throughout the civil war, the British-owned *South American Journal* showed "decided hostility toward the Chilean chief executive," and when Balmaceda fell, it exulted on September 5, 1891: "It is with great satisfaction that we have to record the realization, not only of our hopes, but of the expectations we have throughout ventured to express."[90]

All of this sustains the argument that British capital, with John Thomas North as its apotheosis, was deeply involved in the political opposition and even in the actual armed struggle against Balmaceda. But the latter's sources, as I shall show, were far more complex than this. The narrow thesis that an alliance of North and other foreign capitalists and their paid Chilean hirelings animated "all the opposition" against Balmaceda's policies is vitiated by some rather critical historical facts.

First, whatever North's and his associates' evident political efforts in Tarapacá, and however weighty if not dominant the interlocking North enterprises were in the nitrate industry in that province, "English capital" in Chile was quite split over his railway monopoly. Several leading English firms agreed with Balmaceda's position, including the Clark Brothers nitrate firm, the Campbell Outram railway, the Balfour Williamson merchant-banking house, and Antony Gibbs, Chile's oldest British nitrate company, which also had farflung interests elsewhere in South America. Until North's rise after the war of the Pacific, Gibbs was the most powerful nitrate producer and trader in Chile. Under Balmaceda, the two firms were probably more or less business equals, and they were the leading rivals in the nitrate industry. Gibbs had nitrate-producing interests in both Tarapacá and Antofagasta; in the former province, its two *oficinas* ac-

[89] Blakemore 1974, p. 201.
[90] Rippy 1948, p. 459.

counted for 13 percent of the total nitrate tonnage in 1886 compared with the 14 percent produced by North's five *oficinas*.[91]

In the spring of 1890, the Gibbs house forcefully intervened with the British government *on Balmaceda's behalf*. It protested vehemently when the British ambassador informed Balmaceda's foreign minister that his government opposed "the infraction of the Nitrate Railways Company's monopoly." At the urging of the Gibbs representatives in Chile, the firm's higher officers in London called on the foreign minister personally and informed him that "the monopoly of the Nitrate Railways was weighing unmercifully on the British capital invested in the nitrate works." The Gibbs officers emphasized that many firms supported the Chilean government's efforts to abolish North's monopoly—a monopoly that, as they described it, benefits some "lucky speculators who bought the Railways for a trifle . . . but injures everyone else"—and urged the foreign office to suspend any further activities in the matter. The foreign office, Gibbs argued, should preserve its "customary neutrality" in a *"conflict between British interests abroad."* Responding to these urgent protestations, the foreign office did halt its pressures on Balmaceda and requested the Crown's legal experts to examine the case. In fact, they also later concluded that Balmaceda's revocation of North's monopoly was justified under Chile's constitution; with the civil war already five months in progress, the foreign office refused any futher diplomatic support of the Nitrate Railways Company and so informed the company's representatives. The British ambassador also enjoined neutrality on all British subjects and naval personnel.[92]

Support for Balmaceda from these British nitrate capitalists came, of course, not merely from principle or to set the record straight; the Campbell Outram and Gibbs firms were negotiating with Balmaceda for rights to build and operate their own railway lines to compete with North's Nitrate Railways. In fact, in late March 1890, Bal-

---

[91] In Tarapacá, according to Russell 1890, p. 336, English companies made "more than half of all nitrate." The major firms there, aside from Gibbs and North, were Gildemeister (Peruvian-German), with 7.4 percent of the total tonnage; Campbell (English), 6.5 percent; James, Inglis (English), 5.3 percent; and Folsch and Martin (German and Chilean capital, mainly Francisco Subercaseaux), 4.2 percent (O'Brien 1976, p. 151).

[92] Blakemore 1974, pp. 196–197, 132–134, italics added; Segall 1953, pp. 211–213.

maceda accepted Campbell Outram's bid to construct a competing line from Agua Santa to the port of Caleta Buena and granted the firm a concession for 25 years; as to Gibbs, the civil war broke out before its negotiations with Balmaceda could be completed. In short, these major British companies sought to assist Balmaceda to break the North transport monopoly.

Second, as to the role of North's alleged hirelings in congress, once the civil war ended, the new regime of the victorious Congressionalists—contrary to North's expectations—confirmed Balmaceda's revocation of the Nitrate Railways' monopoly and upheld the concessions granted to Campbell Outram to build a competing railway in Tarapacá.[93] No doubt, as Joseph Brown argues, Balmaceda's conflict with North's interests "was *a factor* in the dispute leading to the revolution of 1891," but it was not the primary, let alone determining, "factor."[94]

Third, focusing on British capitalists and "English imperialism"—or merely on North and his machinations, as the instigators of the civil war—assumes an "anti-imperialist" consistency to Balmaceda's policies and a coherence to his program that neither possessed. For instance, during Balmaceda's administration, British direct investments in Chilean nitrates rose dramatically, but despite his obvious concern about the threat to Chilean capital, his government did not propose specific legislation to congress or use its executive powers to halt or hinder directly the growth of such British investments. Records indicate that 21 British nitrate enterprises were organized in Chile from 1886 through 1890, and this "'boom' in British nitrate investments reached its peak 1888–1889. No less than 18 enterprises were founded in these two years—7 in 1888 and 11 in 1889." No restrictions on their activities were imposed. Even Balmaceda's policies toward the North group aimed mainly at its nitrate transport monopoly in Tarapacá rather than at its investments elsewhere in Chile. In fact, most of these 21 British nitrate firms were founded by North or his close associates; 11 of all 21 (and 9 of the 18) were North enterprises.[95] Even in the midst of the civil

[93] Blakemore 1974, p. 214.
[94] Brown 1958, p. 465, italics added.
[95] Rippy 1948, pp. 460–461.

war, Balmaceda's administration routinely renewed a contract the state had with North's Arauco Company in southern Chile.[96]

The evidence indicates that the Balmaceda government dealt closely with some major British businessmen while opposing the specific interests of others—in particular, North and his associates. It also dealt well with German firms and made serious overtures to American investors and to the American government for support (as Ramírez Necochea himself mentions but ignores analytically).[97] Balmaceda and his leading ministers did not think of themselves as subverting foreign capital in Chile. It was only in the midst of the civil war itself that such a conception, still quite inchoate, began to take hold. Even then the main brunt of the government's rhetorical assaults was borne by North, though occasionally they spilled over into blunt charges that "the English" sought in Tarapacá "a Gibraltar in America, a slice of our country upon which the British flag may wave." Balmaceda was so sure that his government was not a threat to British interests in general, and was not seen as such, that his foreign minister, Domingo Godoy, repeatedly tried to gain *British military assistance to suppress the armed insurrection*; Godoy requested that the British squadron provide support, that the British flag be flown on Chilean cargo ships supplying Balmaceda's army, and that British steamers transport government troops to the northern front.[98] Such actions by Balmaceda and his government's highest officials clearly do not fit a portrait of him as the self-conscious bearer of "marked anti-imperialist sentiments," possessing a "systematic anti-imperialist attitude, which led his government to conduct itself with manifest hostility to the English."[99]

Nonetheless, Balmaceda's visionary nationalism and his government's attempt to spur Chile's independent capitalist development did provoke the movement against him. But that movement arose not primarily, as Brown suggests, because his policies aimed to undermine "the status and power of British capital" in Chile but because they amounted to an unwitting assault on the bastions of

---

[96] Blakemore 1974, p. 205.
[97] Ramírez Necochea 1958, p. 229.
[98] Blakemore 1974, pp. 194–195.
[99] Ramírez Necochea 1960b, p. 134; 1960a, p. 34.

decisive segments of his own class.[100] Balmaceda and his comrades, no less than the Meiji leaders or Bismarck, had no coherent program for capitalist development; nor were they "consistent anti-imperialists." It was only as the Balmacedistas groped toward such a program in practice that they found themselves, almost unawares, engaged in an attempt to subvert their class in order to save it. It was in the face of the unanticipated opposition from within his own class that Balmaceda's state policies took an increasingly radical turn and that, as he antagonized former friends and adherents, he sought the support of former political opponents. Unwittingly, Balmaceda and his closest comrades found themselves taking steps—in the midst of the civil war itself—that, if they had won, would have amounted historically to the imposition of a "revolution from above."

CHILEAN NITRATE CAPITALISTS

Perhaps the central irony, and paradox, of the civil war is that the *Chilean* nitrate capitalists, precisely those whom Balmaceda sought to represent and whose interests he identified with the nation's fate, turned out to be the main base of the insurrection against him. Many of them were among the insurrection's most prominent leaders; most of its financing came from export taxes willingly paid by the *salitreros* (and not only by British and other foreign capitalists) to the Revolutionary Directorate after its forces took control of Tarapacá; the geographical base of the rebel army was in the nitrate terrritories, and its troops were recruited mainly from among the nitrate workers.[101] Thus the question is, what explains the hostility of Chilean nitrate capitalists to Balmaceda's government? What led the leading Chilean nitrate manufacturers, who wanted North's railway monopoly broken and many of whom had long demanded government policies to resist foreign encroachment on the nitrate industry, to turn on a president who articulated just such objectives and attempted to carry them out? What, in the end, united Chile's own nitrate capitalists against the only president who aimed to reinforce and

[100] Brown 1958, p. 465.
[101] Jobet 1955, p. 103; Blakemore 1974, p. 205.

expand their economic base and to stem the ascendancy of their foreign competition?

These questions are crucial to any adequate explanation of the origins of the civil war and its historical significance; but they are virtually absent from the writings on the Balmaceda epoch, including the studies of such Marxian historians as Jobet and Ramírez Necochea, whose almost exclusive focus on the "English imperialists" allows them to ignore these questions.[102] One reason for ignoring these questions is that the answers to them are elusive and, finally, difficult to articulate. Underlying structural determinants, peculiar to their specific intraclass situation, compelled Chilean nitrate capitalists to fight their own president, but only because of the partially contingent historical circumstances in which they and Balmaceda found themselves.

Balmaceda's objectives for the nitrate industry seem fairly clear: to encourage and protect the increased investment of national capital in it; to stimulate its growth and rid it of any restrictions, such as North's railways monopoly; and, above all, to utilize the state's vast nitrate tax revenues to spur Chile's industrialization. But the actual policies his government carried out were often inconsistent; he and his comrades vacillated among specific methods of fulfilling these objectives, and in fact the objectives themselves were partially contradictory.

Early in his presidency, Balmaceda had proposed legislation to congress to finance the state's purchase of the outstanding Peruvian nitrate bonds in the hands of Italian, French, German, Austro-Hungarian, Belgian, and Dutch investors. In mid-June 1887, he announced that the state already had bought 71 *oficinas* (nitrate-operating companies) under the legislation. By annulling the previous

---

[102] Ramírez Necochea (1969, p. 189) finally refers to "the mineowners of the Norte Grande [the provinces of Tarapacá and Antofogasta], *national* and foreign" (italics added) as decisive elements opposed to Balmaceda, but in his lengthy discussion of Balmaceda's nitrate policy and the nature of the opposition to it, he never asks why *Chilean* nitrate capitalists fought against Balmaceda. His all but exclusive focus is on the reasons for *British* opposition (Ramírez Necochea 1969, pp. 64–100). His only implicit answer to this question is wholesale political corruption, but this too, crude as it is, merely dodges the question again: why should the politicians and attorneys working at the behest of *Chilean* nitrate interests have opposed Balmaceda's "anti-imperialist" and "nationalist" policies? Other Chilean Marxian historians also fail to address this crucial question. See, for instance, Jobet 1955.

government's decree authorizing them, the government was also halting any further transfer of nitrate properties to the private holders of Peruvian certificates. What is most significant, Balmaceda declared that his government was "studying whatever measures might be practicable to nationalize those industries in Chile which, at present, primarily benefit foreigners."[103]

What such "measures" might mean was anybody's guess, and in subsequent months throughout 1887 and 1888, there was considerable contention in government circles over the issue of how to "nationalize" (i.e. acquire for the nation) the nitrate industry. One proposal under study—made earlier by several public figures and now urged by Balmaceda's intendant of Tarapacá, Ramón Yavar—was for a state enterprise that would consolidate and operate the state's huge nitrate reserves and the newly acquired nitrate fields and factories.[104] Such an enterprise, argued Adolfo Ibañez (who was later to be Balmaceda's interior minister), could challenge the growing penetration of foreign capital and prevent the formation, already underway in Tarapacá, of "a sort of Indies Company that will soon demand extraterritorial autonomy there." Alfredo Cocq Port, another official in Balmaceda's government, put it bluntly and succinctly in an article on nitrates published in late 1888 by the ministry of finance: "Our absolute ideal can be stated as an aphorism: The State, the only producer, the only transporter, the only seller."[105] Balmaceda's inspector general of nitrates, Guillermo Jullian, also declared himself in favor both "of nationalizing that industry" and of establishing a state nitrate enterprise: "The state should reserve for itself enough nitrate territory of high quality deposits to allow the organization of a national firm to exploit nitrates profitably on its own account."[106]

While such proposals were being debated within the government Balmaceda continued to make some rather pointed remarks in his addresses to the nation. At the National Exposition, on November 25, 1888, he said, referring to the nitrates of Tarapacá: "The for-

[103] Yrarrázaval Larraín 1963, p. 20; Ramírez Necochea 1969, p. 88.

[104] As early as 1880, José Santos Ossa, the man who discovered and pioneered the production of nitrates in Antofagasta, advocated the establishment of a state nitrate enterprise "to exploit these immense riches itself . . . and save the nation" (Pinto Santa Cruz 1959, p. 57).

[105] Ramírez Necochea 1969, pp. 69–70.

[106] Inspección de Salitreras 1888, as cited in Ramírez Necochea 1969, p. 92.

eigner explores these riches and takes the profit produced from . . . our native wealth . . . and the treasures of our soil for the benefit of other lands and unknown peoples." But he also condemned Chilean capitalists for their speculative and unproductive investments, to the detriment of the nation: "Why does [domestic] capital . . . gamble in all sorts of speculative investments . . . but retreat and let foreigners establish banks in Iquique . . . and surrender to them the exploitation of the nitrates of Tarapacá?"[107] Balmaceda's implicit message seems to have been unmistakable: if Chilean private capital could not or would not stem foreign penetration and produce "the riches our nation requires," public capital could and would do so, even impinging if necessary on the immediate interests of Chile's own nitrate manufacturers.

For Balmaceda, "nationalization" meant, at the least, that the state would continue to acquire as many concessions and existing nitrate works as possible from foreign certificate holders, who were prohibited by his presidential decree to own or transfer such properties themselves. What the government would do with its newly acquired nitrate properties, however, was the issue. For "nationalization" could also mean, at the most, the establishment of a state enterprise that would engage in the production, refining, transport, and export of nitrates, as some of Balmaceda's officials advocated. Obviously, such an "exclusively national, great nitrate company," as Senator Luis Aldunate described it in his eloquent pleas for nationalization, would be a threat to foreign capitalists.[108] They would face a rather formidable sort of competition having state power behind it, buttressed by the active support of a government that was committed to breaking the existing nitrate monopolies. This prospect would have aroused concern under ordinary circumstances, but coming as it did during the deepening conflict between Balmaceda and North, it was an even greater source of apprehension in the foreign business community, as editorials in the financial and business press and the comments of other interested observers attest.[109]

---

[107] Ramírez Necochea 1969, p. 87; Blakemore 1974, p. 80.
[108] Yrarrázaval Larraín 1963, p. 20.
[109] Blakemore 1974, p. 80; Russell 1890, pp. 42–43; O'Brien 1976, p. 236. In early 1889, William H. Russell, the famed British correspondent who accompanied North on his travels to and throughout Chile, observed that Balmaceda's "declarations

But precisely for the same reason, the fact that the proposed state enterprise would be "exclusively national" was no comfort to *domestic* private capital, for it would compete with Chilean-owned firms as well as with foreign ones and threaten the immediate interests of both. Furthermore, it would do so in an international market that already appeared to be in trouble, a market that, as we shall see, already faced the prospect of an early glut of overproduction, with no improvement in the situation in sight. Although the Balmaceda government, itself deeply divided on the issue, was still undecided about establishing a public nitrate enterprise, its mere consideration must have deepened the gloom inspired by the market glut and aroused not merely anxiety but also hostility to Balmaceda in the business community. British capitalists and other foreigners heavily involved in the nitrate industry as well as their Chilean compeers must have considered Balmaceda a threat. Gonzalo Bulnes, whom Balmaceda had since replaced as intendant of Tarapacá, made this plain when he bluntly warned of the probable consequences. If government officials formed a state nitrate company "in order to nationalize the wealth of Tarapacá . . . they would *demolish the existing Chilean nitrate industry* in Taltal and Antofagasta. They would imperil the capital of Chilean banks invested with the *salitreros* [nitrate producers] and manage only to provoke a *disastrous struggle.*"[110]

Within Balmaceda's inner council, this same argument against establishing a state enterprise was made by no less than his own interior minister, Enrique Sanfuentes, the man whom Balmaceda still hoped to see succeed him in the presidency. Sanfuentes agreed that the idea of a state enterprise was "generous and patriotic," but he also thought it "chimerical" because it would lead to the dissolution of Chilean nitrate capital. "It is possible that establishing such a great national nitrate company would stimulate the industry," he said, "given the appropriate protection of law—though such a law would be an exception to the general spirit and invariable legislative

---

in reference to the policy of the government in domestic matters, and to its intentions with respect to the great industries of Chile . . . indicated the possibility of important changes, affecting materially the great interests of the strangers within her gates, being at hand, and the mining and nitrate houses, and the railway companies based on concessions, which were chiefly owned by foreigners, were very much exercised by these pronunciamientos" (Russell 1890, pp. 42–43).

[110] Rewritten translation from that by O'Brien 1976, p. 236, italics added.

traditions of this country. But nothing would be able to prevent the dissolution, sale, or cession of the Chilean capitals . . . [already] dedicated to those investments."[111]

"Already in 1888," as Blakemore notes, "informed opinion was uneasy about the proliferation of companies to produce nitrate" because this might bring the entire industry crashing down. There was "disquiet and apprehension" among the leading nitrate houses, as one of their officers put it, that "disaster ere long" might overtake many of them.[112] Given this situation, a state nitrate firm entering the lists as a major producer would not merely be a tough new competitor. What was worse was that it could drastically unsettle the so-called "equilibrium," already endangered, between demand and supply. The threat would be immediate not only to foreign but also to *domestic* nitrate producers, large and small alike. It also would pose a formidable obstacle to the organization of any combination, consignment scheme, or cartel to restrict production and could easily disrupt such a combination even after it was organized. Combination as a "solution" to a depressed market, already tried a few years earlier, was in fact being considered in the industry as an imminent action. But Balmaceda was adamantly opposed to any nitrate combination or "monopoly" because this would squeeze his government's revenue base and tend to dry up the financial fount of his government's drive to modernize and industrialize the country. By 1888, various nitrate duties had already risen from the 27 percent they provided just six years earlier to a current 41 percent of all tax revenue.[113]

Thus even when it became clear in late 1888 that there was scant support in congress for a national nitrate enterprise, Balmaceda's statements on the issue remained studiously vague, perhaps because he himself was undecided about how to proceed or because he thought such a prospect might yet induce foreign nitrate interests to sell off some of their holdings to the state.[114] Furthermore, despite the virtual

[111] Yrarrázaval Larraín 1963, p. 21.
[112] Blakemore 1974, pp. 42–43.
[113] Hernández Cornejo 1930, p. 177.
[114] In January 1888, Balmaceda personally informed a partner in the House of Gibbs that he intended to reduce foreign control of the nitrate industry by establishing a state nitrate enterprise that would be based on the government's existing holdings combined with the planned purchases of additional nitrate lands owned by foreign

absence of support for it in congress, there were still prominent public proponents of a state nitrate enterprise. In early 1889, the newspaper *La Libertad Electoral* warned editorially that the growing British monopoly threatened Chile's very sovereignty and urged Balmaceda to follow through on his original nationalization plan. The influential daily paper ran several articles in February by a "recognized expert on nitrates" reiterating these fears and calling for the establishment of a state monopoly, including an integrated national enterprise with a high capacity for production and refining.[115]

But within the month, those in Balmaceda's government who opposed forming a state nitrate enterprise had apparently won. In early March, in the course of a tour of the republic to rally support for his policies and program Balmaceda made what all historians regard as one of his most significant speeches on nitrates. The speech, in Iquique on March 9, 1889, was a firm reaffirmation of the government's program, which many were now summing up in the slogan, "Chile for the Chilians."[116] Foreign monopoly was the main problem in the nitrate industry, Balmaceda declared, because this virtually allowed foreigners to control prices and, at the same time, through the Nitrate Railways, to impose prohibitive freight charges on other nitrate producers. "Private property [in Tarapacá] is owned almost exclusively by foreigners, and is being rapidly concentrated in the hands of persons of only one nationality. It would be preferable that the property belonged to Chileans also." Balmaceda also raised the prospect of nationalizing North's railroads and operating them as a state enterprise. He hoped, he said, "that at an early date all the railways in Tarapacá will become national property," and he went on to declare that he also aspired "to have Chile become the owner of all the railroads that traverse its territory."[117] Ramírez Necochea calls this speech "a veritable declaration of war on English monopoly

capitalists. Balmaceda apparently thought that the pressure of the Nitrate Railways Company's monopoly would induce Gibbs and other foreign companies to sell their properties to the state enterprise at low prices. Once the enterprise was established, the government would then enforce the 1886 nullification decree against North's railway (O'Brien 1976, pp. 235–236).
[115] O'Brien 1976, p. 239.
[116] Russell 1890, p. 81.
[117] Yrarrázaval Larraín 1963, p. 40; Ramírez Necochea 1969, p. 93.

capital,"[118] and even Encina agrees: "Reading Balmaceda's speech in Iquique, North understood that the orientation of nitrate policy, begun by President Pinto and continued by Santa María, of surrendering the nitrate industry to foreigners and limiting Chile to collecting an export royalty, had changed drastically toward the . . . nationalization of the industry."[119]

Balmaceda took care to say also that he wanted "the question of the railroads to be resolved equitably, without injury to legitimate private interests."[120] But this could scarcely have diminished the "anxiety aroused" not only "among the capitalists of Europe," as a visiting British writer observed, but also among the leading financiers and industrialists of Chile, especially those with heavy personal investments in the nitrate railroads.[121]

Yet Balmaceda's stand remained publicly ambiguous on the question of state enterprise and its role in Chilean capitalist development. He may well have been personally ambivalent. In the same speech in which he remarked on his aspiration for state ownership of the railroads, he also said that the time had come "to declare before the entire Republic that State enterprise cannot hold a monopoly in the nitrate industry. The State's fundamental mission is only to guarantee property and liberty." He added, however, that a monopoly would not be allowed to "private individuals either, whether *national or foreign*; we will never accept the economic tyranny of the many or of the few. The State must always reserve to itself sufficient nitrate property so that it can use its influence to protect production and sales and to frustrate, in any eventuality, the industrial dictatorship of Tarapacá." Balmaceda now proposed "to auction a part of the nitrate territories in possession of the State," including the fields and factories acquired earlier from foreign bondholders, so that Chileans, too, would have a share of Tarapacá's nitrates. "This would open new horizons to Chilean capital, if the conditions in which it operates and the preoccupations holding it back are corrected. The investment of Chilean capital in that industry will bring us the benefits of ex-

[118] Ramírez Necochea 1969, p. 94.
[119] Encina 1952, I, p. 398.
[120] Yrarrázaval Larraín 1963, p. 40.
[121] Russell 1890, pp. 42, 225. On shareownership in the principal railways, see Oppenheimer 1976.

porting our own riches and stabilizing our own production, without the danger of a possible monopoly."[122]

Rather contrasting interpretations have been made of this Iquique speech, and none the least by Balmaceda's own contemporaries. North's traveling companion reported that "it was inferred, especially from his speech at Iquique, that he [Balmaceda] intended, if he could, to close the course to any but native competitors . . . to refuse industrial concessions in the country to non-Chilian [sic] residents, and to reserve the State lands still unappropriated, exclusively and inalienably, to citizens of the Republic."[123] El Mercurio (March 25, 1889) observed that Balmaceda's Iquique speech, which "fully expressed his ideas about the nitrate question and his objectives [for the nitrate industry], might be a bit contrary to Mr. North's goals for Tarapacá and its important industries."[124]

Many, however, heard this speech as a retreat from earlier nationalist positions. An editorial in La Época (March 17 and March 19, 1889), for example, argued that in the face of the growing threat from British penetration (which was a threat because "powerful interests are not only protected by our own authorities and our laws, but also, dangerously, by the . . . force of foreign governments, a force that always accompanies the citizens of a country when they establish businesses and constitute interests in a strange land"), the president failed to propose any concrete action to withstand it. Where were the provisions, the newspaper asked, to ensure that the auctioning of public nitrate properties would really lead to the emergence of a domestic nitrate industry able to compete with foreign capital? It was necessary, La Época again argued, to establish a national nitrate company under state auspices.[125] An article in El Ferrocarril, took a similar line. It attacked the president for not proposing specific steps to stop Tarapacá from becoming a "foreign hacienda . . . a sort of small part of British India exploited by a multitude of corporations organized outside of Chile, without any national interest . . . leaving the nation with a sovereignty more nominal than real."

---

[122] Yrarrázaval Larraín 1963, pp. 27–28, italics added.
[123] Russell 1890, p. 315.
[124] Ramírez Necochea 1969, p. 94. Sometime in the early 1880s, apparently, the "el" became "El" in the name of the newspaper, El Mercurio.
[125] Ramírez Necochea 1969, p. 64; Blakemore 1974, p. 35; O'Brien 1976, p. 24.

In words that Balmaceda himself would shortly take as his own, the article said: "Tarapacá cannot be, it must not be, and it never will be a foreign factory; the Chilean people will not permit it." It urged that if the state was not going to establish its own enterprise, it should assure the creation of viable private Chilean-owned companies by using its nitrate properties and financial resources to underwrite them. The state could also establish mixed companies in which it would have joint ownership with private stockholders. But, above all, these must be companies, the article concluded, "whose management, accountability and majority share-holding would be Chilean, with a prohibition against shares being transferred to foreigners resident outside Chile."[126]

In part, this was a reiteration of the position of Senator Luis Aldunate; alone in the senate the previous year, he had condemned Balmaceda's proposed sale of the state's nitrate properties as a give-away to foreigners. The government, he argued, should offer contracts for the rental of state nitrate properties only to nationals, with the express stipulation that they productively develop them.[127] Indeed, several nitrate capitalists associated with Guillermo Billinghurst also specifically urged the government not to grant new concessions or transfer or sell its properties unless at least 85 percent of the company's capital belonged to Chileans, and then only with an obligatory contractual clause prohibiting the sale or transfer of stock to foreigners.[128] This, in effect, was now the position Balmaceda adopted, with some modification, in his annual message to congress on June 1, 1889, barely two months after his major Iquique speech.

Annual messages on the opening of congress, as Russell observed at the time, were "State documents which announce the line of [presidential] policy." Since such an exposition of the president's "policy in public" was accompanied by "full ability to carry [it] into effect," Russell noted, "as much weight is naturally attached to it as men were wont to give to the New Year's Day announcements

---

[126] *El Ferrocarril* may have been edited at the time by the prominent Balmacedista, Angel Custodio Vicuña. See V. Figueroa 1925–1931, IV–V, pp. 1054–1055. Speech excerpts are from Ramírez Necochea 1969, pp. 65–66; Blakemore 1974, pp. 85–86.
[127] Jobet 1955, pp. 116–117.
[128] Segall 1953, p. 182.

of Napoleon the Third."[129] In contrast to Balmaceda's Iquique speech, this message to congress left no room for guessing about his intentions. Balmaceda proposed that "the nitrate grounds be divided into districts, to be sold at public auction, good, medium and inferior nitrate deposits being included in one lot, and that 4,000 mining concessions [estacas], selected from the best Government land, should be appropriated, to be worked by Chileans, these shares not being transferable for a time, and then to be transferable to Chileans only." Once these 4,000 national concessions were granted, then in every succeeding year, half of each estaca would go to the highest bidder at public auction, but half would be reserved for Chileans, with shares not transferable to foreigners. This would stem "the absorption of small capital by foreign capital"; it would ensure that "the free flow of production would not be impeded, and, at the same time, would guarantee that an industry of Chilean capitals and for Chilean industrialists would take root. . . . It is true," Balmaceda concluded, "that we should not close the door to free competition and production of nitrates in Tarapacá, but neither can we consent to the conversion of this vast and rich region simply into a foreign factory."[130]

This was the forthright statement of concrete government measures to halt continued foreign penetration of the nitrate industry and to resurrect national capital within it. These measures, like Balmaceda's earlier revocation of North's monopoly, were bound to create, as Russell observed, "an unfavourable impression with regard to the equity, in the best sense of the word, of the Government of Chile, in its dealings with vested interests . . . among the capitalists of Europe."[131] No doubt most foreign investors, and North in particular, were hostile to this proposal to sell large reserves of public nitrate lands only to Chileans. But what would such a policy mean, not for "the capitalists of Europe" but for those of Chile? As La Tribuna, one of Balmaceda's most consistent supporters, had recognized even from his Iquique speech, the implementation of these measures would directly threaten the largest nitrate producers by making it very difficult for "a coalition of great capital resources to set up a monopoly

129 Russell 1890, p. 316.
130 Ramírez Necochea 1969, pp. 94–95.
131 Russell 1890, p. 225.

to overwhelm industrialists of modest means''; their implementation would also make the formation of any combination in the industry all but impossible and thereby ensure, as Balmaceda hoped, "the free flow of production."[132]

With its possession of immense unworked nitrate properties, the state had the potential capacity to produce roughly as much as was now being produced by all private firms. The state's holdings represented an estimated potential of 52 percent of total nitrate production. "If these new nitrate properties were put in production, with State financing and the active intervention of the Executive," as Marcelo Segall correctly observes, "a new battle could be launched against the huge British investments."[133]

Opening up these new nitrate properties, however, would vastly increase productive capacity in the industry precisely at a moment when, as noted earlier, the industry was already in a growing crisis of "overproduction" and falling prices. In the fall of 1889, nitrate inventories in Europe already exceeded the previous year's by 200,000 tons, and there were another 400,000 tons "afloat" from Chile to Europe compared with the same period in 1888. Just as Balmaceda was openly edging toward his new policy in the spring of 1889, with all its hazardous implications for nitrate capital, foreign and domestic alike, the price of nitrate shares in London began to fall drastically; by mid-year, when he announced his new nitrate policy, the accumulating surpluses were severely depressing the market and pushing the average annual export price of nitrates to a new low, which continued steadily downward during 1890.[134] Once again, as in the previous crisis beginning in 1884 and lasting to the eve of Balmaceda's inauguration, the precipitous decline in prices not only threatened the profits of the most efficient producers but also the very existence of the smaller and high-cost producers; the latter, who were predominantly Chilean, now faced "speedy and certain ruin," as Francisco Valdés Vergara had put it earlier, unless they could halt the heavy fall of prices by combining to restrict production.[135]

[132] Blakemore 1974, p. 84.
[133] Segall 1953, pp. 208–211.
[134] Blakemore 1974, pp. 107–110; Brown 1963, p. 234; Russell 1890, pp. 341, 372–373.
[135] Brown 1963, p. 234.

Balmaceda's need to assure rising exports to secure the necessary revenue to underwrite his development program and the interests of the nitrate capitalists in restricting production were now immediately at odds. Balmaceda already had let it be known in January 1889 that, as Britain's consul general noted, "any curtailment of production causing a loss of revenue would be met by a corresponding increase in duty on exports." If thousands of nitrate concessions were now opened and put into production—as a leading nitrate merchant put it at the time, "nitrate is *easily* produced. It is easy to *over*-produce"—the consequence for the entire industry would be disastrous.[136]

Thus if, in principle, Chilean capitalists might have welcomed the state's making new concessions available to them and prohibiting any foreign acquistion of the auctioned properties, in practice—*at this specific conjuncture*—this was a direct threat to their immediate interests. Balmaceda's plan apparently had the support of some nitrate capitalists, as we saw earlier, and there was, as Russell observed, "a great schism among nitrate makers" as to how to react to the impending crisis.[137] But even those who agreed with Balmaceda's attacks on North's monopoly, and who advocated the "Chileanization" of the industry, were now jeopardized by his new plan to sell off a huge number of state nitrate properties and by his hostility to any new combination. On the one hand, the Balmaceda government's plan to sell these properties threatened the industry with even greater overproduction; on the other, Balmaceda's "vigorous opposition" to the formation of a combination was a decisive obstacle to the industry's own efforts at salvation.[138] Even in the best of times, as Russell observed, "the interest of the Government in collecting as much revenue as possible from the exportation of nitrate does not accord with that of the manufacturers," but these were the worst of times; if Balmaceda now "insisted on the manufacturers sending down their nitrate to the coast and shipping it *irrespective of consequences*, the Government of Chile would *deliver a heavy blow, and cause great discouragement to capitalists*.[139]

[136] Blakemore 1974, pp. 44, 43.
[137] Russell 1890, p. 209.
[138] Brown 1963, p. 235.
[139] Russell 1890, p. 334, italics added.

Any successful combination required the participation and close cooperation of both Chilean and foreign capitalists, especially the largest of them such as Gibbs, North, Besa, Puelma, and Edwards. By mid-1890, specific terms of a combination were being negotiated by the two major English houses and arch rivals, Gibbs and North. It would be necessary to bring together the major firms in Tarapacá, where North predominated, with those in Antofogasta, where Gibbs and the principal Chilean firms were centered. As a Gibbs partner noted, his firm had "great interests" in Antofogasta and was thus hostile to any combination formed in Tarapacá alone. "A combination for the restriction of production of the northern *oficinas* would not suit us," he wryly wrote, "unless we had the consignment of their produce; as without that inducement we should be obliged as a mere matter of business to cut all their throats." By the summer, Gibbs had become convinced that Balmaceda would not grant them the competing railway concession in Tarapacá they had been seeking from him for much of his presidency. It was impossible for Gibbs to agree to Balmaceda's demand—given the industry's present danger from overproduction—that the firm stay out of any combination and produce and ship a guaranteed minimum from its new Tarapacá works. Now, "as a mere matter of business," Gibbs, North, and Chilean capitalists had to unite to form the combination; under the circumstances, this meant a decisive confrontation with Balmaceda, for everyone understood, as a Gibbs partner reported to London, that the president was determined "to break any nitrate monopoly [whether trust or combination] that is formed."[140] The terms of the combination were agreed on in the last days of 1890 and signed by the participants in mid-January 1891, scarcely a week after the insurrection began. It was in full operation throughout the civil war, solidifying almost the entire nitrate industry, domestic and foreign interests alike, against the Balmaceda government. Here was the dilemma and the tragedy, in these specific historical circumstances, of the Chilean nitrate capitalists. Despite their consistent demands that the state buttress and expand their relative position in the industry vis-à-vis foreign firms, they were now compelled to ally themselves with the same foreign interests against whom they had long contended

[140] O'Brien 1976, pp. 250, 252.

and to fight the first and only president who fully championed their past demands.

In fact, the relationship between Chilean capitalists and foreign capitalists had already put the former in an internally contradictory situation. It was not only that they were momentarily united by their common situation in the depressed world market, but also that in recent years their concrete interests had become increasingly intertwined. Even before the War of the Pacific, much so-called "English capital" had really been Chilean capital exported to what were then Peruvian and Bolivian territories to finance English nitrate works or to exploit the nitrates in joint ventures. In the 1870s, "Iquique and Pisagua had contracted huge debts in the Valparaíso markets," with an estimated financial investment by Chilean banks and other creditors of $8,000,000 in Tarapacá alone. The various English and Chilean houses in Valparaiso frequently floated large loans in common in the larger financial ventures.[141]

Major English and other foreign firms, the German houses of Folsch and Martin and of Otto Hermann, and the English Gibbs and Company, for instance, had common investments with Chileans. The Antofogasta Nitrates and Railway Company, which bulked largest among nitrate producers there, grew out of the original venture of José Santos Ossa and Francisco Puelma Castillo; it expanded in partnership with the Edwards banking family and the English house of Gibbs, whom Agustín Edwards Ross brought into the company. Similarly, Chile's sixth largest bank, Banco Mobiliario, principally owned by the Concha y Toro and Subercaseaux families, heavily invested in partnership with Folsch and Martin and with Hermann. Campbell Outram, the English firm to which Balmaceda's government granted the concession to build the competing railway at Agua Santa as a way of breaking North's monopoly, subsequently reorganized in partnership with Chilean investors, among them Balmaceda's own finance minister, Lauro Barros.[142] (But the Agua Santa Company also later joined the nitrate combination unconditionally.)[143] Banco Valparaíso, Chile's second largest bank, carried major accounts both for North's Nitrate Railways Company and for Gibbs

[141] Billinghurst 1889, pp. 37–38; Jobet 1955, p. 8.
[142] O'Brien 1976, pp. 178, 246; Jobet 1955, pp. 58, 63.
[143] Blakemore 1974, p. 189.

and Company, and the Banco Nacional, in which leading nitrate capitalist José Besa was a principal, also held large Gibbs deposits.[144]

Thus, especially with the proliferation of "joint stock companies" (or corporations) in nitrates in the late 1880s, a rapid merger of foreign and domestic capital took place, and most wealthy Chileans probably were shareholders in these corporations.[145] Plainly (to paraphrase Russell's observations in 1890), although in one sense they were apparently antagonistic, the *immediate* interests of foreign and Chilean nitrate capital were by now indissoluble.[146] As a result, when Balmaceda called for the "nationalization" of the nitrate industry and proposed specific limitations on foreign capital, he was also unwittingly attacking *Chilean* capital.

This close relationship between the foreign and domestic business communities, coupled with Balmaceda's confrontation with both of them over the organization of a nitrate combination at a moment when their market was daily growing more desperate, provoked their common wrath against Balmaceda's government. Their shared concrete interests and the momentary conjuncture in the world market now converged to unite them politically while their underlying symbiotic relationship was also probably the main reason for the inconsistencies, vacillations and overall lack of coherence in Balmaceda's nitrate policies. It was this internal contradiction in the political economy of Chilean nitrate capital that engendered the earlier incoherence in state policy and prevented the Balmaceda government itself from fashioning a coherent development program. In other words, the immediate market interest of Chilean nitrate capitalists contradicted their ultimate interest in liberating themselves from the domination of foreign capital and led to their historical self-interment.

THE BANKS AND BALMACEDA

The major private banks of Chile, as is evident from the previous discussion, formed a crucial financial nexus with foreign capital in the nitrate industry. Any policies to limit foreign capital tended also to jeopardize the banks. This in itself put them and Balmaceda on

[144] O'Brien 1976, pp. 159–160; V. Figueroa 1925–1931, IV–V, p. 193.
[145] See Escobar Cerda 1959 on the growth of the large Chilean corporation.
[146] Russell 1890, p. 335.

an involuntary collision course. In addition the banks were vital to the formation of any nitrate combination, and Balmaceda's insistence that the industry continue its shipments would also have dealt them, as Russell remarked, "a heavy blow." This banking segment of the capitalist class was thus also thrown into opposition to Balmaceda, and several of Chile's principal bankers, among them Agustín Edwards Ross and Augusto Matte Pérez, were leaders of the anti-Balmaceda insurrection.

In many respects, Chile's major banks were at the heart of the nitrate industry. They had been deeply involved in financing the nitrate boom, both as the underwriters of the offerings of shares in the recently organized corporations and as the principal financiers of the nitrate producers. Consequently they had also become, at the least, part-owners of many nitrate works. They provided both the short-term high-interest loans to small producers, through a system of loan "discounting" on sales agreements, and the long-term financing for the major manufacturers, by mortgages against the nitrate works. With the fall in the price of nitrate shares on the stock market and the sinking export prices, the banks found themselves holding considerable commercial paper of doubtful value.[147]

The major nitrate producers and export houses were among the largest depositors in the banks, and much of the latter's operating capital came from such deposits in business accounts. Consequently the continuing depletion of these accounts as the result of the growing crisis immediately threatened the banks' operations. Aside from their joint investments with leading nitrate firms, the banks' foreclosures on mortgages against nitrate works that had shut down or failed, as well as their purchases of these works from heavily indebted clients, also involved them deeply with the immediate fate of the industry. In short, "nitrate capital" was a specific form of "finance capital," the result of the coalescence of loan capital and productive capital in the nitrate industry. Understandably, then, in the similar if less critical world market just a few years earlier, the banks already had been the "major movers" behind the formation of the "First Combination" of 1884–1886.[148] In the present crisis, however, the banks were compelled to confront the dangers of the market, not with the

[147] See Blakemore 1974, p. 90.
[148] O'Brien 1976, pp. 26–27, 159–161, 178.

assistance of the government, as they had in the past, but on the contrary in the face of its opposition to any sort of nitrate combination.

The liquidity problems of the private banks induced by the nitrate crisis also injected still another set of concrete intraclass interests into the escalating conflict between congress and the president over the relative independence of the executive powers of the state. For if the stability of the banks was endangered by the spreading depression in nitrates, their instability also threatened Balmaceda's development program. The banks needed the government to shore them up or at least stand out of the way as they sought to organize a nitrate combination. But the same conditions that drastically reduced the banks' liquidity, if not threatening them with insolvency, made the existing statutes empowering the private banks to act for the state exchequer especially onerous to Balmaceda's government.[149] This relationship with the banks restricted the president's fiscal independence and, perhaps even more important, also narrowed his freedom of maneuver in the sharpening political struggle.

Contentious issues concerning the inconvertibility of the paper currency and what financial reforms, including reconversion to the silver standard, were needed to stabilize the currency and prevent its capricious fluctuations and continuing drop in value had been under discussion in congress virtually from Balmaceda's inauguration, and none of the issues had been resolved. But with the crisis in nitrates, and its general economic threat, they were in need of urgent resolution. Whether and at what rate to retire the paper currency from circulation, how much should remain with the private banks, and how promptly the executive should have access to the public funds on deposit with them were all questions for debate. But the latter question was immediately critical both for the banks and for Balmaceda. Once again, like other concrete political issues whose

---

[149] Temporarily idle public funds were held on deposit in private banks, which were permitted to invest these funds at interest rates higher than they paid the state; private banks also had the right to issue their own paper currency, backed by specified reserves. The irony is that early in his presidency, some observers, including the British envoy to Chile, thought that Balmaceda was "dealing tenderly with financiers." Balmaceda's earlier policies had encouraged "private banks of more or less doubtful solvency . . . to go on issuing notes far beyond their proper means," the British envoy reported in mid-June 1886, "and these have become merged in the general circulation under the protection of the forced currency laws" (Blakemore 1974, p. 74).

resolution would impinge differently on the various segments of the dominant class, these too became posed in terms of congressional versus presidential prerogatives. Was congress or the executive branch of government to control the disbursement of the fiscal funds? Which of them would decide when and how such funds would be accessible to the president?

In his annual message to congress on June 1, 1890, Balmaceda asked the special joint finance commission to resume its deliberations on reorganization of the banking system and to submit its proposals promptly because of the country's pressing monetary problems. The proposed legislation that gained the banking commission's support would have permitted the private banks to continue to issue official currency in specified denominations ($1 to $500) and, most important, would have allowed the government to withdraw the fiscal funds deposited with the banks only gradually in 10 monthly installments of not more than 10 percent of the amount deposited in each bank. If enacted, this law would limit the Balmaceda government's access to state funds and severely restrict its fiscal independence and ability to finance its programs; the law was clearly unacceptable to Balmaceda because of its infringement on executive authority. He also saw it, as he said later, as designed merely to defend the "caprice of bankers and rentiers, [whose] economies are aimed at limiting the public works."[150]

Coincidentally, perhaps, the proposed banking legislation also came at a moment of unveiled and unprecedented attack on presidential authority; on June 14, 1890, the chamber of deputies refused to debate the provisions of the president's tax bill or to authorize the collection of taxes until he appointed a new ministry having "the confidence of Congress." Ironically, the Balmaceda government's earlier financial reforms, at the behest of the banking community itself (which provided the private banks with huge government deposits to use as operating capital), now became, in the midst of the deepening crisis, a potentially lethal weapon against the banks. A leader of the anti-Balmaceda opposition, Enrique MacIver, had seen this at the time; when the legislation was under discussion in the summer of 1888, he had warned that "with huge . . . deposits [in the private banks] under the control of the Government to release

---

[150] Ramírez Necochea 1969, p. 128.

for banking circulation or withhold from circulation, in what kind of a situation does that put the institutions of credit? Isn't it obvious that these institutions and the men of fortune who sustain them and whom they are supposed to serve will now have to be preoccupied with the Government and live in fear of provoking its disapproval?"[151] In response to the senate resolution demanding that Balmaceda appoint a new ministry to its liking, and in anticipation of the proposed banking legislation to curtail dramatically his government's fiscal independence, the president was now to justify MacIver's earlier fears.

Balmaceda issued an executive order notifying the banks that "the deposits of Government money held by the Banks at thirty days notice of intended withdrawal were in future to be considered as deposit accounts at call." Enforcing this decree would have dealt a near fatal blow to the banks in the country's already unstable financial situation and, as the British ambassador observed, would have brought "ruin to persons engaged in industries towards which advances had been made by the banks."[152] Implementing this measure would have resulted in a "catastrophe for the numerous debtors compelled to make immediate payment to the banks," which would have had to call in their loans in order to place the equivalent of the fiscal deposits on call for the government.[153] In effect, this decree and Balmaceda's subsequent veto of the banking legislation proposed by congress not only confirmed the antagonism of the leading bankers but also cemented the alliance between the heavily indebted nitrate producers and the bankers in their common struggle against Balmaceda's government.

THE PROBLEM OF THE LANDLORDS

Balmaceda, aspiring to articulate and to advance materially the interests of national nitrate capital, found himself locked in mortal combat with the very men who were its preeminent personification. But what, then, was the place of Balmaceda's own most immediate class peers, the agrarian aristocrats, in this struggle? In fact, despite

---

[151] Yrarrázaval Larraín 1963, p. 76.
[152] Blakemore 1974, p. 165.
[153] Yrarrázaval Larraín 1963, p. 71.

their structural centrality in the dominant class, it is not clear how central they were in the struggle within it or on what side in the civil war the weight of their opinion and action fell. At the time, in April 1891, *London Times* correspondent Robert L. Thompson, who was "the principal supporter of the *Congressional* cause in the English press," reported unequivocally that "almost all of the landowning families" favored "the fall of the President."[154] Similarly, a contemporary American historian, Anson U. Hancock, who was sympathetic to Balmaceda's cause, wrote immediately after the civil war that the "old aristocratic families" were among the leading participants in the "revolt of interests" against Balmaceda.[155]

Chile's leading Marxian historians also generally assert that the landowners were one of the three pillars of the "all-powerful trinity" that fought Balmaceda. Julio César Jobet, for instance, writes that "The 1891 bloody civil war was the combined action of English imperialism and of the landlords and national bankers united in a close bloc, because [Balmaceda's] reforms and projects hurt their interests." Similarly, Ramírez Necochea argues that "The landed oligarchy understood that the plans of the [Balmaceda government] involved the destruction of the eminently feudal relations of production prevailing in the countryside."[156]

In contrast, although he denies any basic "social nature" to the civil war, liberal historian Heise González makes precisely the opposite claim, namely, that "commanding landowners" were among Balmaceda's closest comrades and partisans in the civil war. "Dozens of landowners as powerful economically as the bankers [who aided the Congressionalist band] . . . were Balmaceda militants. . . . In fact, Balmaceda, who announced in the official press that he was fighting the 'imperious oligarchy,' governed right up to the last minute with genuine representatives of the old colonial aristocracy, which he himself belonged to, and with whom he felt inclined to govern."[157]

Consistent with this view and suggestive is the fact that while

---

[154] Blakemore 1964, p. 428, italics added; Ramírez Necochea 1960b, p. 188.
[155] Hancock 1893, p. 349.
[156] Jobet 1955, p. 103; Ramírez Necochea 1969, p. 112. See also Ramírez Necochea 1960b, p. 199; and Segall 1953, p. 189.
[157] Heise González 1974, pp. 80, 118.

Valparaiso's mercantile and banking community openly fought Balmaceda, Santiago—the home of central Chile's leading landed families—remained comparatively quiescent during the civil war. Of course, with Balmaceda's government and its coercive power intact in that capital city, their inaction might merely have been the better part of wisdom. But at least one prominent leader of the antigovernment insurgents there thought differently. Senator Carlos Walker Martínez, "the head and soul of the Revolutionary Committee" that led the clandestine struggle in Santiago against Balmaceda during the civil war, was so infuriated at the "capital for not having risen against the tyranny, despite his efforts," that he personally ordered the homes of many of its leading families destroyed by organized "mobs" after the fall of Balmaceda's government.[158]

On balance, however, the historical evidence available, although circumstantial, persuades me that Jobet and Ramírez Necochea are closer to the truth than is Heise González. Although their conceptualization of Chile's late nineteenth-century agrarian relations as "feudal" is historically faulty and misleading, their assertion that "the families of the great landowners" opposed Balmaceda is probably correct. Heise González is right to emphasize that "commanding landowners" were prominent in Balmaceda's loyal coterie, and this is an uncomfortable fact generally ignored by leftist interpreters, including Jobet, Ramírez Necochea, and others.[159] But Heise González misperceives who the landed Balmacedistas really were and what they represented and thus misconstrues the historic meaning of their presence at the helm of state with Balmaceda. They represented not "the old colonial aristocracy," as he says, but, as we shall see in the next chapter, a specific historical product of Chile's recent mid-to-late nineteenth-century capitalist development: the coalescence of agrarian property and mining capital.

What impact did Balmaceda's policies have on agrarian interests? Some "commanding landowners" certainly benefited materially from Balmaceda's massive sponsorship of the construction of roads, canals, bridges, viaducts, and railroad lines, traversing the country and tying it together; these not only provided manufacturing and mining

[158] V. Figueroa, 1925–1931, iv–v, pp. 1081–1082.
[159] For instance, Frank 1967, pp. 73–85.

with the "easy and economical transportation" the country had lacked before, but they also now made it feasible and profitable for the products of the great landed estates to reach Chile's expanding internal markets. The railroad lines built or begun by Balmaceda's government were "particularly effective in linking together production, distribution, and consumption centers in the Central Valley and the South."[160] But even the landowners themselves probably were not homogeneous economically and in fact the various agrarian regions were affected unevenly by the "great new network" of roads, canals, bridges, and railways being laid down throughout the country.

Of the roughly 1,200 kilometers of proposed new railway lines that congress reluctantly approved on January 20, 1888, I found that slightly over half was located in the rapidly developing, newly settled, south-central zone from Concepción to Chiloe, and a fifth was in the Norte Chico. In contrast, somewhat less than a third was in the Central Valley. (See Table 3.1.) Similarly, of the four major metal bridges built during Balmaceda's term, three spanned the Malleco, Bío-Bío and Laja rivers in the south-central zone, and one was located in Ñuble, the southernmost province of the Central Valley.[161]

Segall also argues that Balmaceda's public works "favored the southern *latifundistas* . . . [and] in contrast, hurt the other *latifundista* group in the center of the country."[162] But, unfortunately, the available historical studies provide no information on how many of the so-called *latifundistas* had sizable holdings in *both* areas, in the near-south and in the Central Valley; that is, it is not at all clear to what extent they really formed two relatively differentiated agrarian elements at that time, and thus whether or not they responded differently to Balmaceda's policies, as Segall claims. None of these questions is even posed, let alone answered, in the existing historical works.[163]

---

[160] Vattier 1890, p. 1; Kirsch 1977, p. 13. Also see Vattier 1901.

[161] Ramírez Necochea 1969, p. 121; Encina 1952, I, pp. 376–377.

[162] Segall 1953, p. 189.

[163] I analyze the social composition of the leading Balmacedistas and Congressionalists in detail in the next chapter, but it is relevant to note here, at the risk of being accused of vulgar reductionism, that 3 of the 15 landed Balmacedistas in our sample had identifiable south central estates (including Arístides Zañartu, the author of the state bank), whereas, in contrast, none of the 6 landowners among the leading congressionalists had such an identifiable estate. (Further, in anticipation of the analysis below, it should be noted here that the 3 Balmacedist south-central landowners were simultaneously major copper- or coal-mine owners.)

Table 3.1. Railway Lines Constructed Under Balmaceda[a]

Zone[b] and Province	Station to Station	Direction[c]	Kilometers	%[d]
Norte Chico			212	18.2
Atacama	Vallenar to Huasco	EW	48	
Coquimbo	Salamanca to Illapel			
	and Los Vilos	EW	128	
Coquimbo	Ovalle to San Marcos	NS	36	
Central Valley			353	30.4
Valparaiso-	La Ligua and Cabildo			
Aconcagua	to Calera	NS	76	
Santiago	Santiago to Melipilla	EW	59	
Santiago	Santiago to Lo Barnechea	EW	17	
O'Higgins	Pelequen to Peumo	EW	46	
O'Higgins	Palmilla to Alcones	EW	33	
Talca-Maule	Talca to Constitución	EW	75	
Liñares-Maule	Cauquenes to Parral	EW	47	
South-Central			597	51.4
Ñuble-Bío Bío	Coihueco to Mulchen	NS	43	
Valdivia	Antilhue to Valdivia	EW	37	
Malleco[e]-Osorno	Victoria to Osorno	NS	403	
Valdivia-Osorno	Trumau to Osorno			
	y la Unión	NS	50	
Cautín-Malleco	Victoria to Temuco	NS	64	
Total			1,162	100.0

[a] As listed in Encina 1952, I, pp. 376–377, and Ramírez Necochea 1969, p. 118. The construction of these lines was approved by congress on January 20, 1888. Not all of them were actually completed during his presidency.

[b] Norte Chico includes the provinces from Atacama to Coquimbo. Central Valley includes the provinces from Aconcagua to Ñuble. South-Central includes the provinces from Concepción to Chiloé.

[c] EW = east-west line. NS = north-south line.

[d] Percentage of total railway lines constructed.

[e] Malleco and Cautín were established as new provinces in 1887, under Balmaceda's presidency.

The final "pacification" (as the Chileans termed it) of the Araucanian indigenes in 1883 had put a huge new region at the disposal
of the state, open to new forms of agricultural exploitation, and
Balmaceda made its settlement or "colonization" a priority. In his
initial message to congress, he urged the establishment of a Bureau
of Lands, Colonization, and Immigration to survey the territory, fix
the boundaries of Araucanian property, and prepare the area for
settlement. Though this plan was rejected by congress, Balmaceda
established the Bureau anyway by executive order. The Bureau created two new provinces, Malleco and Cautín, in this "frontier" area
and proceeded to encourage settlement by both Chileans and immigrant farmers from Europe. In his second congressional message
a year later, Balmaceda announced that the state would auction lots
there, limited in size to 50 hectares, so that they could be within the
reach of "men of modest fortune" and bring "industrial life to the
vast and fertile portion of Araucania."[164] In the four years of the
Balmaceda government, expenditures on settlement and immigration
expanded 10 times, to a total of nearly $2 million (and dropped
quickly in the years after his government's fall).[165]

Ramírez Necochea, following Segall, also argues that Balmaceda's
settlement program "adversely affected . . . the latifundium of the
Central Zone [because] a new agricultural region was emerging,
whose volume and value of production could gain marked predominance in the national agrarian economy" and that this provoked the
opposition of the great landowning families.[166] Certainly, Balmaceda's colonization policies were vociferously attacked as wasteful
and destructive by the Conservative party and its congressional
spokesmen. Colonization would "bring in useless people," Senator
Carlos Walker Martínez declared, and would have "fatal consequences" for the nation. The Conservative daily *El Independiente*
"protested tirelessly," as it said on March 19, 1889, "against the
system of colonization. . . . Aside from robbing the Chilean worker
of a plot of land that he could live on, it demands tribute in taxes
to pay for the entry and settlement of foreigners who are less capable
. . . and who replace him in working and benefiting from the soil."[167]

---

[164] Ramírez Necochea 1969, pp. 138–140; Segall 1953, p. 189.
[165] Macchiavello Varas 1931, II, p. 83.
[166] Ramírez Necochea 1969, p. 141.
[167] Ramírez Necochea 1969, p. 115.

In the years of Balmaceda's presidency, there was a significant movement of migrants from the rural areas of the central region to the new frontier provinces stretching south from Concepcíon; in addition, some 24,000 foreign immigrants settled there during the same years.[168] It is not known how much of the territory really ended up only in the hands of "men of modest fortune"—Chilean and foreign—as Balmaceda intended. Nor is it known how much land was obtained, either fraudulently or through subsequent purchases, by wealthier Chileans—including Central Valley landowners and near-south grain-mill interests. But the area was, in fact, rapidly transformed into a burgeoning center of wheat production. As Arnold J. Bauer points out, "data on internal [agricultural] production are the most difficult to gather and the least reliable," and the data on exports of wheat to foreign markets are only somewhat better. But bearing this in mind, there appears to have been a very rapid shift of most wheat production from the Central Valley to the new frontier zone. Settlers had pushed out into the Araucanian area bit by bit in the preceding decades, and the near-south was already a major milling and wheat-growing zone before Balmaceda assumed the presidency.[169] Measured by the exports leaving the port of Talcahuano, the area from Concepción southward already produced 65 percent of the country's wheat exports by 1885, but climbed quickly to 90 percent of the total during Balmaceda's administration. At the same time, although the absolute volume exported from the southern area rose somewhat, it dropped precipitously in central Chile, from 382,000 to 86,000 metric quintals.[170]

It is not clear, however, how much this dramatic shift of wheat production from its traditional Central Valley heartland was spurred by Balmaceda's colonization program, with the landed estates succumbing to the competition of the new and more efficient independent producers and grain mills of the south. For this decline of wheat exports from central Chile came precisely when a vast new market for agriculture was growing in the nitrate territories of the north: staples, dried fruit, flour, barley, animal feed, beer, and wine were now being shipped in increasing quantities to the northern desert. It has been estimated that, with fluctuations, the value of such ship-

---

[168] Macchiavello Varas 1931, ii, p. 83; Kirsch 1977, p. 10.
[169] See Hurtado 1966.
[170] Bauer 1975, pp. 71, 85.

ments more than doubled from $1.63 million in 1880 to $3.6 million
in 1888. Merely the need to feed the nitrate territories' "many thousands of mules . . . entirely on barley and hay" brought in from
central Chile, as the British consul observed, would have led to a
shift to these crops from wheat and the latter's consequent decline
on the Central Valley estates.[171] In short, wheat production in the
Central Valley may have declined, not because the estates were
unable to compete effectively with the frontier as wheat growers,
but because they were comparatively better situated to meet the rising
northern demand for the new crops and staples. Thus for now, what
this shift meant to the Central Valley landowners and how they saw
it in relation to Balmaceda's agrarian policy and infrastructure development remains an open question, although it would not be surprising to discover that they thought that this spurred the competitive
rise of the south and thus damned Balmaceda for whatever economic
travail this new competition brought them.

What is clear is that the great landed families of central Chile were
now ever more dependent for their markets on the burgeoning demand
of the nitrate territories. Even before the annexation of Antofogasta
and Tarapacá, the nitrate developments in the Atacama desert just
south of there in the areas adjoining what was then the northernmost
province of Atacama had become an important source of demand
for agricultural products. This was recognized and extolled at the
time by the National Agricultural Association, which wrote that
"each new improvement [in] . . . the industrial and economic life
of the littoral, *whether foreign or national*, is translated immediately
into greater prosperity for our agricultural production."[172] Once the
nitrate territories of Antofogasta and Tarapacá were annexed by Chile,
of course, the new market opened up there for agricultural products
was even more immense and became crucial for Chile's landowners.
This "extremely significant" new internal market came, moreover,
at a moment when prices of Chilean agricultural exports to the world
market were declining steeply; the value of such exports plummeted
from $11.64 million in 1882 to $6.21 million in 1890.[173] Thus the
"greater prosperity" of central Chile's landed proprietors had by

[171] O'Brien 1976, pp. 164–165.
[172] O'Brien 1976, p. 116, italics added.
[173] O'Brien 1976, p. 164.

now become dependent to a considerable extent on the continuing prosperity of the major nitrate capitalists, both foreign and national, and the landowners must have perceived any threat to the latter's immediate interests as, at the same time, a threat to themselves. For these reasons, Balmaceda's nationalist nitrate program itself, if not his agrarian settlement and development policies, probably frightened and aroused the animosity of the owners of the landed estates of the Central Valley.

Aside from the possibility that they were not the primary beneficiaries of Balmaceda's drive to construct a modern agrarian infrastructure, its unintended consequences for the Central Valley landowners would still have frightened them. In prior decades, there had been an increasing movement of population from the countryside to the mining centers and towns, and this was accelerated by the opening up of the nitrate territories. The late nineteenth century saw "the most dramatic population shift in Chile's history," as the "*inquilinos* who had previously labored on the vast estates . . . flocked in unprecedented numbers to northern and central towns."[174] From 1865 to 1895, the rural population stayed almost constant in Central Chile, between 960,000 and 990,000, but in the urban departments of the provinces of Valparaiso and Santiago and the northern metal mining and nitrate districts, the population nearly doubled from 469,000 to 828,000.[175]

Landowner complaint of labor shortage was chronic throughout the second half of the century, as grain production and the consequent demand for agrarian labor rose steadily. Much like their contemporary Junker counterparts in Prussia, Chilean landowners also proposed, but never saw passed, legislation to impose checks on the "land flight of laborers."[176] Under Balmaceda, however, this recurrent landlord lament over the "scarcity of hands" now became shrill and found a political focus. For the rapid flow of agrarian labor to work on the government's construction projects now merged with the more gradual outward stream from the countryside. The public works not only drew off labor from the landed estates, which depended on having available an "elastic labor supply"—a large pool

[174] Pike 1963b, p. 119.
[175] Bauer 1975, p. 152.
[176] Bauer 1975, p. 152.

of itinerant laborers, especially at such times of peak labor demand as the harvest—but may well have undermined peasant docility and pushed up rural wages. Even *El Ferrocarril*, often the voice of leading manufacturers, many of whom were themselves government contractors, worried about "the considerable absorption of hands in the public works, when growing industrial, agricultural, and mining activity demand a greater supply of working men. . . . It is a fact obvious to everyone that today—with the railroads and other public works projects underway, and others that are not yet begun—the conditions of work have been completely transformed. The high costs of day labor and wage workers have reached disquieting proportions, as has, above all, the scarcity of workers, whose availability is necessary to spur the prosperous development and completion of these works."

The large landed proprietors apparently were especially distraught. The *Bulletin* of the National Agricultural Association (May 5, 1889) blamed the deterioration of agriculture directly on "the employment of numerous hands in the public works being constructed" as did *Eco de los Andes*: not only did "the general scarcity of workers" account for "the inferior state of the vines and poor quality of wine products, but . . . vineyard owners are now faced with the imperative necessity of paying the same wage as [the railroad], so as to be able to finish the harvest in time." *La Tribuna* also complained that as the result of "the innumerable public works being constructed in the Republic today, wages have risen in one year enough to demand the attention of our economists." The newspaper reported that typical wages for a railroad laborer went from 60 cents a day without a "ration" (a food allotment) to 90 cents *plus* a ration worth 26 cents, with some construction workers now earning as much as $1.50 daily.[177] Jobet and Ramírez Necochea accept such claims about rising wages. Jobet says, for example, that daily wages for agricultural labor under Balmaceda "rose over 50 percent" because "instead of 30 cents daily [in agriculture], workers could now earn $1.00 or $1.20 on the railroad or other construction projects"; this resulted, he says, in the "de-population" of many large estates by labor emigration.[178] It is

[177] Jobet 1955, p. 100; Ramírez Necochea 1969, pp. 110–111.
[178] Jobet 1955, p. 100.

not clear if average real or even merely money wages for agricultural laborers—who were paid not only in money but in kind, in scrip for the estate store and in perquisites—actually rose during Balmaceda's presidency. One attempt to measure the trend in the wages of agrarian laborers in central Chile shows no change from 1881 to 1890.[179] But of the landlords' *perception* that the tight labor market compelled them to pay higher wages and of their anger at Balmaceda's projects and policies for causing this situation, there can be rather less doubt.

Repeated demands were made in congress that the government reduce the wages paid by government contractors, to which Balmaceda turned a deaf ear.[180] In fact, he spoke in his major speeches of the desirability of "raising wages in proportion to the increased intelligent devotion of the working class" and answered the landlords' complaints about the impact of the public works on agrarian wages by telling them bluntly how to solve the problem. When, for instance, the Conservative politician Macario Ossa met with the president privately to convince him that the labor shortages on the agrarian estates resulted directly from "the much higher wages being paid in the public works," Balmaceda's reply must scarcely have been endearing: "Don Macario," he said, "you have the remedy in your hands: pay the *campesinos* what the laborers earn in the public works and you can be sure your laborers will stay in the countryside."[181]

Aside from the problem of labor scarcity and the possible rise in agrarian wages, there were the unsettling effects that the presence of construction and railroad workers, many with experience in the nitrate fields and mines, must have had in the countryside. Seeing them, talking to them, working alongside of them, the sons of peons and estate tenants probably found the example of such "free" workers instructive and thus became less docile. There is no record of any serious rural struggles at this time.[182] But the mere availability of the new opportunities for work outside the estates, as well as the example of growing militance among workers in the nitrate fields and construction sites, must have undermined the tenantry's docility

[179] Bauer 1975, p. 156.
[180] Ramírez Necochea 1969, pp. 110–111.
[181] Ramírez Necochea 1958, p. 112; 1969, p. 206.
[182] Bauer 1975, p. 222.

and subverted labor discipline, just when the landlords most needed enhanced discipline to expand production. Finally, it will be recalled that Balmaceda's administration also built schools from one end of the country to the other, and the expansion of the primary and secondary educational system to such an extent must also have had disquieting effects in the countryside. The expanded school system was viewed with alarm by conservatives, who worried about how such public secular schools—such "palaces for instruction," as the *Estandarte Católico* called them—would weaken the piety and acquiescent Catholic conscience of the rural population.[183] At best, the commanding landowners were surely made anxious if not unnerved, by the sudden social changes being wrought in the countryside under Balmaceda's aegis.[184]

[183] Ramírez Necochea 1969, pp. 112, 115. Also see Winter 1912, p. 342.

[184] Indeed, even the agrarian capitalists who were the outstanding beneficiaries of the state's largess in the deep south in the Patagonian hinterland had reason to fear Balmaceda's policies. He continued and even quickened the practice of his recent presidential predecessors of auctioning off public lands in Magallanes at a pittance, or ceding them on long-term lease. In the past, these concessions were authorized to foreign purchasers without restriction, and many foreign immigrants had come to participate in the development of the sheep industry there—the sheep population grew from 30,000 head in 1883 to 400,000 by 1890 (Jobet 1955, pp. 70–72). But Balmaceda reversed this policy of allowing foreigners to purchase concessions freely, and he issued an executive order requiring all companies organized to exploit these concessions to have at least 80 percent of their capital controlled by Chileans. An obligatory clause to this effect was written into all contracts for the purchase of the concessions, and the executive order also stipulated that violation of this clause could result in the expropriation and resale of these properties. It was disclosed later, however, that several of the largest companies in the province, including the recently organized Tierra del Fuego Exploitation Company and the Gente Grande Cattle Company which ranked as the two largest, had the majority of their shares held by British investors. Tierra del Fuego Company was established in 1890 by a combination between Duncan Fox, the English trading firm, and the concessions owned by the Portuguese immigrant José Nogueira, his Livonian wife Sara Braun, and her brother Mauricio. Duncan Fox held 50.3 percent of the company's shares. It is not clear if John T. North's Bank of Tarapacá also participated in that company's founding (its successor, the Bank of London and South America, later held principal shares in it). But Segall reports that North's bank did have "great . . . concessions" in the province also, some of which were held in partnership with the Menéndez and Campos families who, as it happens, were also closely intermarried with the Brauns. The Gente Grande Company had 66.7 percent of its capital in the hands of British investors (Segall 1953, pp. 193–195). Quite obviously, these investments were endangered and could be expropriated if Balmaceda's government were to discover and enforce its order against the controlling British holdings in these ostensibly Chilean companies. Here, again, there was a confluence, rather than a conflict, of interests between domestic and foreign capitalists

Thus the cumulative if unintended impact of Balmaceda's policies on his own aristocratic peers—the differential improvements in the agrarian infrastructure, the emergent competition of the south-central zone and newly settled frontier, the immediate threats to the nitrate industry and thus of reduction in demand for the landed estates in one of their most vital markets, the pull of labor from the land, and the consequent labor scarcity, erosion of peasant docility, and possible rise in agrarian wages—must have aroused among them considerable antipathy to his government. But in contrast to the deadly threat of Balmaceda's policies to the bankers and nitrate capitalists, and the sense of desperation this provoked in them, none of his policies appears to have posed the same sort of imminent danger to the great landed families. Not "the landed oligarchy" but these specific capitalist elements of the dominant class became Balmaceda's most desperate enemies. Thus the paradox: that it was a successful capitalist insurrection that put an end to Balmaceda's own unwitting capitalist "revolution from above."

---

and between agrarian capitalists and so-called "feudal landlords," in opposition to Balmaceda's policies.

Chapter 4 ➤ THE REVOLUTION FROM ABOVE UNDONE

Balmaceda's government impinged heavily, if often inadvertently, on the material interests of decisive segments of the dominant class and provoked their common wrath against him. Thus the causes of the civil war—contrary to the prevailing view that it arose for "political and sentimental" reasons alone—were as we have now seen, profoundly "social and economic." The question, however, is not only whose interests Balmaceda's government threatened and what elements of his class overthrew it, but whom it represented. Was there a segment of the dominant class whose demands the Balmacedistas met and whose interests they served—a class segment that became their social base in the political struggle and whose active historical agents they were? Or was it that the Balmacedistas, in commitment to their own political principles and while independently striving to fulfill their vision of the nation's destiny, alienated all segments of their class and won the backing of none?

Chile's leading Marxian historians argue that Balmaceda was isolated in his own class but was supported by the "national bourgeoisie," whose interests he championed against both the so-called "feudal-plutocratic oligarchy" and "imperialism."[1] Although in this interpretation Balmaceda won support from the new "middle strata" in the growing state bureaucracy, from artisans and nitrate workers, and from a variety of beneficiaries of his agricultural settlement program, it was above all the "incipient industrial bourgeoisie" whose advocate he was. "Balmaceda was," Hernán Ramírez Necochea argues, "the spokesman of nascent industrial capitalism. He took as his own the positions of the national bourgeoisie, which aspired to tap Chile's economic potential by establishing manufacturing activities and pushing the development of the productive forces in general." Balmaceda thus interpreted, seconded, and nourished

[1] Jobet 1955, p. 105.

"the marked anti-imperialist sentiment of the incipient national bourgeoisie."[2] Or as Julio César Jobet puts it: "Balmaceda represented the industrial vanguard of Chilean capitalism. In defense of the national industrial bourgeoisie, he attacked the usurious bankers and English commercial monopoly in Tarapacá. Balmaceda fell in defeat because national industry was still weak."[3]

This is surely a plausible interpretation, but the evidence presented to support it is scanty and unconvincing. For instance, the names of several men mentioned by Marcelo Segall as "forgotten heroes" of the industrial bourgeoisie—as its "last antilatifundist knights," or as the actual "nascent Chilean industrial vanguard"—turn out, as often as not, to have died long before the civil war, or to have fought against rather than supported Balmaceda.[4] Ramírez Necochea, to show that there were many advocates of economic independence and industrialization on the eve of the Balmaceda presidency, cites several speeches and articles over the prior decades but, like Segall, neglects to investigate how their authors later aligned in the struggle. For example, he quotes extensively from the 1883 inaugural *Bulletin* of the manufacturers' association, *Sociedad de Fomento Fabril* (SFF), as the embodiment of the aspirations of the nascent "industrial bourgeoisie," whose clarion call it was that "Chile can and must industrialize." "Balmaceda," Ramírez Necochea concludes, "accentuated this tendency."[5] But the manufacturers' association's first

---

[2] Ramírez Necochea 1969, pp. 108, 199–210; 1960b, p. 134.

[3] Jobet 1955, p. 94.

[4] Segall 1953, pp. 171, 268, 178. The specific members of this "industrial vanguard" whom Segall mentions are Isidoro Errázuriz, Carlos Lambert, José Francisco Vergara, Felipe Matta, Ricardo Lever, and Maximiano Errázuriz Valdivieso. But, in fact, Isidoro Errázuriz was one of the leading Congressionalist opponents of Balmaceda. Carlos Lambert, senior, died in England in 1876, and I have found no information on the allegiances of his son. Carlos A. Vergara died in March 1889; his biographer reports that he remained aloof from politics during the Balmaceda years and that his son, Salvador, a colonel in the army, went over to the Congressionalists in the civil war, "despite his friendship with President Balmaceda." Felipe Matta died in 1876, and his sons fought against Balmaceda (V. Figueroa 1925–1931, III, pp. 70–74, 627–628; IV–V, pp. 1021–1022, 216). Despite such chronic factual inaccuracies in his essay, however, I think that Segall intuitively grasps the bases of the intraclass struggle under Balmaceda, as my analysis below will demonstrate. For aside from the so-called "industrial vanguard," Segall also suggests that Balmaceda sought and found support—as he became isolated from his original political allies— among the copper-mine owners (Segall 1953, pp. 171–173).

[5] Ramírez Necochea 1969, p. 146.

president and signatory of that editorial was Agustín Edwards Ross, who, although he served as finance minister in Balmaceda's first cabinet, later became one of his main antagonists.

The manufacturers' association itself, political nucleus par excellence of the "incipient industrial bourgeoisie," gave Balmaceda no support in the intraclass struggle and civil war. Although it had the organizational resources "to launch a strong campaign of public support in behalf of Balmaceda," Henry Kirsch points out, "the SFF discontinued publication of its monthly *Boletín* until Santiago came under rebel control. Then in the first issue after its reappearance, the journal referred with a certain disdain to the 'dictatorship' which the country had just experienced. . . . The repudiation of his cause on the part of the association is clearly seen in the meetings of the executive council. On its own initiative, the council refused acceptance of the state subsidy which was due it 'during the period of the dictatorship'; it [declared] . . . that those funds had to come from an administration legally constituted by Congress, i.e., Balmaceda's adversaries.''[6]

The fact is that the manufacturers' association, misnamed the "Society for Industrial Development," consistently had shown little interest in, and was even antagonistic to, state assistance to the development of basic industry and a capital goods sector. Apparently, the association represented light manufacturers who produced consumer goods mainly with imported machines and production techniques; they therefore preferred to keep such imports relatively tariff-free, since protection of the emergent heavy equipment industry in Chile would have increased their own short-term costs. The "Society for Industrial Development," against the explicit and repeated demands of domestic heavy equipment producers, pushed for the abolition of existing duties on imported machines and tools. It sponsored a bill, passed by congress over Balmaceda's opposition, to repeal even the weak tariffs on imported manufactures. The law of September 10, 1889, specifically exempted "all machinery, tools, pipes, wire, telegraphy, and railroad equipment" from import duties.[7] Such, then, was the historical role of the so-called "national

---

[6] Kirsch 1977, p. 109.
[7] Pregger Román 1979, p. 229; Kirsch 1977, pp. 150–151.

industrial bourgeoisie" at this critical moment in Chilean capitalist development!

To compound the paradox, some of the most powerful protagonists of the protection and underwriting of domestic basic industry were "foreign capitalists," mainly Scots and Englishmen, settled in Chile, whose firms produced heavy equipment for the railroads, agriculture, and mining. Apparently, they considered "their businesses more as integral parts of the Chilean domestic economy than as segments of a foreign one." It was they who took the lead in "protesting the placing of orders with manufacturers outside of Chile" and whose petition for support the SFF rejected.[8]

Two of the largest of these heavy equipment manufacturers, for instance, were Lever Murphy and Balfour Lyon; both were ardent advocates of state protection and stimulation of domestic industry and were the recipients of large government contracts for the construction of locomotives, engines, flat cars, metal bridges, and other Balmaceda projects. Balmaceda's government surely subsidized and encouraged domestic manufacturing. But it also let some contracts to foreign manufacturers and imported heavy equipment from England and the United States—including flatcars and locomotives—which could have been, and was, locally produced.[9] To protest this import policy, Lever Murphy, for example, published a public "memorandum" to the president in his first year in office, pointedly objecting to the continuation of such foreign purchases of heavy equipment. The firm noted that its workers had already produced 18 locomotives and 100 flatcars under government contract (including the 22-ton "José Manuel Balmaceda," the first such engine produced by private capital in South America), which "offered considerable advantages over foreign material. The provision of contracts for public works to foreign capitalists," it stated, "has not given any protection to [domestic] industrial establishments. The liberality with which foreign capitalists are exempted from import tariffs makes it almost impossible for diverse industries to flourish here. *Only with the direct assistance of the government,*" Lever Murphy concluded, "*can the way be paved for national industry.*"[10]

[8] Pfeiffer 1952, p. 139; Kirsch 1977, p. 150.
[9] Kirsch 1977, p. 102.
[10] Pinto 1959, p. 42, italics added.

The latter, of course, was the cardinal commitment of Balmaceda's government, and at least some of these major manufacturers were among his outstanding partisans. In the civil war, "Ricardo" Levy, head of Lever Murphy, is said to have financed personally the Balmacedist troops encamped on his property while his workshops forged weapons for the army.[11] Similarly, Roberto Lyon Santa María, the Chileanized son of an immigrant Englishman and founding partner of Balfour Lyon, also was a partisan of Balmaceda in 1891.[12] On balance, then, how the so-called "industrial bourgeoisie" aligned itself in the struggle against Balmaceda remains somewhat obscure. It may well have split along rather paradoxical lines, in a way not comprehended by the orthodox Marxian thesis or its a priori categories: "foreign" rather than "national" manufacturers appear to have been the champions of Chilean heavy industry and among the leading partisans of Balmaceda's development program.

THE SPECTER OF COMMUNISM

The Balmaceda epoch was a period of unprecedented working class insurgency. Between 1884 and 1890, the country witnessed dozens of strikes and workers' uprisings. The northern *pampas* and nitrate cities of Iquique and Pisagua, the port of Valparaiso, and the south-central coal-mining area around Lota, Coronel, and Concepción were often the scene of bloody clashes between workers and the police, civil guard, and army troops—in battles reaching almost civil war proportions. By 1890, there were some 50 "workers' societies" organized throughout the country. In that year, the workers went out on "the first general strike of South America," which began in Iquique and spread southward in a cumulative wave of strikes, to all major towns, ports, and cities, including Valparaiso and Santiago. Among the largest strikes of the nineteenth century anywhere, it was probably the most bitterly fought and severely repressed in Chile's history.[13] In consequence, throughout the sharpening intraclass conflict under Balmaceda, there were repeated warnings of the emergent

[11] Segall 1953, p. 178.
[12] V. Figueroa 1925–1931, IV–V, p. 136.
[13] Segall 1953, pp. 29, 225–233.

menace from below. The conservatives warned, as did *El Estandarte Católico* (April 30, 1888), that "liberalism" would undermine the docility of the masses, whereas the liberals warned, as did *La Unión* in Valparaiso (May 6, 1888), that "a new element is arising on the horizon of our political contests. . . . The socialist movement is no mere specter in Chile; it is a growing menace and a very grave problem."[14]

Thus the working class was in its most insurgent phase precisely when the Balmacedistas were struggling to transform their country against the will of their own class. Involved in deepening intraclass political strife at a moment when that class was also threatened from below by workers' insurgency, the Balmacedistas were caught in an insoluble contradiction. Although Balmaceda courted the workers, especially of the nitrate *pampas*, who early in his government greeted his travels through the north and his nationalist slogans with great acclaim, he vacillated sharply in his actions toward them. He was torn between trying to win them to his banner and maintaining order in the face of their growing militancy. When he wavered in repressing them Balmaceda was met with scorn and outrage among the men of his own class, especially the nitrate capitalists, who faced the most combative and insurgent workers in the country.

The available evidence on the stance of the workers toward Balmaceda and his program is quite thin, but it seems doubtful, as Ramírez Necochea claims, that "aside from the active support given [Balmaceda] by the industrial bourgeoisie and middle class, he also counted on the adherence—if only passive—of the working class."[15] When the extraordinary strike wave of July 1890 began in Iquique, and the association of the owners of the *oficinas* sought the support of government troops, Balmaceda at first refused to dispatch them and sent a famous telegram asking to be informed "of the demands of the strikers and of what steps you have taken for a reasonable and equitable understanding with the workers."[16] The outraged response of many in his class was epitomized in an editorial in *La Libertad Electoral* on July 7, which was widely reprinted in the press. "From the elevated throne of the presidency, Mr. Balmaceda has constituted

[14] Ramírez Necochea 1956, pp. 291, 205–207.
[15] Ramírez Necochea 1969, p. 208.
[16] Segall 1953, p. 227.

himself as an official agent and obsequious mediator for the insurgent strikers and nihilistic bands in the streets. . . . Bravo, Mr. President! What an example our Republic sets for South America, with such a discreet Executive."[17] In congress, Balmaceda was condemned for letting the strikes and street riots continue. Speaking of Valparaiso, for instance, where on July 1, fighting at the barricades and repression by the army left 500 workers wounded and over 50 dead, the congressional commission of inquiry reported on July 26 that "the hordes of looters and pillagers could have been contained had the authorities taken opportune measures of repression." Indeed, Balmaceda did try to portray himself to the workers as their friend. On July 20, he told the convention of the newly formed Democratic party, organized by his supporter Malaquias Concha with its base mainly among urban artisans, that "the opulent classes" opposed him because of his "special solicitude for the interest of the people."

In the event, however, Balmaceda's government was finally responsible for the massive repression of the strikers in the northern *pampas*. In the summer of 1890, some 10,000 nitrate strikers marching in Iquique were fired on by soldiers armed with automatic weapons, and over 2,000 workers died. Here and throughout Chile, workers' leaders were arrested and imprisoned; many were summarily executed on charges of sedition, and the workers' guilds and unions were forced to dissolve. The defeat of the strike wave with the repressive assistance of the Balmaceda government probably won him no significant new support in his own class, and it must have also served to dissolve whatever so-called "passive adherence" the workers may have been giving him. In fact, early in the civil war itself, the Balmaceda regime had to confront renewed workers' insurgency. In January and February 1891, the nitrate zone again witnessed huge demonstrations, as well as food riots and even attempts to seize trains bringing provisions to the *pampas*. With the zone still under government control, Balmaceda sent troops against the workers, some of whom were killed, and ordered the imprisonment of their leaders. Coupled with his government's repression of the general strike months earlier, in the summer of 1890, this probably solidified the workers' antagonism to Balmaceda's cause

[17] Ramírez Necochea 1956, p. 310.

in the civil war. Many joined the Congressionalist army raised against him.[18]

Caught in the cross fire of class and intraclass struggle in the midst of the civil war, the Balmaceda regime excoriated "the exploitative oligarchy," in league with "the foreign enemy," and urged the workers to fight to destroy that oligarchy. At the same time its editorialists contemptuously denounced "the abject and ferocious popular masses" and condemned "the political aberration of exaggerated electoral power and popular sovereignty, which legitimates the right to revolution."[19]

MINING CAPITAL IN CRISIS

Did Balmaceda have a major base in his own class or not? Was he, as virtually all historians argue, throroughly isolated and compelled, as Jobet and Ramírez Necochea put it, to "confront that monumental crisis almost alone" and "without a powerful, solid, and cohesive cadre to count on"? Was he, as Luis Vitale argues, dependent on the "functionary bureaucracy" and the army, abandoned entirely by his class?[20] The evidence, when properly examined, reveals that on the contrary the courageous dissidents who supported Balmaceda were the personification of the historically specific interests of powerful copper-, silver- and coal-mine owners. They represented, that is, not so much an "incipient" bourgeoisie as one, born nearly a half century earlier, now facing premature senility and rapid decline.

From the mid-nineteenth century on, copper was Chile's major export; it exceeded all other export products in value until the rise of nitrates in the 1880s. Chilean copper mines, almost entirely owned and controlled by Chileans, were already producing a fifth of the world's production by the 1840s, and Chile soon displaced England as the world's leading copper producer, now reversing their previous relative positions in the world market. Whereas Chile's mines ac-

[18] Jobet 1955, pp. 102–103, 98, 138; Segall 1953, p. 232; Heise González 1974, pp. 117ff.
[19] Heise González 1974, pp. 121–122.
[20] Jobet 1955, p. 123; Ramírez Necochea 1969, p. 197; Vitale 1975, p. 229.

counted for 20 percent of the world's copper production in 1841–
1850 compared with England's 31 percent, by the 1851–1860 decade,
Chile was producing 32 percent and England 21 percent of the total.
In the next decade, 1861–1870, Chile enjoyed overwhelming pre-
eminence in the world market, with 44 percent of total copper production compared with England's mere 11 percent and with the 9
percent share of the new entry in world competition, the United
States. Their relative positions changed only slightly in the 1871–
1880 decade, when Chile accounted for 36 percent, England (largely
from its new Río Tinto mines in Spain) for 15 percent, and the United
States for another 15 percent. But in the next decade, 1881–1890,
Chile's place in the world market fell abruptly, its share reduced to
16 percent, behind England with 22 percent, and the United States,
beginning its reign as the world's largest copper producer, with 32
percent of world production. Chile's share of the British copper
market, in particular, also fell severely, from 75 percent of Britain's
total imports in 1873 to less than half that, or 37 percent, in 1881,
and to a mere 10 percent in 1891.[21]

Continually rising world demand, sustained especially by European military consumption of copper (for cartridges, shell cases, and
ships) brought major new producers into the market. British interests
reopened the Río Tinto mines in Spain in 1876, and copper production
in the United States (which had been a net importer) jumped fivefold
between 1876 and 1889. As world copper production—now also
spurred by the spread of electricity—rose steadily between 1879 and
1890, however, the price of copper dropped, and with it, Chilean
output. Demand for copper during the Bismarckian wars of German
unification and the Franco-Prussian war had pushed the price of
"Chili bars" (the standard on the London Metals Exchange) to £90
(pounds-sterling) in 1866 and to its apogee of £99 in 1872.[22] After
that, the price fell steadily and steeply, as United States production
alone leaped from 12,500 tons in 1872 to 103,240 tons in 1888. By
the summer of 1887, the world price was at the unprecedented low
of £38 per ton.[23]

---

[21] Przeworski 1972, pp. 392, 397; 1974, pp. 1, 13.
[22] In that decade, the exchange rate was typically 4.8 U.S. dollars per English
pound sterling (Przeworski 1978, p. 300).
[23] Abrams 1931–1932, p. 412.

At this point, in October 1887, there appeared a putative savior in the form of a French copper syndicate organized by Eugene Secretan, head of the Société Metallurgique du Cuivre. To drive up the price of copper Secretan and his associates (including American, British, and Cape producers) bought all the copper available on the London exchange and at the same time speculated in Spanish and other mining shares in the now rapidly rising stock market. In response to the artificial boom, new copper mining companies appeared on the London market almost every month, from December 1887 through 1888. The price of copper rose to £80 a ton in the first half of 1888, a figure over twice the previous year's low, and nearly all the major copper companies, including those in Chile, paid "greatly increased" cash and stock dividends that year.[24] The corner on the market was impossible to hold for long, however, because there were copper deposits around the globe, many of which could now be profitably, if briefly, exploited by small inefficient mines, as well as by the largest low-cost producers. Previously invisible stocks of copper now inundated the market, and the copper syndicate, after some 18 months of activity, collapsed in March 1889, and world prices plummeted.[25]

Copper output had been falling steadily in Chile since 1885, on the eve of Balmaceda's presidency, except for the brief syndicate-induced flurry of 1888, when production rose somewhat. But the collapse of the syndicate now led to a profound crisis in the industry and near-paralysis of the country's copper mines. In 1889, copper production in Chile fell to its lowest point in 30 years.[26] Why did Chile's copper production *drop* as the price dropped? Elsewhere in the world, the major new producers—the United States and England in the lead—*raised* the volume of their production consistently and dramatically, even while the price of copper fell as the result of increased supply in world markets.

The collapse of the Secretan syndicate, which had momentarily raised the price of copper enough to stimulate renewed Chilean pro-

---

[24] Chile, however, was "the only important thorn sticking into the Syndicate," as a partner of the Gibbs house noted, and was alone among major producers in staying out of it (Przeworski 1978, p. 55).

[25] Abrams 1931–1932, pp. 410, 413–417; Andrews 1889, pp. 508–516.

[26] Przeworski 1972, p. 397.

duction, coincided with an act of God, an act that was uncannily symptomatic of a tendency already manifest in the Chilean economy for more than a decade. In the spring of 1888, the principal coal mines in Chile were virtually paralyzed by heavy rains, flooding, and on top of that a cholera epidemic among the coal miners. The cholera epidemic had hit the coal regions the previous year, but "its decimating effects" were felt in 1888. The sudden shortages and the precipitous nearly fivefold rise in the price of both the remaining available domestic coal and the imported coal led to the shutting down of the furnaces of many of Chile's largest smelters. Just when the syndicate had pushed copper to its highest price internationally, the price paid by the major smelters in Chile was lowest, since the shortage of coal compelled them to keep their copper purchases to a minimum.

This natural disaster hit domestic coal production in the midst of an already gathering crisis for the copper-mine owners. Even when Chile enjoyed a virtual monopoly of the international market in copper, its mining bourgeoisie had continually complained of the burdensome costs of fuel and transport, which cut into their profits. But with the United States, Britain, and other major rivals now on the world copper scene, these costs were all the more deeply felt. Costs that could be profitably absorbed when Chile had no significant international competition now became oppressive, as the world price of copper fell.

In addition, the sudden rise of competitive foreign copper producers coincided with the rapid growth of the nitrate industry at home, which now competed with copper mining not only for coal but also for other crucial imports, provisions, credit, manpower, and transport facilities. "The production of nitrates," as Joanne Fox Przeworski's fine analysis reveals, "had destructive consequences for copper mining and refining. . . . Rather than following upon the heels of a moribund or decaying copper industry [the growth of nitrate production] did much to supplant it by competing for a limited infrastructure and by preempting scarce resources."[27]

Much of the smelting industry in copper (as well as in silver) heavily depended on imported coal, but that coal had been increas-

[27] Przeworski 1978, pp. 118–119, 195–202.

ingly diverted from the Norte Chico mining ports, since the late 1870s, to the newly burgeoning nitrate areas further north. From 1885 on, the price per ton of coal arriving at the copper mining ports was by far the *highest in the world*. The nitrate regions increasingly attracted the sailing ships and steam vessels that used to ply the copper ore trade between the ports of the Norte Chico and the major importing countries. Not only did this drain the copper and silver smelting industry of imported coal, but it also diverted the shipping fleets necessary to export copper and pushed up and made prohibitive what the mineowners already considered "absurd" transport costs.

Ships that had been equipped especially for carrying copper—a dense and dangerous cargo—were now rebuilt to accommodate the relatively easy transport of nitrates. The ships would arrive with coal as ballast, which was then consumed as fuel in the processing of nitrate ores, and leave laden with nitrates. The devastating result was that the number of vessels and the total tonnage *arriving* in Atacama and Coquimbo provinces from abroad fell precisely at a moment when Chile's copper mines faced formidable and growing international competition. Chile's small merchant marine, in any event largely ill-equipped for transoceanic voyages, could not fill the gap in transport for the copper industry.[28]

Nitrate production not only immensely burdened Chile's inadequate infrastructure at copper's expense but also drew on the contiguous copper and silver mining regions for manpower and competed for foodstuffs. Already by 1883, the year that the War of the Pacific formally ended with the annexation of Antofagasta and Tarapacá, "the scarcity of hands" and "the rise of wages and the cost of food for the miner to twice and three times what it was in previous years" had become a critical problem for the copper capitalists.[29] The population of the Norte Chico rose steadily through most of the nineteenth century and peaked in 1885 at just over a quarter million; from then on it declined, in both Atacama and Coquimbo provinces. The slowdown in copper mining and the rapid growth of nitrate production interacted to push and pull wage labor from the Norte Chico. "Migration to Antofagasta and Tarapacá," as Leland Pederson notes,

[28] See Przeworski 1978, pp. 118–167.
[29] Vicuña Mackenna 1883, pp. 494, 586.

"undoubtedly accounts for much of the Norte Chico's loss of people" in the late nineteenth century.[30] Thus mediated by the convergent effects of an inadequate infrastructure, the preemption of fuel and supplies, and rising labor costs, the growth of nitrate production (much of it under foreign control) was the proximate cause of the stagnation of copper mining in Chile. Here, surely, was a palpable and immediate "objective contradiction" between the nitrate and copper capitalists.

Parallel with Chilean copper's stagnation, and for much the same immediate reasons, there was also a fall in Chile's production of silver, which was second only to copper among its metallic exports. Chile ranked third among the world's silver-producing countries in 1887, when it recorded its all-time high, and had been a leading silver producer for half a century. Its long-term production curve had been remarkably similar in shape to copper's, and a steep downturn in silver output now also coincided with the decline in copper: the volume of production fell by 28 percent and its value by 23 percent from 1887 to 1890.[31] "It became clear that silver could not absorb the slack in mining caused by copper's fall."[32]

Not only were their production curves similar and their geographical loci in Norte Chico almost identical, but many if not most mining magnates had interests, often colossal holdings, in mines and smelters producing both metals. For example, Ramón Francisco Ovalle Vicuña, described by his biographer as "one of the most powerful mineowners of Chile," was both the country's "prime producer of copper" and one of its major silver magnates from mid-century to his death in 1885. Similarly, his contemporary, José Ramón Ossa Mercado, who founded the Bank of Ossa and was the progenitor of "one of the richest and most powerful trunks" of the Ossa family, made his fortune in Copiapó in both silver and copper.[33] The simultaneous decline of copper and silver thus had a cumulative and convergent effect on essentially the same mining segment of the class.

The mining industry involved many hundreds, perhaps thousands,

[30] Pederson 1966, p. 176.
[31] Encina 1952, i, p. 408.
[32] O'Brien 1976, p. 228.
[33] V. Figueroa 1925–1931, iv–v, pp. 443, 425.

of producers, but it was the largest Chilean-owned silver and copper mines and smelters that dominated production. The number of major copper smelters had shrunk steadily from the 1860s on, from over 250 to 69 in 1886.[34] In the 1880s, on the average, the top 10 producing mines accounted for well over a third of total output, even reaching over half the total in some years.[35] In fact, many individual "mines" were integral parts of the same mining operation; probably not more than five companies, controlling 150 or more highly mechanized mines between them, produced at least half of Chile's copper in that decade and employed well over a quarter of all copper miners. Silver output was even more concentrated and came mainly from a few large mines.[36] It was in these large copper and silver mines that "the greater part of the fortunes in Chile" were made, and it was their owners who formed the core of the mining bourgeoisie that now found itself endangered.[37]

In a country that was predominantly rural (in 1885, two out of three Chileans lived in the countryside), and in which the large landed estates of the Central Valley were the decisive units of production, not agricultural products but copper and silver bulked largest by far in the value of exports.[38] During the 1860s and 1870s, before nitrates also became a major "mining export," copper and silver amounted to at least $6.00 out of every $10.00 of the combined value of mining and agricultural exports, and in the preceding two decades the proportion was even higher.[39] No wonder, then, that mineowners formed the largest plurality among the nation's richest individuals on the eve of the Balmaceda presidency.

Four years before Balmaceda's election, and before the final conquest and annexation of the northern nitrate territories, *El Mercurio* (April 26, 1882) published a list of Chile's 59 "millionaires," along with their declared "occupations"; 34 listed one such occupation and another 6 listed two; of these 40 "millionaires," and allowing for double counting, 15 identified themselves as mineowners, 18 as

---

[34] Segall 1953, p. 163.
[35] Przeworski 1974, p. 4.
[36] Pederson 1966, p. 197.
[37] Ortuzar 1907, p. 96.
[38] Pérez Canto 1912, p. 172.
[39] Calculated from figures in Oppenheimer 1976, p. 463.

landowners, 3 as bankers, 3 as merchants, 3 as industrialists, and 1 as a brewer. The remaining 19 on the list either referred to themselves, as 11 of them did, by the generic term "proprietor" or "capitalist" or they provided, as 8 did, only a vague self-identification (e.g. "benefactor") or none at all. My analysis of biographical data on these 19 individuals who did not identify their "occupations" reveals that 11 of them were mineowners or belonged to mineowning families. Further, even a cursory glance at the 25 names of those who did list an occupation but did not identify themselves as mineowners reveals another 2 (one landowner and one landowner-banker) who were also copper-mineowners.[40] In all, therefore, at least 28 of the 59 millionaires of Chile, on the eve of Balmaceda's presidency, belonged to the mining bourgeoisie.[41]

Thus this was not a "weak" but an especially powerful, thoroughly national, bourgeois segment of the dominant class, whose interests no Chilean government could easily ignore. It was, moreover, a peculiarly cohesive and self-conscious class segment, in part because of its regional concentration. "The great nineteenth-century booms in copper and silver were phenomena of the Norte Chico and its immediate fringes." Comprising the provinces of Atacama and Coquimbo, running some 450 miles long by less than 100 miles wide in most places (narrowing to 60 miles between the coast and Andean divide in southern Coquimbo), the compact area of the Norte Chico,

[40] "Cursory glance" because extensive analysis was not warranted (or, if warranted, can be done by someone else).

[41] Among the 34 who declared one "occupation," the distribution was as follows: landowner, 16; mineowner, 11; merchant, 2; industrialist, 2; banker, 2; and brewer, 1. Among the 6 who listed two distinct occupations, the distribution was: landowner and banker, 2; landowner and mineowner, 1; industrialist and mineowner, 1; merchant and mineowner, 1; *salitrero* and mineowner, 1. No biographical data were available on 7 of the 19 millionaires who listed no occupation, and an eighth had no identifiable mining interests. The 11 individuals whom I found to be mineowners or members of mineowning families (copper, silver, or coal) were, by rank order: Juana Ross de Edwards, Emeterio Goyenechea Gallo, Carmen Quiroga de Urmeneta, Adolfo Eastman, Luis Pereira, Diego Ovalle, José Francisco Vergara, Magdalena Vicuña de Subercaseaux, Bruno González, Carmen Cerda de Ossa, and María Ana B. de Ossa. The principal biographical source was V. Figueroa 1925–1931, but several other references were also consulted. On April 28, 1882, *El Mercurio* listed the names of another 20 millionaires, with no other identification. An analysis of their interests was not undertaken. All 79 names are listed in Oppenheimer 1976, pp. 490–491. A list of the first 59 names and their self-identification also appears in Bauer 1975, pp. 246–247.

as I emphasized in my analysis of the meaning of the abortive mid-century revolution, long had a "certain historical unity" and distinctiveness as the center of Chilean mining development. From the 1850s on, the area's population had grown steadily, based on the sustained boom in silver and copper, and more than two thirds of it was concentrated in Coquimbo. After the annexation of the northern nitrate territories and the ascendance of the nitrate industry, however, the Norte Chico, and the national mining bourgeoisie for whom it had long been the economic (and political) base, was "reduced to a secondary status in mining for the first time in Chile's history."[42]

[42] Pederson 1966, pp. 15–17, 172–174. Annexation of the nitrate territories and the rapid growth of nitrate production in the new provinces of Tarapacá and Antofogasta had devastating consequences not only for copper and silver mining but also for *nitrate* production in Norte Chico. The infant Norte Chico nitrate industry in the southern Atacama desert districts of Taltal and Aguas Blancas soon collapsed in the face of the competition from the new "Norte Grande" ("Big North"). The Chilean-controlled industry in the Norte Chico worked deposits that were both inferior in quality to the northern deposits and located further from the coast. It still lacked adequate transfer and port facilities (aside from those run by the ubiquitous John Thomas North interests), and its production costs were an estimated 40 percent higher than in the Norte Grande. But paralysis of Norte Chico nitrate production was the result not only of the cold winds of competition blowing from the north but also of the failure of the state to give it shelter.

Chilean producers in Taltal and Aguas Blancas were compelled to pay the same export taxes as their northern neighbors, foreign and Chilean alike, despite their ardent—and strident—demands for a "proportional duty" that would tend to offset their natural competitive disadvantages. In 1880, congress passed a "uniform duty" on all nitrate exports—and simultaneously all but destroyed the nitrate industry in Norte Chico and dealt another severe blow to the already reeling mining bourgeoisie. Confirmation awaits future research, but the owners of the copper and silver mines and of the nitrate fields in the Norte Chico were probably, if not one and the same, close business associates, friends, and relatives. They were surely close political allies in the struggle for state protection and assistance for the region's economy and for domestic against foreign capital.

The fact is that (as Thomas F. O'Brien notes without realizing its deeper significance) "only northern mining interests protested the affirmation of foreign control at the expense of Chilean nitrate producers" (1982, p. 61). It was "a handful of Congressmen from the northern mining areas whose constituencies included or bordered on the Chilean nitrate regions" that fought for protection of the fledgling Chilean-owned nitrate enterprises of Taltal and Aguas Blancas. Their "only support came," says O'Brien, from men like Justo Arteaga Alemparte, who espoused a protectionist economic policy on nitrate matters" (1982, p. 58). This was the son of Justo Arteaga Cuevas and the cousin of Juan Alemparte Lastra, both of whom we encountered earlier as mineowners and leading 1850s insurrectionaries (and the latter of whom also lived to become a leading Balmacedista). Justo Arteaga Alemparte argued that protecting Norte Chico nitrates was not merely in the private interest but was, in reality, a

Thus in the spring of 1889—at a time when Balmaceda found himself under sharpening attack by nitrate capitalists, bankers, and central landowners—another segment of the class was suddenly thrown into the fray, as its own market grew more menacing daily. Already in critical condition, the copper-mine owners now desperately sought the state's assistance to survive their latest, near-fatal, blow (i.e. the collapse of the copper syndicate and the plummet of the world price of copper). Balmaceda's program for using the state's immense new revenues from nitrates to push the country's industrialization now coincided with the urgent needs of the endangered mining bourgeoisie. In its midst, Balmaceda sought and found the necessary and powerful partisans he had hitherto lacked.

The president had been courting their support for some time, and already had responded concretely to the demands of the Norte Chico for state assistance, as its mining bourgeoisie's place in the world market worsened. The mineowners' recurrent political lament, heightened sharply as Chilean copper production began to decline in the late 1870s, had long been that the government had abandoned their mining provinces to "private initiative" while spending "mil-

national imperative. Failure to act in defense of the industry in Taltal and Aguas Blancas would, he warned, result in the creation of a nitrate monopoly on Chilean territory controlled by "foreigners or enemies." As Justo Novoa also scathingly remarked in the congressional debate over the "uniform export tax" on nitrates: "The capital employed in the establishments of the south [in the Norte Chico] belongs, . . . with few exceptions, to Chileans or foreigners residing in the Republic. Is it possible, then, to dictate a law that will mortally wound our capital and our industry?" It was, another embittered opponent of the uniform duty exclaimed on July 17, 1880, not congress but the "bankers and great landowners who make the laws in Chile and [enforce] them at their whim" while lacking the slightest "degree of abnegation, prudence, and patriotism" (O'Brien 1982, pp. 59, 60).

Here, then, was one more sharp political battle pitting the compact mining bourgeoisie and its representatives, nationalist in both interest and conviction, against the rest of their class, scarcely a decade before these internecine struggles erupted in civil war. Indeed, that battle was so hard fought that, as O'Brien remarks while again missing its portent, "fears were expressed [in congress] that a uniform duty would split the country socially and politically" between the mining bourgeoisie and "the agricultural, financial, and commercial interests [who] were willing to sacrifice the southern nitrate regions" to foreign control (O'Brien 1982, pp. 58, 60). (Yet, after himself revealing such clear evidence of sharp intraclass contradictions and political clashes, O'Brien then goes on to conclude that "despite this conflict, the *entire* elite could take comfort from the fact that a solution of Chile's worsening crisis had been found"! [O'Brien 1982, p. 62, italics added]. On O'Brien's conception of the civil war of 1891, see Chapter 3, note 7, above.)

lions south of Aconcagua" in the Central Valley. In particular, the National Mining Society, established in 1883, made heated and repeated attacks on the "disastrous effect of the high railroad rates on the copper industry."[43] The Norte Chico mineowners "clamored for lower [railroad freight] rates, government ownership, and extension of roadways south to link the discrete transverse systems, hoping thereby to revive decayed *minerales* and the decaying industry."[44]

The brunt of the mineowners' political attack was aimed at the "almost absurd rates" of the British-owned railroads of Coquimbo and Tongoi.[45] Even the huge Tamaya mine (whose co-owners, the

[43] For instance, in the *Boletín*, January 2, 1884, July 15, 1887, April 30, 1889, May 31 and August 31, 1890.

[44] Pederson 1966, p. 222. Under the presidency of Domingo Santa María, Balmaceda, as minister of public works, had urged congress to support the construction of a northern line into the copper mining regions. His unfulfilled plan for "a central and strategic line with numerous branches to the mountain range and to the coast" was, as we know, to become a major objective of his development program as president. This earlier preoccupation had also been a rather direct response to the "vocal and persistent campaign" of the copper-mine owners and their spokesmen, who also urged the government to nationalize these foreign railroads that charged "intolerable" freight rates (Przeworski 1978, p. 248).

[45] Although the press often referred to the Coquimbo Railroad as "English dominated," it appears likely that, in fact, the Edwards banking house either controlled it outright or controlled it in association with English capitalists. Most shares were *owned* by Chileans, but a sizable block was also owned by shareholders registered in England, which amounted to 16.4 percent of the total in 1873, and 29.2 percent in 1875 (the two years on which such ownership data by nationality are available). A block of such proportions could have constituted an English controlling interest, depending on the relative dispersion of the ownership of both the Chilean and English shares. The authorized agent for the English shares, however, was Edwards and Sons, and they also held the major block of Chilean-owned shares; in 1873, they held 23.1 percent of the shares; in 1875, 28.4 percent, and by 1883 (for which no data on foreign-held shares are available), they held nearly half (45.1 percent) of the outstanding stock that paid dividends in Chile. Moreover, they also held the dominant interest, aside from shares held in England, in the Copiapó Railroad Company (Przeworski 1978, pp. 234, 246). Since these data were recorded in the annual reports of the railroad companies, it is not unreasonable to assume that informed men in the mining community knew of the principal if not controlling interests held by the Edwardses in these companies—whose monopoly position and "absurd" rates were anathema to the mining bourgeoisie. If so, this would have constituted a rather crucial underlying contradiction of their immediate interests and a concrete source of conflict between them and the Edwardses, as the incarnation par excellence of the banking segment of their class. To this must be added the apparently dominant position the Edwardses also held in Atacama smelting and refining, which constituted another source of irritation to the mineowners, especially to the lesser ones who did not possess their own smelting facilities. Indeed, Przeworski notes that an issue of the National Mining

brothers-in-law Adolfo Eastman Quiroga and Maximiano Errázuriz Valdivieso, were soon to be among Balmaceda's staunchest supporters) found transport costs prohibitive. Mining in Elqui and other promising mines in Cerro Blanco and Atacama were closed down by their owners because of the "insuperable freight rates." This was true even when the copper market was briefly booming because of the syndicate's copper corner. In early 1888, for instance, the English house of Gibbs itself, which owned mines in Atacama and also favored Balmaceda's attempt to break North's nitrate railways monopoly in Tarapacá, had "rebuffed" their British compatriots for charging burdensome transportation tariffs.[46]

In response to copper capital's enduring lament and persistent campaign, Balmaceda had inaugurated the construction, in January 1888, of three major railroads in the Norte Chico, two in Coquimbo and one in Atacama, which were to be the first railroads built there by the state, entirely at public expense. (See Table 3.1 in the previous chapter.) In October of that year he presented legislation to congress to authorize the expropriation of several British railroads in Norte Chico. "Since these railroads are private property," Balmaceda declared, "and thus necessarily serve, above all, to the advantage of the owners of these enterprises, the freight rates are three to four times higher than those fixed by the State railroads in the center and south of the Republic. Such rates lead to the stagnation of mining and agriculture, which are also preyed on by large-scale speculators. This is to the grave and manifest detriment of large and small industrialists and of industry and production in general."[47]

Immediately after the collapse of the copper syndicate in March 1889, the president traveled through the provinces of the Norte Chico, and in a speech on March 22 in La Serena, Coquimbo's copper mining capital, he declared that it was necessary now "to assist the copper industry financially, through the State." Protection of the industry and, most important, spurring its conversion into an inte-

---

Society's *Boletín* had "decried the Edwards monopoly" of Atacama in the early 1880s—and this was repeated again within years of Balmaceda's defeat in 1896 and again in 1900, when "the tutelage of the Edwards banking house" was again charged with being one reason why "mining in the Copiapó valley . . . languishes" (Przeworski 1978, pp. 245, 247).

[46] Przeworski 1974, pp. 10–11.

[47] Ramírez Necochea 1969, p. 119.

grated mining, smelting-refining, and metal manufacturing industry was the order of the day, with government assistance. "The oscillations in the copper market from which the province [Coquimbo] is now suffering the effects," he told his listeners, "persuades me that both the mining industry and agriculture have to be converted into manufacturing industries. This would rid them of dependence on foreign firms or on syndicates that gamble in—or even precipitate—speculative activities. *The assistance of the State may be necessary to lay the foundations of a copper fabricating industry. I believe that the moment has arrived to put the public fortune on the side of the copper industry.* This would save it for our posterity and preserve the productive bases of Chilean foreign commerce."[48]

The same theme was highlighted in an analytical essay in the influential daily *El Ferrocarril* several weeks later. The author, writing under the pseudonym Julius y Mayo, argued that Chile's abundant iron and copper mines should serve as the basis, not only of the "growth of many already existing industries, but of the birth of new ones, as well. Great metalworks and cauldron factories can be established. All types of equipment necessary in the mines and nitrate fields, and the implements and tools of agriculture [can be produced here] . . . thereby stimulating manufacturing industry and emancipating ourselves from Europe and the United States."[49]

On June 1, 1889, Balmaceda delivered his annual message to congress. (Such messages bore profound political weight in Chile, as a contemporary British correspondent remarked, akin "to the New Year's Day announcements of Napoleon the Third" in France.)[50] In that message the president reiterated his government's urgent commitment "to the need to stimulate (*alentar*) the copper industry by all reasonable means," and he specifically linked such assistance of the copper industry to the continued growth of nitrate production on whose revenues state capital investment depended. This was the speech, it will be remembered, in which Balmaceda announced his plan to auction public nitrate properties just when the world market was becoming saturated and the leading nitrate firms were trying to form a combination to restrict production.

---

[48] Segall 1953, pp. 169–171; Silva Vargas 1974, p. 66, italics added.
[49] Ramírez Necochea 1969, p. 69.
[50] Russell 1890, p. 316.

Thus in one and the same major policy pronouncement, Balmaceda simultaneously (but probably unwittingly) antagonized nitrate capital and offered mining capital its salvation. Again, in October, when presenting his plan to congress for the reform of the constitution and the decentralization of government, he emphasized also that this would fulfill his commitment to bringing about "the decentralization of the national wealth." In scarcely veiled allusion to the Norte Chico's plight, and responding to its long-term sense of regional discrimination, Balmaceda declared that his government would continue to use "the treasures of Chile in *all* of Chile, thereby putting an end to a political economy in which the center of the Republic was . . . everything, while the country's extremities were *tributary regions* of the capital and its environs."[51]

Balmaceda's public policy commitment to provide the copper industry with state protection and financial assistance encouraged the renewed campaign of the mineowners to have the government take over the railroads in Norte Chico. Since it was "economically utopian to ask lower freight rates from private firms for the benefit of the community," as a National Mining Society editorial put it in the spring of 1890, the government either had to impose the reduction of such rates so that the mining of low-grade copper ores could be made profitable, or actually purchase and run the railroads as a public enterprise so as to assure equitable rates. At the end of May, rumors that nationalization of the northern railroads was imminent were "ecstatically reported" in the National Mining Society's *Boletín*.[52]

The simultaneous collapse of copper and the spreading depression in nitrates were depleting the operating capital of the major banks; it made them cautious, to say the least, about providing further copper mining credits or loans. "Capital for mining investment dried up."[53] Such investment capital could now be supplied by the government alone, especially since the president wanted "to put the public fortune on the side of the copper industry," not just for the short term but to subsidize its rapid conversion into an integrating mining and fabricating industry.

But much of the "public fortune" was deposited in the coffers of

[51] Ramírez Necochea 1969, pp. 128, 158, italics added.
[52] Przeworski 1978, pp. 223, 224.
[53] O'Brien 1976, p. 228.

the private banks. This, as we have already seen, imposed narrow limits on the president's access to fiscal funds; in particular, it restricted his ability to channel them promptly into public capital investment. To pursue his program, to gain room for political maneuver, and to fulfill his commitment to provide the mining bourgeoisie with immediate assistance, control of these public deposits was essential. Thus, it will be remembered, in mid-June 1890, "in the midst of the continuing political convulsions, [Balmaceda ordered] the return within a maximum of 30 days of all [public] funds deposited in the banks."[54] All government deposits, the banks were instructed, were now to be considered "deposits at call."

With the banks and Balmaceda locked in battle, and in the quickening political crisis, Balmaceda now apparently leaned toward the establishment of a state bank, to hold all deposits of temporarily idle public funds. Establishment of the state bank would, above all, as Congressman and coal magnate Arístides Zañartu had argued, put an end to the "surrender of the nation's general business equilibrium to the calculations and convenience" of private bankers. Through the state bank, it would be possible to centralize the public expenditures and capital investments necessary for the nation's development.[55]

The project for the establishment of the state bank was not promulgated, however, until early in the civil war itself. One of Balmaceda's first acts after the Congressionalist revolt began, since "the majority of the banks supported the revolutionary movement," was to appoint "interventors" to oversee the banks' affairs. This was meant to prevent their disbursement of funds to support the rebel forces and to assure the government's access to its remaining deposits. Balmaceda also issued an executive decree requiring the intervened banks "to loan the government a sum equal to the amount of their own currency issue outstanding, to be placed in the charge of the State, as if the banks' private emissions were really State currency. This was an operation," as Guillermo Subercaseaux correctly remarks, "equivalent to contracting a no-interest loan."[56] It was indeed, as Balmaceda's finance minister José Miguel Valdés

[54] Yrarrázaval Larraín 1963, p. 99.
[55] Zañartu Prieto 1940, p. 192.
[56] Subercaseaux 1920, pp. 181–183.

Carrera said bluntly, an "act of expropriation."[57] But it put at the government's immediate disposition only $8.9 million; the government thus found it necessary to issue new currency, in the amount of $20.8 million, to be put into circulation. Leaving public funds on deposit with the private banks was obviously inexpedient for the besieged government, and a state bank now became a wartime necessity, if not a political imperative, to assure the continuing support of Balmaceda's new-found mining allies.

In early May of 1891, shortly after requiring the banks to lend their funds to the state, Balmaceda also appointed a commission to study the ways and means for "establishing a State Bank that would serve the general interests of commerce and industry and, through the guidance and action of the State, would provide the necessary stability and appropriate conditions to assure moderate discounting and interest rates."[58] Daniel Balmaceda, the president's brother, declared in the constituent congress that "it is imperative to break the fetters of the banks. The only way to make certain of this is to order the establishment of a State Bank." This would, as another member of the constituent congress put it, "liberate us from the exigencies of banking usury."[59] The official formation of the state bank was announced on July 9 by Arístides Zañartu, the banking legislation's main author and newly appointed finance minister.

The state bank was slated to be endowed with $60 million in net capital assets, partly drawn from revenues earned by the state railroads and partly from annual nitrate taxes, fully 20 percent of which were to be allocated for the bank. It was also to receive half of the state's nitrate reserves and to be consolidated and run as a public enterprise. (The other half was to be sold at auction, both to provide additional public capital and to preserve "free industry and competition.") Credit would be provided at a maximum interest rate of six percent, and such credit was to be not a privilege but a "right," so long as the borrower satisfied the state bank's statutory requirements.[60] Here, at last, was a guarantee of public investment capital to subsidize the copper mining and smelting industry. It would fulfill

[57] Yrarrázaval Larraín 1963, p. 106.
[58] Encina 1952, I, p. 426.
[59] Yrarrázaval Larraín 1963, pp. 108–109.
[60] Yrarrázaval Larraín 1940, II, pp. 257–258.

the long-sought but previously frustrated policy objectives of the mineowners. State railways would reduce transport costs, and state financing would assist the copper industry to rationalize and modernize its mining and smelting facilities. This would enhance Chilean mining's competitive edge in increasingly competitive international markets; long-term public stimulation of the development of an integrated mining-manufacturing industry would also supply important new domestic markets for copper.

In one act, the promulgation of the state bank reflected and condensed the contradictory interests and opposing political needs tearing apart the capitalist class itself. Much of the "public fortune" that the Balmaceda regime now planned to allocate through the bank in order to protect, subsidize, and develop the copper industry was to be appropriated, directly and indirectly, from integrated nitrate and banking capital. With the establishment of the state bank, perhaps their single most radical act, the Balmacedistas would also have put an end—had they won—to "the epoch of a system of free banks . . . in Chile. . . . In this Institution," as Arístides Zañartu declared, "there will be no place for the banking and oligarchic classes."[61] Not the Balmacedistas, however, but "the banking and oligarchic classes" were to win the civil war and impose their rule on the nation. What, then, was the historic impact of the defeat of the Balmacedistas?

THE MEN AT THE HELM: A SOCIOLOGICAL PROFILE

This is the decisive historical question, but before I offer my "answer" to it a closer look has to be taken at the real men who led, organized, and fought on the opposing sides of that bloody conflict. For who they were must bear heavily on the choices they made and thus on what their winning or losing meant for Chilean historical development. The civil war originated in the contradictory impact of Balmaceda's program and policies on different segments of the dominant class, but what of the men who took the lead in that struggle and who openly chose sides as it sharpened? Were they

[61] Encina 1952, I, p. 426; Yrarrázaval Larraín 1940, II, p. 257.

personally in the same intraclass location as the segment of the class whose interests their political activities tended to advance?

There is no a priori reason why the real individuals who take the lead in any political struggle must be drawn from the same social origins or share the same class or intraclass situation as those whose interests they represent in practice. Indeed, it could be argued that they perceive those interests more clearly the farther removed they are from them personally. Even with limited political suffrage, those who populate the executive and legislative branches of the parliamentary republic may well be selected and recruited by social criteria and personal characteristics that are quite different from the ones defining the classes they serve. Further, any political struggle, especially one so sharp as to split asunder a dominant class, surely has its own relatively independent motion, dictated by its own inherent contingencies. Political survival may become its own imperative. The leading participants in a political struggle are bound to find allies and supporters wherever they can, within principled limits, and whatever the struggle's original source. The real clashes and confrontations in which they are involved might compel them to make choices and take actions they never expected, with consequences they never intended. They might, indeed, find themselves acting against their own immediate class or intraclass interests, especially as their own involvement in the political struggle itself creates new comradeships, loyalties, and adherents, as well as making enemies of former friends and allies.

This, indeed, must have happened to many of the participants on both sides in the intensifying political strife and actual civil war. It must certainly have happened to Balmaceda himself. "A democrat by conviction and a noble by birth," as Figueroa aptly notes, he sought a national renascence by imposing imperative structural changes "from above" in spite of the opposition of his own class peers.[62] His social vision surely transcended his own concrete interests, which could scarcely have motivated the struggle he led and the final sacrifice he made. In striving to fulfill that vision, he found himself beset by unanticipated choices and with a desperate need for new allies. This must have been true of many of the men, no less than

---

[62] V. Figueroa 1897, p. 2.

of their president, who grouped themselves around him for the final contest. As the political polarization sharpened, these men might well have answered to the demands of the mining bourgeoisie *in practice*, not because of a coherent program or of a community of interest with them but because political exigencies compelled them to do so. For the mineowners were powerful men, indeed, to win to their side. Even if it were true that the personal motivations and political principles that originally inspired the Balmacedistas to defend the president were remote from the specific interests of the mineowners, in the circumstances they could, in fact, have chosen to make a trade for the mineowners' political support in order to enhance their chances of winning their own political objectives.

Thus the possibility remains that, whatever the practical consequences of their political action for given intraclass interests, the Balmacedistas could have been "free-floating" historical agents, dissident elements drawn at random from the various segments of their class; as visionary patriots, the null hypothesis would read, they recognized that they were alive at a crucial historic moment for their nation, and that only resolute action by the state could stem Chile's subordination to foreign capital and ensure its independent capitalist development. But they differed from the men who fought them only in this conviction and the will to act and not in their own intraclass situation or specific material interests. In short, it is quite possible that the men at the helm of state with Balmaceda and for similar reasons those who formed their opposition, as political strife erupted into civil war, were not *personally* representative of the class segments they represented *in practice*.

There are, however, specific historical reasons why this hypothesis is doubtful, particularly in the context of the intraclass struggle as it developed. This was a dominant class that *governed* as well as ruled its country, and active participation in "politics" and actually holding congressional office were an obligation and honor widely assumed by its men. The nation's great families placed their sons in parliament in every generation, and a roll call in congress would doubtlessly have paralleled any list of these families, which, in their interweaving, formed the integument of the dominant class itself. Although the suffrage already had been extended to all literate men, without income or property qualification, an independent income

was still indispensable to serve in congress, since its members received no public salaries. In short, every major segment of the dominant class was probably represented in congress by its own members
during these years (though detailed research would be required to
reveal its specific intraclass composition). Thus the differential impact of Balmaceda's policies on the constituent elements of the dominant class was probably felt in congress not only indirectly, as their
representatives heard from them, but directly and immediately, unmediated by any intervening political process.

This was also, of course, a dominant class whose mineowners of
the north had already engaged it in bloody combat in the civil war
and abortive revolution of the 1850s. The mineowners had long
possessed a sense of their own unique identity, in part regionally
nourished, and they were fully conscious of the distinctive community of interest that set them apart from others in their class. As
young men, many of them had personally scoured the wilderness,
risked its dangers, and won its riches, working with their own hands
and developing an authentic bourgeois individualism, if not a radical
bourgeois political outlook. Of course, a generation later, these experiences of their youth may no longer have continued to influence
them. But the spatial separateness and the specificity of copper mining's internal labor relations and world market situation probably
still nourished in them a distinctive social self-awareness and recognition of common interest.

A conception of themselves as "tributaries" of the state, under
the domination of the lords of the Central Valley, recurs throughout
their half-century history. Thus they had special reasons to participate
in politics and to seek and gain public office, which their regional
base facilitated, in order to represent their particular interests in
congress personally and to try to obtain the state's intervention on
their behalf. Once a struggle ensued within the class, even if its
initial wellsprings lay elsewhere—that is, in the threat of Balmaceda's policies to others rather than in any actions taken on their
behalf or at their behest—the mineowners must have been politically
conscious enough to seize the time to gain the president's backing
for themselves, spurred especially by the economic crisis they were
then experiencing with such severity. In turn, of course, they provided him with the political allies he now needed for his own cause.

For these specific historical reasons, I suggest, the mineowners should have been heavily overrepresented among the active Balmacedistas in congress.

That is, in answer to the question of whether "the revolution," as Harold Blakemore asks, divided "Chilean politicans along social and economic lines,"[63] I suggest that the intraclass divisions at the focus of the present historical analysis were also reflected in the divisions among the political struggle's leading participants themselves. But the bearing of such a finding or its absence on my historical argument should be clarified. If, in fact, no significant "social and economic" differences were to be found between the "politicians" on the opposing sides, this finding would not, per se, be negative evidence against my historical-sociological interpretation of the causes of the civil war. For, as already emphasized, the relative autonomy of any political movement also makes it possible that the leading participants in this struggle were not personally representative of the intraclass interests they represented in practice. Finding that they were, in fact, drawn more or less at random from the dominant class as a whole, rather than being distinctively composed of members of its politically relevant segments, would not in and of itself constitute evidence against my thesis that the origins of the civil war lay in the contradictory effects of Balmaceda's policies on that class' constitutent segments.

In contrast, if we found that "the economic and social interests of [the] . . . Balmacedists [did differ] . . . from those of the Congressionalists against whom the government thundered during 1891"— if we found that "Chilean politicians" *were* relatively "divided along social and economic lines," reflecting the intraclass divisions that I have argued were at the root of the civil war—then this *would* at least show that so-called "personal and political allegiances within the governing class were [not] the principal determinants of conduct."[64] In fact, that finding would also directly contradict the general historical thesis that the intraclass strife under Balmaceda was not a "conflict of interests" but was, as Franciso Antonio Encina puts it, essentially "political and sentimental."[65] If the "politicians" on the

63 Blakemore 1974, p. 418.
64 Blakemore 1974, p. 418.
65 Encina 1952, I, p. 396.

opposing sides of the political struggle were themselves found to be divided by contradictory social-economic interests or characteristically drawn from different class segments, then the deeper source of the conflict between them could scarcely have been only "political and sentimental." That finding would not only provide significant negative evidence against the accepted interpretation but would also be consistent with my own interpretation of the origins of the civil war and lend it added credence.

So, then, who were the men who led and actively participated on the contending sides in that historic conflict? Compelled by circumstances to rid themselves of political ambivalence, to put an end to temporizing, and to make the terrible choice between their president and congress, were their actions also rational and explicable in terms of their own specific intraclass location?

Method

Before addressing this question, there is the prior one of "method": what are the appropriate populations of antagonistic "politicians" to study, how are they correctly sampled, and what data on them are essential? One possibility would be to compare those who voted for and against the unprecedented resolutions that, in retrospect, made the breach between the president and congress irreparable— first by declaring him unfit, and second by depriving him of budgetary authorization to govern. But such a procedure could provide us, not with a selection of the leading antagonists in the conflict, but with ephemeral groupings based either on momentary political considerations or on the particular, limited constitutional issues involved. In contrast, the constituent congress set up by Balmaceda and his adherents to conduct government and prosecute the civil war was undoubtedly made up of men who cast their lot with the beleaguered president, and thus deserve to be considered leading Balmacedistas. It was, in fact, Blakemore's suggestion many years ago that "a detailed investigation of the economic interests of [Balmaceda's] . . . supporters" should focus on "the membership of the rump Congress of 1891."[66] Therefore, I began with a select group of this "rump

66 Blakemore 1965, p. 418.

congress," specifically the nine members whom Blakemore himself listed and at whose "economic interests" he had given "a cursory glance," as the basis of his tentative conclusion that they were not socially unlike their insurrectionary adversaries. To this list I added one more name drawn at random from the full list of constituent congress members, which provided a "sample" of an even 10.[67]

Aside from the members of the constituent congress, the Balmaceda government's ministers were, of course, crucial political actors, both in the intensifying struggle prior to the organized revolt, as well as in the civil war itself. Here, the resignation of the Belisario Prat ministry and Balmaceda's dissolution of the extraordinary session of congress was the decisive political rupture between congress and the president; subsequent cabinets were "composed exclusively of his personal followers."[68] There were 16 men who served in Balmaceda's personal cabinets after this final breach with the congressional majority, from the appointment of Claudio Vicuña Guerrero as minister of the interior, October 15, 1890, until the end of the civil war.[69] These men are described by Blakemore as Balmaceda's "unswerving personal adherents."[70] From these 16 names I drew a random sample of 10.[71] Of these 10 ministers, all but one (Claudio Vicuña Guerrero, who was, in fact, to become the rump president of the country) also served in the constituent congress. One of the 10 ministers selected (Cruzat) was already on the first rump

[67] The names are listed in Valencia Avaria 1951, II, pp. 326–336. The nine members of the constituent congress discussed by Blakemore were, as he named them: Ricardo Cruzat, Victor Echaurren, Manuel García de la Huerta, Juan Mackenna, Alejandro Maturana, Alfredo Ovalle, Ruperto Ovalle, Santiago Pérez Eastman, and Ignacio Silva Ureta. To them I added the randomly selected name of Adolfo Eastman. But Blakemore mistakenly included Manuel García *de la Huerta Pérez*, who died on June 9, 1889, much before the civil war and establishment of the constituent congress. The actual rump deputy was Manuel García *Collao*, who was also Balmaceda's comptroller in 1891. Had I retained Blakemore's García, the mining capitalist quotient among the leading Balmacedistas in my sample would have been raised because Manuel García de la Huerta was married to Ceferina Izquierdo Urmeneta, a close relative of mining magnate José Tomás Urmeneta.

[68] Winter 1912, p. 344.

[69] Valencia Avaria 1951, II, pp. 348–350.

[70] Blakemore 1974, p. 184.

[71] Julio Bañados, Lauro Barros, Rafael Casanova, Ricardo Cruzat, José Francisco Gana, Domingo Godoy, Guillermo Mackenna, Ismael Pérez, Claudio Vicuña, and Arístides Zañartu.

list named by Blakemore, so these two samples netted a sum of 19 men.

Of course, there were also prominent Balmacedistas who were not necessarily members either of congress during Balmaceda's presidency or, later, of the constituent congress itself, but who were nonetheless known to be among his outstanding partisans. To include such men in this analysis, I gleaned the names mentioned in this sort of context from various historical works; some of these names, as would be expected, simply duplicated ones already on the previous two lists. Included among these "prominent Balmacedistas" were, for example, leading ministers who served in Balmaceda's cabinets prior to but not during the Vicuña ministry and who continued to support him afterwards; men who served as his leading advocates and supporters (e.g. jurists, provincial governors and intendants, a senator who did not join the rump congress); and several influential businessmen who (as far as the available record shows) held no formal posts in the Balmaceda government but were identified as among his principal public supporters. This "gleaning" netted another 21 names that had not already been selected in the two earlier samples. In sum, the total sample of 40 leading Balmacedistas includes (double-counting) 25 members of the constituent congress, 16 ministers, 4 jurists, 21 "prominent" Balmacedistas, and 10 men who later were among the founders and early leaders of the new Balmacedist Democratic Liberal party, which met in its first convention two years after the civil war ended. The names and selected theoretically relevant attributes of these 40 "leading Balmacedistas" are listed in Table 4.1.

The "leading Congressionalists" were selected as follows. In the midst of the civil war, on April 12, 1891, "the leaders of the opposition . . . organized a Provisional Government, centered [in Iquique], governed by a junta [or directorate], which consisted of Jorge Montt, designated president, Waldo Silva, Ramón Barros Luco, and Enrique Valdés Vergara, who was appointed Secretary."[72] In addition, named as the provisional government's ministers were Manuel José Irarrázaval, Isidoro Errázuriz, Joaquin Walker Martínez, and Adolfo Holley.[73] Immediately after the "Congressionalist

---

[72] Yrarrázaval Larraín 1940, II, p. 224.
[73] V. Figueroa 1925–1931, III, p. 539. Yrarrázaval Larraín (1940, II, p. 224) erroneously refers to "Alfredo" rather than Adolfo Holley.

Table 4.1. Leading Balmacedistas: Their Individual Intraclass Situations and Political Activity

Balmacedistas	Intraclass situation									Political activity					
	a Mineowner	b Mineowner Kin	c Industrialist	d Nitrater	e Merchant	f Banker	g Landowner and Mineowner	h Landowner	i Norte Chico Resident	j 1850s Activist	k Rump Congressman	l Minister	m Jurist	n Prominent Balmacedista	o Party Leader
Luis Aldunate Carrera	x	x							x					x	
Juan Alemparte Lastra					x		x	x	x	x			x	x	
Julio Bañados Espinosa									x	x	x	x	x	x	
Lauro Barros Valdés			x					x			x	x			
Rafael Casanova Casanova											x	x			
José Fructuoso Cousiño		x							x					x	
Ricardo Cruzat Hurtado		x					x	x			x	x	x		
Adolfo Eastman Quiroga	x										x				
Victor Echaurren Valero									x		x				
Maximiano Errázuriz Valdivieso	x						x	x						x	x

Table 4.1. (cont.)

| | Intraclass situation | | | | | | | | | Political activity | | | | | |
| | a | b | c | d | e | f | g | h | i | j | k | l | m | n | o |
Balmacedistas	Mineowner	Mineowner Kin	Industrialist	Nitrater	Merchant	Banker	Landowner and Mineowner	Landowner	Norte Chico Resident	1850s Activist	Rump Congressman	Minister	Jurist	Prominent Balmacedista	Party Leader
Baldomero Frías Collao											x			x	
José Francisco Gana Castro		x									x	x			
Manuel Garciá Collao											x	x			
Domingo Godoy Cruz											x	x			
Manuel Goyenechea		x							x					x	
Ricardo Lever			x											x	
Eusebio Lillo Robles	x					x				x		x		x	
Juan Eduardo Mackenna Astorga	x						x	x				x			
Guillermo Mackenna Serrano		x									x	x			
Alejandro Maturana Feliú			x		x			x			x				x

Alfredo
Ovalle Vicuña

Ruperto
Ovalle Vicuña

Santiago
Pérez Eastman

Ismael
Pérez Montt

Enrique Salvador
Sanfuentes
Andonaegui

Vicente
Sanfuentes Moreno

Vicente
Sanfuentes Torres

Ignacio
Silva Ureta

Santos
Tornero Montero

Recaredo Santos
Tornero Olmos

Table 4.1. (cont.)

| Balmacedistas | Intraclass situation | | | | | | | | | Political activity | | | | | |
---	a Mineowner	b Mineowner Kin	c Industrialist	d Nitrater	e Merchant	f Banker	g Landowner and Mineowner	h Landowner	i Norte Chico Resident	j 1850s Activist	k Rump Congressman	l Minister	m Jurist	n Prominent Balmacedista	o Party Leader
Adolfo Valderrama Saenz									x	x	x			x	x
Ambrosio Valdés Carrera		x					x	x	x	x				x	x
José Miguel Valdés Carrera		x					x	x		x	x	x		x	x
Angel Custodio Vicuña Vicuña		x	x											x	x
Claudio Vicuña Guerrero		x					x	x	x	x		x		x	x
Nemesio Vicuña Mackenna		x									x				x
Benjamín Videla Pinochet	x		x							x	x	x		x	
Joaquín Villarino Cabezón		x							x					x	
Manuel Arístides Zañartu Z.	x						x	x			x	x			x
Juan Zavala Aguirre		x							x				x	x	

Note. For explanation of the letter designations at the top of each column, refer to the Key that appears beneath Table 4.2.

triumph," a post-civil-war cabinet of September 7, 1891 was formed, whose ministers were Manuel Antonio Matta and Augustín Edwards Ross in addition to Irarrázaval, Errázuriz, Walker, and Holley.[74] Each of these 10 members of the provisional government were also included in the sample. In addition, the historian José Miguel Yrarrázaval Larraín refers to "some of the most active revolutionaries" and to "civilians who were of the greatest utility to the opposition cause" as well as to the provisional government's three most active agents abroad (Agustín Edwards Ross, Augusto Matte, and Ricardo Trumbull).[75] I added to the list all 15 of these "prominent anti-Balmaceda activists," four of whom were already included above, providing a total "sample" of 21 "leading Congressionalists." Their names and selected theoretically relevant attributes are listed in Table 4.2.

To obtain data on the class situation and other relevant social attributes of the men in the two samples of leading antagonists, I drew from many historical works and relied heavily, in particular, on the indispensable multivolume major historical and biographical dictionary compiled by Virgilio Figueroa [Talquino], as well as on other such dictionaries, compiled by Pablo Figueroa, and by Jordi Fuentes and Lía Cortés.[76] My assistants and I recorded any information on the location of the leading antagonists within the structure of the dominant class and on the comparative intraclass composition of the contending political camps. This included any data indicating that they had mining, industrial, nitrate, mercantile, banking, or landowning interests. We also sought data on a few other social and political "variables"; these will be discussed below in the appropriate analytical context. Since my historical analysis focuses on the specificity of the crises in which the nitrate, banking, and mining capitalists found themselves, and on how Balmaceda's activities differentially affected these class segments, we sought information on the immediate families and close kindred of each individual. Thus where

---

[74] V. Figueroa 1925–1931, III, p. 539.
[75] Yrarrázaval Larraín 1940, II, pp. 211, 226, 229. Also see Blakemore 1964.
[76] The main works were Encina 1952; O'Brien 1976; Yrarrázaval Larraín 1940, 1963; Ramírez Necochea 1969; Blakemore 1965, 1974; Segall 1953; Przeworski 1978; Galdames 1941; Bauer 1975; V. Figueroa 1925–1931; P. Figueroa 1897–1901; Fuentes and Cortés 1963, 1967.

Table 4.2. Leading Congressionalists: Their Individual Intraclass Situation and Political Activity

Congressionalists	Intraclass situation									Political activity			
	a Mineowner	b Mineowner Kin	c Industrialist	d Nitrater	e Merchant	f Banker	g Landowner and Mineowner	h Landowner	i Norte Chico Resident	j 1850s Activist	p Junta Member	q Minister	r Prominent Rebel
Ramón Barros Luco											x		
Ventura Blanco Viel				x		x		x					x
Alfredo Délano				x		x							x
Gregorio Donóso Vergara				x				x					x
Agustín Edwards Ross		x	x	x	x	x	x	x				x	x
Isidoro Errázuriz Errázuriz			x		x	x				x		x	x
Adolfo Holley												x	
Manuel José Irarrázaval Larraín		x					x	x				x	x
Demetrio Lastarría				x									
Enrique MacIver Rodríguez													x
Manuel Antonio Matta		x							x	x		x	x
Augusto Matte Pérez					x	x							x

	a	b	c	d	e	f	g	h	i	j	k	l	m	n	o	p	q	r
Montt Álvarez												x						x
Belisario Prats																		x
Agustín Ross Edwards		x			x							x						x
Waldo Silva Algüe												x						
Ricardo Trumbull																		x
Enrique Valdés Vergara	x	x				x						x			x			
Carlos Walker Martínez		x													x			x
Joaquín Walker Martínez	x	x		x										x				
Julio Zegers Samaniego	x			x										x				x

Note. The following individuals were employed as legal counsel by John Thomas North: Enrique MacIver Rodríguez, Ricardo Trumbull, Carlos Walker Martínez, and Julio Zegers Samaniego. For explanation of the letter designations at the top of each column, refer to the Key that appears below.

Key to Tables 4.1 and 4.2

Intraclass situation

a. Copper-, silver-, or coal-mine owner
b. Copper-, silver-, or coal-mine owner, kin or associate
c. Industrialist
d. Nitrate manufacturer, trader, kin, or associate
e. Merchant
f. Banker, kin, or associate
g. Copper-, silver-, or coal-mine owner, kin, or associate *and* landowner
h. Landowner
i. Norte Chico resident or representative

Political activity

j. Leading activist in the 1850s
k. Member of Balmaceda's "rump" or constituent congress
l. Minister in Balmaceda's government
m. Jurist under Balmaceda
n. Prominent partisan of Balmaceda who was not necessarily a member of his government or of congress, or later of the "rump" congress during the civil war itself
o. A leader of the Balmacedist Democratic Liberal party founded after Balmaceda's death
p. Member of the Revolutionary Directorate (Junta)
q. Minister in the post-Balmaceda provisional government
r. Prominent anti-Balmaceda "revolutionary," who was not necessarily a member of the "provisional government" during the civil war or of the immediate post-civil-war regime

no information on the individual was found, the available information on his close relatives was used to characterize his intraclass situation. For instance, if the individual in question was not identified personally as a landowner, say, or as a banker, or a mineowner, was he from an identifiable landowning, banking, or mining family? Was his father or uncle or any other close relative a landowner, banker, or mineowner? To make such an identification, the prerequisite, of course, was extensive research on the kinship relations of each individual, especially those on whom personal social-economic data could not be located. Then the same research in the biographical and historical works had to be conducted on them as had been conducted on the leading activists themselves.

The rationale for such kinship analysis in order to delineate adequately the internal structure of any dominant class is that, in general, as Joseph Schumpeter observes, "the family, not the physical person, is the true unit of class and class theory," and that classes are internally constituted socially of freely intermarrying families.[77] In particular, this is characteristic of dominant classes, both now and in the past; within them, individuals may "own" property—whether in land or capital—only insofar as they are family members; individual and family standing in "upper" or propertied classes are virtually inseparable. Of necessity, the individual members of a family have a common stake in its combined economic interests. Of course, such family members can also politically differ and fight among themselves, perhaps even more bitterly than strangers. Surely, the 1891 civil war violently split many of the great families and was, on occasion, a literally fractricidal conflict. Yet, as the wisdom of the ages sums it up, "blood is thicker than water." Interwoven ties of kinship form tough and durable, if occasionally breakable, social boundaries to intraclass social cleavages. These bonds are the most primordial bases of personal loyalty, and they sustain and are sustained by their intertwining with concrete interests and controls that give them pragmatic nourishment. In any case, it is surely a critical empirical question as to whether or not the real men in the forefront

---

[77] Schumpeter 1955, p. 113. For an extensive discussion and demonstration of the relevance of kinship analysis to grasping the internal structure of a dominant class, see Zeitlin and Ratcliff 1975.

of the warring camps were more or less typically drawn from identifiably different types of propertied families.

But there is an additional consideration, which is at once "methodological" and "theoretical." To what extent did the great families of Chile have extensive interests that cut across the various economic categories? Given what is known of Chile's economic development, the wealth and social standing of some families could have derived simultaneously from trade and industry, finance, mining, and land-ownership. For "practically from the beginning of European settlement," as Arnold J. Bauer notes, "the economic interests of the Chilean elite overlapped. Sons of landowners went into trade, miners bought land, bankers owned dairies; and as we move through the nineteenth century, this process of economic intermingling was simply accelerated . . . [and reinforced by] closely-woven social relationships."[78]

Although unfortunately, as Bauer notes, "we do not have anything near to a comprehensive historico-quantitative study" of the nineteenth-century dominant class in Chile, Bauer himself has at least examined in some detail the estate inventories of a few prominent wealthy families at that century's end. In general, he found that "despite all that has been suggested about overlapping or interlocking economic interests by many writers," the several estate inventories that he examined typically lacked diversity. The 1888 estate of a principal figure in "the enormous Larraín clan," for example, which "represents better than any other the oligarchy of nineteenth-century Chile," had a total nonagricultural wealth of only 1.5 percent. In striking contrast, however, was the quintessential capitalist family, the Edwards, which had diverse interests spanning commerce, industry, mining, finance, and agriculture. Though even here, in 1898, the personal fortune of Agustín Edwards Ross, its leading figure, was mainly concentrated, according to Bauer, in urban and rural land and in stock in the Edwards family's bank and newspaper.[79]

I did not gather detailed data on specific estates, so my information does not allow any quantitative estimates of the composition of an individual's fortune. But I did record information on whatever

[78] Bauer 1975, pp. 206–207.
[79] Bauer 1975, pp. 185–194.

interests appeared in the biographies and other historical works consulted. Thus, for example, such sources revealed that Agustín Edwards Ross personally had interests in industry, nitrates, trade, finance, and land, and that his family also owned copper mines and smelters.[80] Such a diversity and range of holdings, however, was, as revealed by my data (see Tables 4.1 and 4.2), atypical of the leading antagonists in the drama of 1891—although, as shall be seen, the combined ownership of capital and landed property was a distinctive quality of certain of its actors.

The Findings

What, then, do we find concerning the social location of the leading antagonists? To what extent and in what way did the identifiable interests and intraclass situations of the opposing political camps differ?

To begin with the so-called "national industrial bourgeoisie," were they, as Chile's leading Marxian historians have generally argued, the quintessential Balmacedistas? Did individual members of this "industrial vanguard" stand out among the leading political comrades of Balmaceda? My findings are mixed: there were proportionately twice as many industrialists among the "prominent Balmacedistas" as among their Congressionalist counterparts; and the percentage of industrialists among these "prominent Balmacedistas" was sizable enough to have mattered in that small coterie: fully a quarter of them were industrialists. But when we consider all of the men in the leadership of the opposing camps, this difference between them tends to disappear. Among *all* of the leading Balmacedistas and Congressionalists, the proportion of industrialists is about the same, that is, roughly a fifth on each side. (See Tables 4.3–4.5.)

Industrialists fought industrialists. But it is quite possible, as is suggested by my brief historical analysis above, that ranged against each other were industrialists whose concrete interests and types of manufacturing investments were distinctive and contradictory. For instance, to what extent the Balmacedistas tended to be engaged in the heavy equipment industry whereas the Congressionalists were in

[80] V. Figueroa 1925–1931, iii, pp. 18–20; Przeworski 1978, pp. 245–246.

light manufacturing is a critical question that my data are unfortunately not detailed enough to answer.

The banks, as my historical analysis has shown, were endangered by Balmaceda's policies, and his final political act toward them, on the eve of the civil war itself, was all but confiscatory. Such leading bankers as Augusto Matte and Agustín Ross were, as is well known, active Congressionalist agents in Europe during the civil war; Agustín Edwards, the incarnation of Chilean banking, was also a leading Balmaceda adversary who served in the insurrectionary provisional government.[81] In fact, of the 15 "prominent anti-Balmaceda activists," a third were from banking families, although when all 21 of the leading Congressionalists are considered, the proportion decreases to 24 percent. In contrast, only 2 of the 40 leading Balmacedistas, or 5 percent, had any identifiable banking connections.[82] (See Tables 4.3–4.5.)

It was above all, I have argued, the unwitting threat to nitrate capital posed by Balmaceda's policies that underlay the widespread hostility to his government and led to the subversive movement against it. How many of the leading Congressionalists themselves were nitrate manufacturers or traders?[83] Remarkably, 7 of the 15 "prominent anti-Balmaceda activists," or 47 percent, and 9 of the entire group of 21 leading Congressionalists, or 43 percent, had identifiable nitrate interests. In addition, 4 of these 9 Congressionalist *salitreros* were also from banking families (which means, of course, that 4 of the 5 Congressionalist bankers had nitrate interests). These men personified the coalescence of banking and nitrate capital. They

---

[81] See Blakemore 1964.

[82] The two "bankers" among the Balmacedistas, it must be noted, were not at all as integrated into or as significant members of the banking fraternity as were those among the Congressionalists. Eusebio Lillo's banking interests were in Bolivia, where he founded the Banco de la Paz sometime in the 1860s as an adjunct to his mining activities, and it is not apparent from the works consulted whether or not he retained those banking connections years later. Santiago Pérez Eastman was associated with the Banco Nacional for ten years as a "counselor" (*consejero*), but this appears to have been in the period beginning *after* the civil war (V. Figueroa 1925–1931, III, p. 500).

[83] Separating "manufacturers" from "traders" in the nitrate industry was not possible based on the data used—and doing so may have been analytically misguided anyway, since production and trade appear to have been inseparably integrated business activites in the principal nitrate houses.

included Agustín Edwards, the founder and director of the Antofogasta Nitrate Company; his first cousin, the noted financier
Agustín Ross, who also had his own investments in nitrates; and
Alfredo Délano, whose banking family had been established in Tarapacá nitrates since the boom of the 1870s. Not incidentally, the
families of all three men had been closely associated for years in
both banking and nitrates and were also intermarried—with Délanos,
Rosses, and Edwards all involved in the founding of the banking
House of Edwards and participating in the management of Antofogasta Nitrates.[84]

Thus 10 of the 21 Congressionalist leaders, or 48 percent, were
nitrate capitalists or bankers. It must also be admitted that just enough
of the others, 4 of the total 21 (all of whom appear in the group of
15 "prominent anti-Balmaceda activists"), were employed as ad-
visors or attorneys by the North interests, so it is not only the cred-
ulous who might be convinced by Balmaceda's deathbed "conviction
that he had been defeated by a miserable coalition . . . without roots
in the country, and by English gold."[85]

The heavy presence of men with nitrate interests among the
Congressionalist leaders strikingly contrasts with their complete absence from the entire coterie of 40 Balmacedistas. Such a finding,
it must be said, is worrisome, even if welcome; it suggests that our
social economic data are incomplete, which they may well be, given
the primitiveness of our sources. But, of course, if they had such
interests, these should also have been disclosed by the sources used
to disclose them among the leading Congressionalists. No doubt,
subsequent historical research as a follow-up to my hypotheses will
probably change particular aspects of this finding as well as others.
But it is not likely that such research will substantially alter the vast
intraclass differences revealed here concerning the nitrate interests
of the men on the two sides. (See Tables 4.3–4.5.) Given the collapse
of the Norte Chico nitrate industry in the early 1880s after the annexation of the Norte Grande and the ensuing ruinous competition
this brought with it, the absence of identifiable nitrate interests on
the Balmacedistas' part is, at least, understandable. If, as seems

[84] V. Figueroa 1925–1931, ii, p. 553; iii, pp. 18–19; iv–v, pp. 716–717; O'Brien
1976, pp. 194, 241.
[85] Encina 1952, i, p. 164.

Table 4.3. Number of Leading Balmacedistas in Specified Intraclass Situations by Political Position[a] (Separately Sorted)[b]

Political Position	Mine-owners	Indus-trialists	Nitraters	Mer-chants	Bankers	Landed Mine-owners	Land-owners	Norte Chico Residents	(N)
Members of "rump" congress	14	4	0	2	1	8	11	7	(25)
Ministers	10	2	0	1	1	5	7	3	(16)
Jurists	3	0	0	1	0	1	1	4	(4)
"Prominent" Balmacedistas	13	5	0	2	1	5	6	9	(21)
Democratic Liberal party leaders	8	1	0	1	1	6	7	4	(11)
All leading Balmacedistas	25	8	0	3	2	12	15	15	(40)

Note. N = total number of leading Balmacedistas in each category.
[a] See Key to Tables 4.1–4.2 for more detailed descriptions of the categories here.
[b] Each individual is separately sorted on each category, so an individual can appear, depending on his attributes, in more than one intraclass category.

Table 4.4. Number of Leading Congressionalists in Specified Intraclass Situations by Political Position[a] (Separately Sorted)[b]

Political Position	Mine-owners	Indus-trialists	Nitraters	Mer-chants	Bankers	Landed Mine-owners	Land-owners	Norte Chico Residents	(N)
Members of revolutionary *junta*	0	1	1	0	0	0	1	0	(4)
Ministers in the provisional government	3	3	2	2	1	2	3	1	(6)
"Prominent" anti-Balmaceda activists	3	2	7	2	5	2	4	1	(15)
All leading Congressionalists	3	4	9	3	5	2	6	1	(21)

Note. N = total number of leading Congressionalists in each category.
[a] See Key to Tables 4.1–4.2 for more detailed descriptions of the categories here.
[b] Each individual is separately sorted on each category, so an individual can appear, depending on his attributes, in more than one intraclass category.

Table 4.5. Percentage of Leading Balmacedistas and Congressionalists in Specified Intraclass Situations by Political Position[a] (Separately Sorted)[b]

Political Position	Mine-owners	Indus-trialists	Nitraters	Mer-chants	Bankers	Landed Mine-owners	Land-owners	Norte Chico Residents	(N)
"Prominent" Balmacedistas	62	24	0	9	5	24	29	43	(21)
"Prominent" Congressionalists	20	13	47	13	33	13	27	7	(15)
All leading Balmacedistas	62	20	0	7	5	30	37	37	(40)
All leading Congressionalists	14	19	43	14	24	9	29	5	(21)

Note. N = total number of individuals in each category.

[a] See Key to Tables 4.1–4.2 for more detailed descriptions of the categories here.

[b] Each individual is separately sorted on each category, so an individual can appear, depending on his attributes, in more than one intraclass category.

likely, any nitrate enterprises owned by the copper-, silver-, or coal-mine owners were located mainly in the Atacama desert districts of Taltal and Aguas Blancas, then their nitrate interests were probably wiped out or they abandoned the nitrate industry much before the Balmaceda presidency. (See note 42 in this chapter.)

Not only were the leading Congressionalists "typically" involved in the nitrate industry, whereas none of the Balmacedistas were, but *most* of the latter were drawn from the mining bourgeoisie. Well over half of the members of Balmaceda's constituent congress and nearly two-thirds of the government ministers and "prominent Balmacedistas" had identifiable copper-, silver-, or coal-mining interests.[86] Among the 10 men in the *junta* and cabinet of the Congressionalist regime, however, only 3 were in mining, and the same number appeared among the 15 prominent anti-Balmaceda activists. All told, 3 of the 21 Congressionalists, or 14 percent, had identifiable mining interests compared with 25 of the 40, or almost two-thirds, of Balmaceda's leading adherents.

Further, the regional contrast between them is also marked; the "prominent Balmacedistas," in particular, typically were or had been residents or congressional representatives of the mining provinces of Norte Chico: 9 of these 21 prominent men, or 43 percent, were from

---

[86] Copper and silver mining were, as I noted earlier, closely bound up with each other, their ores often coming from the same or contiguous lodes. In addition, copper output and domestic coal production for smelting and refining were vertically integrated among the largest of the copper- and silver-mining companies. Domestic coal production, until the efflorescence of nitrates, was almost entirely consumed in the furnaces of the copper foundries, and the companies of the coal-mine owners and copper capitalists were closely integrated economically. Evidence of coal-mining interests was, therefore, also a criterion here for inclusion in the "mining bourgeoisie." An analysis of the integration of coal mining and copper mining, smelting, and refining, with abbreviated case studies of their integration in the enterprises of the Urmeneta-Errázuriz, Cousiño, Schwager, and Rojas Miranda families, appears in Przeworski 1978, pp. 172–190. In her discussion of José Rojas Miranda, who does not appear in my sample, Przeworski provides details that indicate him to have been one more exemplary personification of the Balmacedist mining segment. A Liberal deputy and later senator from the coal-mining region of Concepción, and then a member of the constituent congress (whose home was razed and his family's possessions destroyed by the victorious insurgents), he had made his fortune in coal mining, after being "schooled in copper mining in his birthplace of La Serena, Coquimbo." His coal company consistently ranked among the top three national producers in the decade from 1878 to 1888, supplying between one-fourth and one-fifth of domestic coal output.

that region. Not surprisingly, Balmaceda's constituent congress also had a heavy regional component, with 7 of the 25, or 28 percent, drawn from the Norte Chico. Again, the contrast with his antagonists is sharp: whereas 15 of the 40 leading Balmacedistas, or 37 percent, were from the Norte Chico, only 1 man in the Congressionalist band (who was also a mineowner) came from there.[87] Of the 15 Balmacedistas from the Norte Chico mining provinces, 3 had no identifiable mining interests; all three of them were members of the rump congress, one was also a minister and another was a "prominent Balmacedista." This means, in sum, that 17 of the 25 rump members, 11 of the 16 ministers, and 14 of the 21 prominent Balmacedistas, thus 28 of the 40 leading Balmacedistas (i.e. 70 percent) either were mineowners or came from the mining provinces of Norte Chico. (See Tables 4.3–4.5.)

It is now clear that this was a remarkably homogeneous group of men, drawn from the same mining segment of their class (or from the same compact mining region of the country) that stood with Balmaceda to the end. In addition, 10 of the 40 leading Balmacedistas came from the same *tightly intermarried core of mineowning families*, based mainly in the Norte Chico. They also included, in particular, 28 percent of the 25 members of Balmaceda's constituent congress and a quarter of the 16 ministers. Among them, also, were both Balmaceda's chosen "president" of Chile, Claudio Vicuña, who was elected by the constitutent congress during the civil war, and the president of that rump congress itself, Adolfo Eastman.

Alas, because of space exigencies, Figure 4.1, which shows the kinship relations among 10 leading Balmacedistas, has been split in two, with the halves shown on facing pages. Readers must, then, "splice" these two halves of the diagram in their mind's eye so as to see it whole: the two halves belong next to each other, on the

---

[87] Manuel Antonio Matta, whom we encountered earlier as a leading radical representative of the mining bourgeoisie in its abortive mid-century revolution, now found himself fighting many of his former comrades. As Pedro Pablo Figueroa remarks in his biography, Matta's leading role in the Congressionalist cause against Balmaceda "was a trespass that Mr. Matta committed at the end of his life. . . . By associating himself with the reactionary clerical elements and with the financial and social oligarchy that carried forward the insurrectionary movement [against Balmaceda], he entrapped himself in the immense national political disaster for the Republic caused by the revolution of 1891" (P. Figueroa 1897–1901, p. 283).

same level, and the lines abruptly ending at the right end of the half shown on the top facing page (p. 184) should be seen as continuing on to connect the lines beginning at the left of the half shown on the bottom facing page (p. 185). Thus splicing the two halves reconnects Carmen Mackenna Vicuña to her brothers Juan and Felíx and their wives, children, and kin and, in the next generation, reconnects Carmen's sons Nemesio and Benjamin to their brother (and her other son) Juan, and so forth.

Each of the 10 closely related Balmacedistas shown in Figure 4.1 was either personally a powerful copper- or silver-mine owner, or the son, nephew, first cousin, or in-law of one or more such mineowners. The uncle of Claudio Vicuña, for example, was the copper-mine owner Pedro Félix Vicuña Aguirre, who brought him up when his father died. Claudio Vicuña was also simultaneously the first cousin and brother-in-law of the brothers Ramón and Ruperto Ovalle Vicuña, the latter a member of the constituent congress and was, therefore, also the uncle of another member of the constituent congress, Alfredo Ovalle Vicuña. Claudio's wife Lucia was the daughter of Ramón Subercaseaux Mercado. The Ovalles and Ramón Subercaseaux were among Chile's "most commanding miners." Ramón Ovalle, for instance, established "mining operations and silver foundries of such importance that towns and villages arose around them"; he also built the Port of Carrizal Bajo and established a huge copper smelter at Carrizal Alto to process the more than 50,000 metric tons of copper delivered monthly from his Mondaca mine at its height. Similarly, Ramón Subercaseaux's discovery of silver in Arqueros near La Serena made him the country's first millionaire as early as 1831, and his widow Magdalena (Claudio Vicuña's mother-in-law) was listed among the nation's top 59 "millionaires of old Chile" a half-century later (as was Claudio himself).[88]

Adolfo Eastman, who presided over the constituent congress, married (after the death of his first wife) Claudio Vicuña's cousin, María del Carmen, the sister of another rump senator, Juan Eduardo Mackenna Astorga. Adolfo Eastman's first wife, Manuela, was the daughter of José Tomás Urmeneta, the discoverer and owner of the huge

[88] V. Figueroa 1925–1931, IV–V, pp. 443–444, 867, 1040–1041; Pederson 1966, pp. 189–190.

copper lode at Tamaya. Adolfo Eastman, his father-in-law José Tomás Urmeneta, and his prominent Balmacedist brother-in-law Maximiano Errázuriz Valdivieso, who married another Urmeneta daughter, jointly developed Tamaya into Chile's (and in the 1870s perhaps the world's) preeminent copper-mining center; in its time, it produced over $100 million worth of copper.[89] Adolfo Eastman, Maximiano Errázuriz, and their widowed mother-in-law Carmen Quiroga were among the richest of the 59 "millionaires of old Chile," with a combined fortune of $6 million in 1883.

Aside from the 10 men in the interwoven core of mineowners, there were another 9 men who were related to at least one other leading Balmacedista.[90] If we consider them as a group, then roughly two-fifths of the rump congressmen (11 of 25) and of the ministers (6 of 16) were close relatives of other Balmacedistas; the same was true of over half the group of prominent Balmacedistas (11 of 21) and nearly half (19 of 40) of the entire group of leading Balmacedistas. Thus this was an extraordinarily cohesive group of men, bound together by common mining interests and closely knit familial ties, who constituted the cadre of leading Balmacedistas of 1891.

Finally, there remains the question of the comparative relationship of the leading antagonists to the ownership of large landed property. Of the 10 members of the rebels' provisional government, I identified 3 as landowners compared with a considerably higher proportion of the men in the Balmacedist rump congress (i.e. 11 of 25, or 44 percent, and of the ministers, 7 of 16, or 44 percent). Of the 15 prominent anti-Balmaceda activists in the Congressionalist band, 4 were identifiable landowners, compared with 6 of the 21 prominent

---

[89] V. Figueroa, 1925–1931, II, p. 617; III, pp. 65–66; IV–V, pp. 935–936.

[90] Vicente Sanfuentes Torres, a Liberal senator who was a prominent Balmacedista, was the father of Vicente Sanfuentes Moreno, a deputy in the rump congress. Adolfo Valderrama Saenz, a native of La Serena, Coquimbo's major city, and a senator in the rump congress, was the father-in-law of Julio Bañados Espinosa, who was a leading jurist, the founder of the Balmacedist newspaper *La Nación*, Balmaceda's interior minister, and a member of the rump congess. Recaredo Santos Tornero, who founded the Valparaiso daily *El Comercio* in 1890 to support Balmaceda, was the son of the prominent Balmacedista Santos Tornero, the founder and director of *el Mercurio* of Valparaiso. The aunt of the brothers José Miguel and Ambrosio Valdés Carrera (the latter, Balmaceda's governor of Coquimbo, and the former, his minister of industry and a deputy in the rump congress) was the mother of Senator Luis Aldunate Carrera, the leading advocate of the nationalization of nitrates.

Figure 4.1. Kinship Relations Among Ten Leading Balmacedistas from Mineowning Families

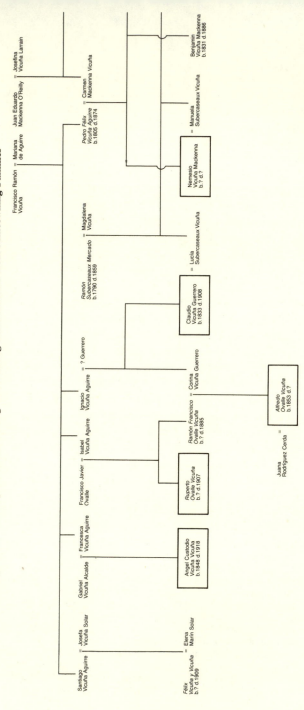

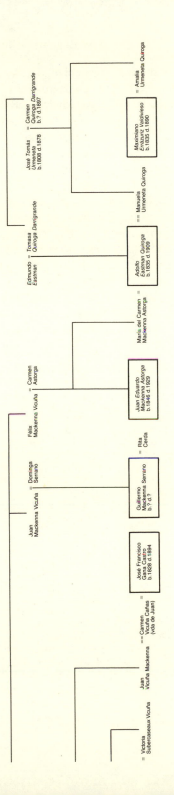

Victoria
Subercaseaux Vicuña =

Juan
Vicuña Mackenna

== Carmen
Vicuña Cañas
(vda de Juan)

José Francisco
Gana Castro
b.1828 d.1894

Juan
Mackenna Vicuña

== Dominga
Serrano

Félix
Mackenna Vicuña

= Carmen
Astorga

Guillermo
Mackenna Serrano
b.? d.?

= Rita
Cerda

*Juan Eduardo
Mackenna Astorga*
b.1846 d.1929

María del Carmen =
Mackenna Astorga

Edmundo = *Tomasa*
Eastman *Quiroga Darrigrande*

José Tomás
Urmeneta
b.1806 d.1878

= Carmen
Quiroga Darrigrande
b.? d.1897

*Adolfo
Eastman Quiroga*
b.1835 d.1909

== Manuela
Urmeneta Quiroga

*Maximiano
Errázuriz Valdivieso*
b.1835 d.1890

= Amalia
Urmeneta Quiroga

Note: The names of mineowners are italicized,
and the names of the ten leading Balmacedistas
are enclosed in boxes.

=   Marriage

==   Remarried widow or widower to deceased spouse

⊢   To children of marriage

⌐⌐   Siblings

Balmacedistas. In sum, 37 percent of the leading Balmacedistas compared with 29 percent of their Congressionalist counterparts were identifiable landholders. Thus, if anything, Balmaceda's loyal political coterie had a somewhat *higher* overall percentage of landed proprietors in it than was in the Congressionalist band. In this sense, then, Julio Heise González was correct in his observation that there were "commanding landowners" among Balmaceda's leading partisans.[91]

But their aristocratic appearances belied the landed Balmacedistas' distinctly bourgeois reality. For most of them were also, if not preeminently, the owners of major mining enterprises. Of these 15 landed Balmacedistas, 12, or 80 percent, were also the owners of copper, silver, or coal mines, and this predominance of mineowners among them is also true of each of the political subgroups: 8 of the 11 landed constituent congressmen, 5 of the 7 landed ministers, and 5 of the 6 landed "prominent Balmacedistas" were also mineowners. But, in contrast, only 2 of the 6 landed Congressionalists also had mining interests.

[91] Parenthetically, this presence of many "commanding landowners" among Balmaceda's partisans suggests a major—and paradoxical—reason why the army remained loyal to the president, even though the navy joined the insurrection against him. The mercantile community and its English elements in Valparaiso had close personal ties to the naval officers resident there, and the army general staff must also have had similar ties to the landed aristocracy. The Central Valley's large landed proprietors were scarcely enamored of Balmaceda's policies and, on balance, probably sought his downfall, even if they did not lead the insurrection against him. Despite this—and despite the cloak of legitimacy an army mutiny against the president could have worn, given the congressional majority against him—most of the highest officers of the army remained loyal throughout the civil war, and two generals gave their lives defending the Balmaceda regime on the field of battle. Why?

Balmaceda definitely wooed the military with increased emoluments: higher salaries, new and modern equipment, a military academy, and professional training. Together with this, the ideological appeal of a strong if not authoritarian executive against the claims of its parliamentary opposition may also have been an important ingredient in the army's loyalty. But given what appears to have been overwhelming hostility to him among the "respectable elements of society," with whom the officers corps must have identified, these alone do not seem sufficient reasons for their support. The higher officers' support for the president may have been solidified by the presence within Balmaceda's loyal coterie of many men who were the epitome of the "aristocracy" and among its most vaunted landowners. Their presence, I suggest, provided the necessary social garb for Balmaceda's government and legitimated the army's loyalty to it. The presence of these landed Balmacedistas in the constituent congress and at the head of Balmaceda's ministries must have, at least, neutralized Congressionalist efforts to suborn the officers' loyalty to the president.

These Balmacedistas personified the historical coalescence of land and capital in Chile through the reinvestment in commercial agriculture of the capital accumulated in mining. For it was the mining bourgeoisie, above all, that had transformed the old haciendas and furthered the penetration of capitalist productive relations in the Chilean countryside by constructing some of the most technologically advanced grain mills in the world to compete in international cereal markets. If anyone was exemplary of the "progressive agriculturists" among the landowners, who "put a great deal of money and effort into the modernization of their estates . . . [and] built irrigation works, dairies, and impressive new vineyards, and [introduced] new varieties of plants and livestock," it was the country's major mineowners. Maximiano Errázuriz Valdivieso, for instance, "one of the pillars of Balmacedismo," was a quintessential figure in this process.[92] He not only owned and developed copper and coal mines and built what was then the world's largest copper smelter, but also—like his mining-magnate father-in-law, José Tomás Urmeneta—invested heavily in commercial agriculture. He founded the Panquehue Vineyards and "pioneered new systems of [agricultural] exploitation."[93] This, on the most personal of levels, may also have been one reason for the sense of kindredness shared by Balmaceda and his new political adherents. For he, too, was personally an exemplary "progressive agriculturalist," as was his father.[94]

But whatever the particular personal motivations and political principles that inspired them individually, my analysis has shown that the role of the leading antagonists in the intensifying political conflict and ensuing civil war was both rational and explicable, given their

[92] Bauer 1975, pp. 40, 181, 209; Segall 1953, p. 253.

[93] V. Figueroa 1925–1931, III, pp. 65–66. Maximiano Errázuriz Valdivieso is included in our sample of "prominent Balmacedistas," based on Segall's description of him as a Balmaceda partisan. But Errázuriz died in 1890 before the outbreak of the civil war, and his brief biography makes no mention of his stance toward Balmaceda (V. Figueroa 1925–1931, III, p. 65–66). During the civil war, his properties and the mine at Lebu were sacked by the army, according to Yrarrázaval Larraín (1940, II, p. 382); this suggests the possibility that his *heirs* were known to be hostile to the Balmaceda regime, though, of course, in the midst of civil war, the decision to raze what could have been a tactically critical site if it had fallen into rebel hands might have been made independently by commanders in the field. Kirsch (1977, p. 104) considers the sacking of Errázuriz's properties a principal reason for rejecting Segall's characterization of Errázuriz as a "pillar of *Balmacedismo.*"

[94] Encina 1952, I, p. 15.

specific contradictory intraclass interests at that historic moment. Nearly half of the men who led the armed insurrection against Balmaceda were nitrate capitalists or bankers, whereas the overwhelming majority of his own leading partisans were drawn from the tightly knit copper-mining bourgeoisie.[95]

INTRACLASS POLITICAL HEGEMONY, STATE POLICY, AND CAPITALIST DEVELOPMENT

What were the historic consequences of the Balmacedistas' defeat in the civil war? What, in particular, were the consequences of that defeat for the economy, for the state, and for the nature of the dominant class itself? Like all major historical questions, this one breaks down into two others: what happened as the result of the Balmacedistas' defeat, and what *might have happened* if they had won?

Contrary to what John Thomas North expected, and to any thesis that interprets the civil war as his "orchestration," the victors *confirmed* Balmaceda's revocation of the Nitrate Railways transport monopoly in Tarapacá. That monopoly had been opposed, it will be remembered, by some British as well as Chilean nitrate firms, which agreed that it "weighed unmercifully" on all of them. After Balmaceda's fall they again sought, this time successfully, the breakup of that monopoly and urged the construction of competing railroads

[95] A few years after the civil war ended, when the Balmacedistas were once more allowed to participate freely in political life, some of them founded the Democratic Liberal party and ran candidates for Congress, advocating presidential government, administrative decentralization, and protective tariffs for industry. The party quickly split into two factions, one led by Claudio Vicuña, the other by Juan Luis Sanfuentes, brother of a former Balmaceda interior minister. "The faction led by Sanfuentes," Monteón remarks, "was particularly unprincipled" (1982, p. 56). A careful analysis of the intraclass locations of the Democratic Liberal leaders and congressional members (who were considered among "the most progressive elements in Congress in the mid-1890s," as Monteón notes) and of the party's contending political factions might be revealing. Among the 40 leading Balmacedistas in my "sample," for instance, 11 were later founders or early leaders of the Democratic Liberal party; 8 of them were mineowners or from mineowning families. What is more, another 2 of them were from the Norte Chico provinces, so 10 of these 11 Balmacedist party leaders after the civil war were from mining families or from the copper-mining region of the country.

in Tarapacá, one of which was Campbell Outram's Agua Santa railroad, which had been chartered by Balmaceda himself.

Aside, however, from this important continuity with Balmaceda's policies, his successors in government made no effort to stem foreign ascendance in the nitrate industry or to integrate it into the national economy. The state's nitrate reserves were auctioned off to private capital, with no clause limiting how much could be acquired by foreign investors. Despite Senator Luis Aldunate's prescient and eloquent warnings of "the dolorous consequences" such a sale would have for Chile's development, 38 nitrate complexes and 23 fields in the state's possession were sold at auction on November 29, 1893. The new regime rejected "the idea that the nitrate industry should be nationalized" or, as Aldunate demanded, that "the machinery of the state" be used to assure conditions for the successful competitive growth of the domestic nitrate industry.[96]

The existing firms, Chilean and British alike, despite their misgivings about the new competitors and increased capacity that such auctioning of nitrate properties would add to the industry, were no longer in a desperate but indeed a vastly improved market. As a result the combination was already coming unbound, and its demise had already been announced in September of that year. Both Chilean and foreign firms shared the immediate and primary objective, as the British ambassador observed, of preventing the renewal of "vexatious state interference" in the nitrate industry, and they saw the auction of state properties as providing a guarantee against it.[97]

This auction was merely the opening act in the restoration of essentially the same nitrate policies that, under previous governments, had led to foreign nitrate hegemony in the first place. As Encina puts it, "the governments that succeeded Balmaceda restored the nitrate policy of [Presidents] Pinto and Santa María, i.e., to deliver the nitrate industry to foreign capital and limit themselves to collecting export duties."[98] The result, as Senator Luis Aldunate had predicted, was to consolidate "the establishment of an enclave in Chilean territory, a species of colonial industrial factory, for foreign exploitation and utilization, granting us the seignorial right of col-

[96] Jobet 1955, p. 116; Blakemore 1974, p. 223.
[97] Blakemore 1974, p. 229; 1965, p. 419.
[98] Encina 1952, I, p. 400.

lecting rents but reserving for itself the monopoly of Chile's rich production."[99]

The defeat of the Balmacedistas put an end to their program of massive public investment in infrastructure and the state's "resolute and active encouragement of national industry." No remotely comparable expenditures to spur modernization and industrialization were made by any subsequent governments. The "robust growth" experienced by Chilean industry in the Balmaceda epoch was followed by a decade of stagnation and by the neglect of basic industry by the state for a half-century after Balmaceda's death. At best, the efforts to protect national industry were faltering and inconsistent, and then the emphasis was on the manufacture of consumer goods rather than capital goods. The technically advanced heavy equipment industry, which had flowered in the Balmaceda epoch, was shortly to disappear, as subsequent governments provided only sporadic and limited demand through public works expenditures, and virtually no protection or assistance to generate a relatively self-sustaining process of industrial growth. What remained of a metalworks industry in later years was confined mainly to consumer durables, produced by imported machines and equipment.[100] It was not, however, only the absence of sufficient and consistent state demand and coherent protection measures that struck a mortal blow against Chile's rapid industrialization. For, in addition, perhaps its most vital source was cut off when copper mining in Chile was allowed to stagnate and then, like nitrates, to fall quickly under the control of foreign capital.

Until then, despite the fact that much equipment and machinery was imported from abroad, mining—in both metals and nitrates—provided the country's heavy equipment industry with its major domestic market. Most of the foundries of Santiago and Valparaiso and all of them in the northern copper and nitrate areas depended on mining for "a great portion" of their business.[101] They produced narrow-gauge locomotives, railways, copper and iron cauldrons, steam pumps and other such machinery, overhead cable transports, mine-

[99] Pinto 1959, p. 56.

[100] Kirsch 1977, pp. 27, 33, 14, 52.

[101] Kirsch 1977, p. 141. The phrase "great portion" is Kirsch's and is indicative of how much is yet to be learned about the history of Chile's heavy industry despite the pioneering studies by Kirsch, Pfeiffer, and Rippy.

shaft ventilators, and equipment for mineral smelting and refining. Various types of blast furnaces, purifiers, converters, and amalgamators were all produced in late nineteenth-century Chile; some of the largest producers, such as Balfour Lyon and Lever Murphy, were also competitive enough to export substantial amounts of machinery and equipment to the neighboring countries of Peru, Bolivia, and Argentina. Even imported heavy equipment often went to domestic metal shops for considerable rebuilding and modification to adapt it to local mining needs, and many of its components and spare parts were also fully produced in Chile.[102]

Of course, copper mining also could have become the immediate basis for its own *copper*-fabricating and manufacturing industry. But, it fact, Chile's direct consumption of its own copper was negligible. Worse, the country imported not only machinery and equipment with components made abroad from copper that probably originated in Chile, but also intermediary products such as copper slabs and rolled sheets, as well as wire and tubing. "Leaders in the mining industry had long argued," as Przeworski observes, that at least such basic metallurgical inputs as copper sulfate and sulfuric acid should be protected against foreign imports and be produced domestically.[103] Their awakening understanding that they had to find domestic outlets for Chile's copper production was expressed in the pages of the *Bulletin* of the newly organized National Mining Society, after the onset of Chile's depressed copper markets in the 1880s.

In 1883, Minister of Finance Luis Aldunate appointed Román Espech Medeiros, one of the nation's leading copper-mine owners and later a noted Balmacedista, to prepare a "study of the conditions for the development of manufacturing industry"—one immediate result of which was President Santa María's sponsorship of the organization of the national manufacturers' association, the SFF. It was Espech's view, as he wrote in the Mining Society's *Bulletin* in 1884, and later elaborated in his book *Industrial Propaganda* in 1887, that "*Chile must be the consumer of Chilean copper.*" It should be utilized, he argued, wherever possible in place of imported iron in the machines and engines already being manufactured in Chile. This,

[102] Kirsch 1977, pp. 14–15; Pfeiffer 1952, p. 140; Segall 1953, pp. 176–177; Pérez Canto 1893, pp. 1–16.
[103] Przeworski 1978, pp. 40–41.

of course, was precisely what Balmaceda himself was shortly to advocate, though defeat and death overtook him before his government could act to stimulate and protect domestic copper fabrication.[104]

No subsequent government was to face this "great problem of the day," as Samuel Valdés Vicuña called it shortly after Balmaceda's overthrow.[105] Again urging Chile's use of its own copper in manufacturing so that it could become "independent of the [foreign] market that has become the arbiter of our being," he unknowingly wrote the epitaph not only for the unborn copper-fabricating industry but also for the infant basic industry itself. Unless Chile consumed its own copper in domestic manufacturing, Valdés Vicuña correctly predicted, the country would remain "no more than a simple commercial colony of the European nations." The paralysis of national copper mining, the conversion of nitrates into "a species of colonial industrial factory," the sporadic and limited state demand for domestic capital goods, and the eventual rise of a self-sufficient American enclave in copper mining were to be cumulatively malignant for Chile's heavy industry.

THE QUESTION OF CHILEAN COPPER'S DECLINE

What accounts for the demise of national copper mining, and what might the retention of state power by the Balmacedistas have meant for its renewed vitality?

The mining of copper developed in Chile throughout the nineteenth century as a national industry, with domestic capital predominant in its extraction, processing, and refining, although both foreign and Chilean interests shared in its actual sale and transport abroad. England was the major destination of Chilean exports, and until the British-controlled Río Tinto mines in Spain became major producers, most of England's copper imports also came from Chile. As a result, not only Chilean but also Welsh and English houses were among the principal commercial intermediaries in the consignment, sale, and

---

[104] Przeworski 1978, pp. 37–39, italics added; P. Figueroa 1888, pp. 180–181; V. Figueroa 1925–1931, III, pp. 90–91.
[105] Valdes Vicuña 1895, p. 189.

shipping of copper abroad for the mining companies. There were also a number of German and American trading houses, but among the major firms in copper marketing, British and Chilean houses were dominant. Two major mines were also developed early in the nineteenth century by English companies, one near Copiapó in Atacama, the other at Panulcillo in Coquimbo, and their output consistently placed them among the 10 largest mining operations in the country. Most production of copper, however, came from mines developed, owned, and controlled by domestic private capital. Further, although foreign ships predominated in numbers and tonnage among the vessels going in and out of Chilean ports, the leading Chilean copper companies also ran their own shipping fleets at the height of copper production in the 1870s; indeed, over a fourth of the ships in Chile's merchant marine in that period were built in the country's own shipyards.[106]

What explains Chile's late nineteenth-century displacement from the lead in world copper markets and the subsequent stagnation, decline, and foreign penetration—and eventual foreign control—of its copper-mining industry? To answer this question, I suggest, is tantamount to deciphering the riddle of Chile's retarded capitalist development. And this, as I have argued, presupposes a correct grasp of the social forces and political struggles under Balmaceda and of the historic meaning of his government's overthrow. But the standard interpretation of Chilean copper's demise focuses elsewhere, offering an ahistorical and narrowly technological or economic explanation for the decline and dissolution of national capital and the rise of American capital in Chile's copper mining.

The reigning explanation, in essence, is that the nineteenth-century copper boom in Chile was based on "copper . . . mined only from veins of rich ore," averaging from 10 percent to 15 percent in copper content, which could be profitably exploited with the prevailing labor-intensive techniques. As these rich veins were depleted, however, competition from the new American and European producers put an end to Chile's world copper ascendancy. To exploit Chile's low-grade ores, especially its porphyry (nonvein) deposits, it became necessary to employ "the revolutionary methods of extraction and

[106] Przeworski 1978, pp. 24–25, 44, 103–107, 148–149.

processing" introduced in the western United States in the early twentieth century. But Chileans lacked "the technology, capital and managerial skills necessary for large-scale low-grade mining."[107] Such mining operations "demanded a complex technology and management and a capital investment which were far beyond the capacity of the Chilean business community to supply. Accordingly, when Chilean copper production began to pick up after 1900, it did so largely as a foreign-controlled industry."[108]

Was it the absence of the technological capacity and large aggregates of capital necessary to mine low-grade ores that explains the decline of national mining in Chile and its displacement by American firms? This is doubtful for several reasons. First, the decline began long before the actual penetration of large American investments in Chilean copper and—most important, as Przeworski notes—before the major technological advances that spurred copper mining's rebirth under foreign control.[109] The electrolytic refining process was developed only in 1892 (coincidentally the year after Balmaceda's death), and the breakthrough in mining low-grade porphyry ores did not come until 1904 (which was, again coincidentally, the year the first copper mining property in Chile was acquired by an American company).

Of critical importance, moreover, is the fact that "the use of mass mining techniques," as Pederson points out, "and of hydrometallurgical techniques are not unique to the twentieth century, to the exploitation of porphyry deposits, or to the large [American] mining operations. Panulcillo, a massive shallow deposit of oxidized copper pyrites near Ovalle, was worked profitably by open-pit methods during the late nineteenth and early twentieth centuries for ores that averaged only 3-½ percent copper."[110] The real distinctiveness of the American operations in Chile was not so much in the technique used as in their scale and mode of integration, a point we return to below.

At its height, Chilean mining went through its own technological revolution; its earlier smelting technology was replaced with the most

[107] Moran 1974, pp. 20–24.
[108] Glade 1969, p. 327.
[109] Przeworski 1978, p. 2.
[110] Pederson 1966, p. 244.

advanced methods used at Britain's smelting center in Swansea "and all of its trappings, including reverberatory furnaces, multiple firings, large scale of operations, high technical standards, specialized equipment, and tremendous fuel requirements." The large mines at Carrizal, Tamaya, and elsewhere in the Norte Chico were highly mechanized operations. At Tamaya, José Tomás Urmeneta, and his sons-in-law and partners Adolfo Eastman and Maximiano Errázuriz achieved the "memorable triumph" of successfully penetrating "the deeply buried, enormously rich pockets of sulphide ore on Tamaya's steeply dipping main vein by cutting vertical shafts and horizontal adits through hundreds of meters of sterile rock, permitting the systematic and effective exploitation of the deposit with methods that were considered comparable to the best in Europe and the United States. . . . The Tamaya of the 1870's and 1880's [was] a model of efficiency and productivity."[111] Yet by the time William Braden made his first modest purchase of copper properties southeast of Santiago, Tamaya—the pride of Chile—had long been abandoned, its fires stilled, its pits flooded.[112]

Chile's copper bourgeoisie was in close touch with international technical developments in mining; its leading elements recognized clearly that they had to be able to mine low-grade ores to survive and expand. This was, from its inception in 1883, a high priority of the National Mining Society. The Society sent its own engineers, technicians, and mineowners to the world's principal copper-mining sites, in Río Tinto, in Lyon, in the western United States, and elsewhere to monitor and report on the procedures used. Its *Bulletin* regularly carried extensive descriptions of the workings of the industry in the major copper-producing countries, reporting in detail on the most important technical advances and, in particular, featuring methods applicable to the extraction of copper from abundant low-grade sulphide ores and metallurgical techniques using fuel other than coal, such as the wet process and electrolytic refining. It regularly published translations of articles from the world's principal mining journals. In fact, Chile's copper-mine owners made a plethora of efforts to apply the latest mining and smelting techniques, including

[111] Pederson 1966, pp. 206, 192, 189.
[112] Ortuzar 1907, p. 115.

new methods of concentration of ores, reduction of minerals, the use of machinery in mining itself, and so forth.[113]

The American "solution" to the problem and challenge of mass mining of low-grade ores, when it was finally implemented and when American firms began large-scale production during the First World War, conformed "in most respects" Pederson concludes, "to the prescriptions offered for the ills of Chilean copper mining in the late nineteenth and early twentieth centuries" by the leading Chilean mineowners themselves.[114] What was lacking, then, to prevent Chilean mineowners from following their own prescriptions and establishing a technically advanced and integrated mining industry that extracted, processed, refined, and transported Chile's copper, not under foreign but under national control?

Was it because of the absence of the necessary amounts of capital in Chile to construct the huge integrated mining complexes with concentrators, smelters, and railroads located in the midst of the northern Atacama desert or in the Andes? Was the magnitude of the required investment beyond the reach of Chilean capitalists? William Braden bought his first properties at "El Teniente," covering more than 1,200 acres in central Chile, in 1904, for some $100,000, and the capital stock of the Braden Copper Company that was formed to exploit them amounted to less than $2.5 million; similarly, the Chile Exploitation Company was organized with a subscribed capital of $1 million. Before these mines could be brought into production, however, enormous long-term capital investments had to be made by the American companies. At El Teniente, more than $25 million was spent before the mine turned a profit. To develop the largest open pit mine in the world at Chuquicamata, an estimated $100 million was poured into the desert over a dozen years. Andes Copper Company put out $45 million for construction costs and equipment over a decade before production began.[115] That these were formidable investments is obvious, but that Chileans had the money to invest in such amounts is also clear, "if for no other reason," as Clark Reynolds points out, "than the existence of extremely high profits

[113] Przeworski 1978, pp. 46–48, 97–99.
[114] Pederson 1966, p. 246.
[115] Vera 1961, pp. 45, 47; Bohan and Pomeranz 1960, p. 40; Przeworski 1978, pp. 278–285.

from nitrates which were accruing to Chilean entrepreneurs well into the twentieth century.'' The estimated Chilean investments in Bolivian tin mines alone, just as the major American mines were going on stream, was $100 million.[116] Why, then, did Chilean capitalists not invest in the resurgence of their own mining industry?

Doubtless, as Theodore H. Moran argues, ''the high risk and relatively low profits . . . were . . . disincentives'' to domestic capital, which ''gravitated toward the more speculatively profitable nitrate industry, the rich copper-veins mining, urban commerce, or toward conservative cattle-raising in the fertile valley.''[117] But why should Chilean capital have ''gravitated'' there while American capital flowed into ''high-risk'' mining in Chile? Why were these ''disincentives'' not bars to American capitalists also? Przeworski emphasizes that the already existing large mining corporations in the United States tied together financial, industrial, and mining interests and provided access to massive and centralized pools of risk capital. Corporate business organization in Chile, which had recently burgeoned in nitrates, was nonetheless still comparatively incipient in other industries. Most important, the diverse operations and multiple holdings of these American corporations made it possible for them to afford to wait until their Chilean ventures paid off. Their other profitable investments in the United States and abroad subsidized these ventures and also permitted them to pay their shareholders substantial dividends in the interim.

What this implies, therefore, is that what was lacking in Chile at that historical moment was not the technical capacity or sufficient aggregates of capital necessary to develop the mining industry but the political will.[118] For what could have integrated financial, industrial, and mining activities, provided access to a mass of cen-

---

[116] Reynolds 1965, p. 220. Macchiavello Varas (1923, p. 110), is the immediate source of this estimate, citing the research reported in an article by Santiago Marin Vicuña, in the *Boletín Minero* of 1920. Aside from the roughly $100 million invested in Bolivia by Chilean *corporations* alone, Marin Vicuña says that perhaps another $400 million was invested by private individuals and unincorporated firms!

[117] Moran 1974, p. 20.

[118] This was, *mutatis mutandis*, precisely the view articulated in 1920 by a distinguished descendant of the great mining families of the north, the writer Santiago Marin Vicuña: ''If the financial problem [of copper mining] is analyzed correctly, then it is not capital that is lacking as much as it is men and decisions'' (Macchiavello Varas 1923, p. 111).

tralized risk capital, and assured the security and amortization of long-term private investments in copper mining, *in that specific historical context*, was the state. It was the state that could have rescued national mining capital and made its resurgence possible, and this was precisely the most consistent demand of the organized mining bourgeoisie.

What the copper-mine owners needed and wanted above all was the construction, at public expense, of the infrastructure necessary to reduce the cost of transporting and processing ores and of bringing in equipment and the coal and foodstuffs otherwise shipped in by sea from the Central Valley or imported from abroad. Once the nitrate areas began to compete with copper for fuel and ships, however, diverting them increasingly from the copper ports, then both government expansion and modernization of the transport system and the protection and assistance of the domestic coal industry became imperative. The first was always clear to the mining bourgeoisie, but on the second they often vacillated or split.

Where copper smelting and domestic coal production were integrated, as in the largest operations, the confluence of coal and copper interests was immediate and obvious. But for mineowners whose access to domestic coal was limited, foreign imports promised cheaper fuel and reduced costs. But even the integrated mining operations suffered from increased copper-export shipping costs during the years when, briefly, domestic coal production was protected. After Chile's imposition of heavy duties on coal imports in 1864, for instance, the European shipping companies increased their freight rates sharply because coal constituted the overwhelming bulk of their Chile-bound cargo. The government then rescinded the protective tariff on coal.[119]

The political alternative, of course, would have been public expenditures to protect and expand Chile's merchant marine and turn it into the premier oceanic transporter of its own production, thereby breaking the hold of foreign shippers. Even many of the ships carrying copper ores from the north to southern smelters and refineries were foreign. In 1887, half the volume of Chile's entire coastal trade was carried by foreign (mainly British) ships, and they carried two thirds of the country's total exports and imports. One of the foremost

[119] Véliz 1961, pp. 202, 296; Vicuña Mackenna 1883, pp. 530, 533.

advocates of state protection for the merchant marine was Félix Vicuña y Vicuña, a leading copper-mine owner (and, not incidentally, nephew of Pedro Félix Vicuña Aguirre, the 1850s revolutionary and early champion of public financing and protection of the copper industry). Félix Vicuña y Vicuña traced "the annihilation of [Chile's] merchant marine" to the "freedom of navigation" that was granted to foreign ships in Chilean coastal waters, and he advocated restricting Chile's internal commerce to Chilean-owned ships alone. Along with this, he urged the state to underwrite the purchase of a fleet of "first-rate ships" and provide Chilean shippers with the regular "subvention of the state."[120]

The National Mining Society also called for measures to stimulate domestic coal production, including changed regulation of subsoil rights and staking of mining claims. But legislation to permit alienation of subsoil rights was successfully resisted by the landed proprietors. The Mining Society also persistently urged, to no avail, that the state undertake exploration and development of the carboniferous lands of the Central Valley and near-south provinces. It urged the construction in the southern coal regions, just as in the mining provinces of the north, of the necessary roads and railways to lower the costs of transport from the mines so as to cheapen the price of domestic coal. Indeed, Balmaceda himself, when he was minister of the interior in the Santa María government, had unsuccessfully urged congress, in 1884, to support a concession to build a railroad from the Bay of Arauco to the coal mines at Lebu.[121] Why drain the country of millions to pay for imported coal, he asked, when the country could produce its own coal? But it was not until it was too late, and American capital had already become dominant in copper, that protection was afforded domestic coal producers almost a half-century later in 1928.[122]

The mineowners long emphasized that the prosperity of copper mining depended on the exploitation of Chile's low-grade deposits, not only in the Atacama desert but also in the south and far north. The *Bulletin* of the National Mining Society observed as early as

---

[120] Vicuña y Vicuña 1887, pp. 278, 340–346.
[121] Przeworski (1978, p. 206) quotes "the Minister of Interior" in 1884, who was, according to Valencia Avaria (1951, I, pp. 341–342), José Manuel Balmaceda.
[122] Przeworski 1978, pp. 203–209.

1883 that "the rich copper and silver deposits justifiably called 'lucky mining' are largely exhausted. The minerals that we possess in truly extraordinary abundance are low-grade minerals. If we attend to our industrial technique and reduce our high costs of production, these are the minerals that can serve as a stable base for a true industry."[123] To achieve this, however, the *Bulletin* declared that state policy had to be radically changed. Even the so-called "rich veins" could not profitably be exploited in competition with the new international producers unless the copper-mine owners were freed from excessive tax burdens and provided state assistance. "Are the mines now in bad shape because of the exhaustion of the ones possessing rich minerals? Not by any means!" exclaimed the author of a report to the finance ministry in 1883. To make the outlays necessary to reach the deeper veins, to transport and process the ores cheaply enough to be competitive, there had to be an end to the "asphyxiating taxes that weigh on the copper industry and . . . burden the great majority of copper miners in the country with so much injustice." Above all, what the mining industry needed but had "never received [was] the protection of the state."[124]

Minimally, the government had to extend public roads and railways to integrate the separate privately owned transverse systems in the mining regions and, of decisive importance, build a public railroad stretching from Calera near the port of Valparaiso to the nation's northernmost tip at Tacna. Such a main longitudinal line, publicly owned and run and providing subsidized freight rates, "would make it possible," Benjamín Vicuña Mackenna argued, "to put on a profitable footing the industrial exploitation of the innumerable known veins and the veritable mountains of low-grade copper located in the successive valleys of the great north, which compare with the ones at Río Tinto in Spain and in the Copper-Polis of the United States. Such [state assistance] could provide the impetus necessary to revive the fatigued mining industry of the north and restore its . . . old exuberance." But rather than assistance, the mining industry was subjected, Vicuña Mackenna concluded, to "the accelerated and

[123] Vicuña Mackenna 1883, p. 533n.
[124] Quoted by Vicuña Mackenna 1883, pp. 523, 526, 529.

almost violent extraction of some $500 million, ceded to the national treasury . . . in this century"—and not the mineowners but the large landed proprietors were the beneficiaries of these taxes.[125] As an 1883 National Mining Society report to the finance ministry put it, "an eloquent statistical contrast" in public infrastructure expenditures indicated how fully the interests of the mining bourgeoisie were subordinated to those of the Central Valley landowners: "The state has constructed 949 kilometers of railroads in the south of Chile for the development of agriculture, at a cost of $43,534,800, while in the mining provinces of the north, the miners themselves have constructed 906 kilometers for the export of their minerals, which is almost the same amount constructed by the state in the south."[126]

Only under Balmaceda did the state begin to construct the roads and railways long demanded by the mineowners, including two sections of the major longitudinal line, from Calera to La Ligua and Cabildo in Aconcagua and from Ovalle to San Marcos in Coquimbo. For nearly two decades after Balmaceda's overthrow, despite persistent demands from the mining bourgeoisie for its completion, the extension of the longitudinal railroad from Calera to the north was paralyzed.[127] This was, of course, precisely the critical period during which the rapid penetration of American capital in copper mining took place, and the American corporations themselves constructed the roads and railroads needed to exploit profitably the low-grade ores of Chile's north.

The interests of the copper-mine owners were ignored even on the rare occasions when they had an effective representative in the executive office. Thus, for example, in 1903 and 1904, the finance minister, who had been a staunch Balmacedista, called again for the "prudent protection of the mining industry" and unsuccessfully urged the construction of new public roads, railroads, and port facilities in the northern mining regions to allow the profitable exploitation of the low-grade deposits.[128] Not until the outbreak of World War I,

[125] Vicuña Mackenna 1883, pp. 589–590.
[126] Quoted by Vicuña Mackenna 1883, p. 528.
[127] Przeworski 1978, p. 249.
[128] Przeworski 1978, p. 254. I am assuming that this was Manuel Salinas González, Balmaceda's intendant in 1887 in Atacama and in Tarapacá in 1890, and then his

however, did a public railroad join with the transverse lines running between the mines and ports of the north. Extension of the public railroad from south to north continued slowly in the following years, both through new construction and absorption of some private lines. But by the time this integral railroad system was completed, "the copper carrying trade in these regions had dwindled substantially," as Przeworski remarks, and the American ascendancy in Chilean copper was already secure.[129]

This same pattern of neglect characterizes state policy toward the copper smelting industry. It went without state assistance throughout the epoch of domestic capital's dominance in copper, despite the early recognition by the mineowners themselves that this "principal branch of mining" needed the "prudent protection" of the state if it were to "combat the monopoly of the English smelters" at Swansea successfully. State protection and low-interest loans to domestic smelters had been a principal demand of the young bourgeois revolutionaries in the civil war of 1859 and was repeated time and again afterward, but without success. The mineowners repeatedly urged the abolition of export taxes on refined copper bars and intermediate (regulus) ingots, even the payment of a state "premium" for their production, and the retention of export taxes only on crude ores. This would "benefit copper smelting," the National Mining Society said in an 1883 petition to the ministry of finance, "and also foment the exploitation of the coal mines."[130]

Linked to the protection of the smelting industry was another always frustrated demand, namely, the establishment of a state bank to provide loans and credits for mining so that the financial hold of the English houses and domestic *habilitadores* (merchant bankers) over the industry could be broken. First voiced in the abortive 1850s revolution, the demand reappeared in various forms in subsequent years. Generally, the mineowners, especially the smaller ones, sold their ores to private purchasing agents or those in the employ of the major trading houses. These were often also their only source of

---

confidential agent abroad during the civil war (V. Figueroa 1925–1931, IV–V, p. 754; Valencia Avaria 1951, I, p. 368).
[129] Przeworski 1978, p. 256.
[130] Vicuña Mackenna 1883, pp. 518, 530.

loans and credits for foodstuffs, supplies, and equipment. The loans were guaranteed against consignment of the mine's production, at the prevailing market price. This meant that if the price rose later, the mineowner lost out while the merchant banker gained, since the former's production had already been consigned at a lower price. The interest rates charged were also "frequently phenomenal," and the mineowner was also subject to handling and brokerage fees, as well as commissions, which took still another sizable chunk of the mineowner's profits.[131] Even in the 1870s, after the growth of several domestic banks into formidable financial institutions (some, like the Bank of Edwards and Bank of Ossa, deriving directly from profits earned in the *habilitación* of mining) and the establishment of a formal money market, mineowners found it difficult to get loans and credits.[132]

Few banks made direct loans for copper-mining ventures, given their risky nature, and most private credit went overwhelmingly to landowners and traders. The public *Caja de Crédito Hipotecario* was founded in 1855 to provide long-term investment loans, but throughout its existence it acted primarily as a source of mortgage funds for the owners of the large estates of the Central Valley, who typically received over 80 percent of its outstanding loans.[133] The *Caja* was always, as Borde and Góngora remark, "a docile instrument in the hands of the landed proprietors,"[134] whereas the copper-mine owners were deprived even of such public financing.

The latter's antagonism toward the "usurers" and bankers was, therefore, understandably strong, summed up expressively in 1883 by one of their foremost spokesmen and representatives, Benjamín Vicuña Mackenna: "The bankers roast and burn the industry in the slow fire of their usurious capital," he wrote, "and make [the copper-mine owners] live in perpetual misery and deprivation." Usury is

[131] Przeworski 1978, pp. 100–101; Segall 1953, pp. 70–76.

[132] In 1875, according to Segall 1953, pp. 76–77, there were 61 registered corporations in railroads, commerce, banking, insurance, mining, and industry, with an aggregate capital of $53.5 million, of which $19.3 million (36 percent) was held by banks, $11.5 million (21 percent) by railroads, and $13.7 million (26 percent) by silver-, copper-, and coal-mining companies.

[133] Bauer 1975, pp. 90–91.

[134] Borde and Góngora 1956, p. 126.

"an ancient and vicious cause of the permanent depression of metal values in the country . . . [because] the moneylenders generally have monopolized the production of copper from the mouth of the mine to the hold of the ship carrying the [copper] bars. . . . They have profited in this speculation one hundred percent at the cost of the sweat of the producer. . . . Little has changed in this situation . . . with the transformation of many moneylenders into corporations." The foreign commercial houses were also the target of the same antagonism leveled against domestic bankers, whose burdens the mineowners saw as inseparable. "Devoured by credits and loans," Vicuña Mackenna observed, "the industrialist has come to be no more than an unhappy source of nourishment for foreign capital."[135]

Despite their awareness, their acute sense of "exploitation," and their consistent demands, if not supplications, the mineowners' call for public financing of mining and smelting was ignored by successive governments. Such financing, provided either directly or through a state bank, or by private mining banks formed with state support, was necessary, as an 1875 mineowners' statement pleaded, "to liberate the mineowners who have the least resources from the power of the *habilitadores*."[136] Not, however, until the state bank was promulgated by Balmaceda in the midst of the civil war itself did any government make a significant effort to fulfill this demand.[137] After Balmaceda's death, the idea was revived again, but the government's action came, as usual, too late with too little. A *Banco Minero* was established by presidential decree on March 29, 1906, but "collapsed within two years" after receiving only scanty state support. Its assets never exceeded $1 million. This niggardly appropriation, coming "at a time when mining ventures required large financial resources," amounted to far less than one sixtieth of the real assets with which Balmaceda had endowed the state bank a decade and a half earlier.[138]

---

[135] Vicuña Mackenna 1883, pp. 147–148.
[136] Vicuña Mackenna 1883, p. 602.
[137] Furthermore, opposition to its establishment reportedly came even from some outstanding Balmacedistas, including José Miguel Valdés Carrera, recently appointed minister of finance, who defended the private banks as "elements of progress and well-being among us . . . when honorably administered" (Yrarrázaval Larraín 1963, pp. 109–110).
[138] Przeworski 1978, p. 116.

REVOLUTION FROM ABOVE, CAPITALIST DEVELOPMENT,
AND POLITICAL DEMOCRACY

Inscribed in Chilean history was a distinct pattern of state policy toward copper, now revealed by my analysis but always visible and palpable to the most advanced elements of the mining bourgeoisie itself. The mineowners' reiterated demand that the government intervene "to revive the fatigued mining industry . . . and restore its . . . old exuberance" was never fulfilled. They were subjected instead, as Vicuña Mackenna had exclaimed in 1883, to the almost "incurably debilitating hostility of the State and its agents, taxes, and laws." No government but Balmaceda's committed itself to the historic task that the most self-conscious mineowners recognized and demanded of the Chilean state: to protect and stimulate the development of copper mining, as the basis of an integrated mining, smelting, and fabricating industry. No other government would respond to their demand, already articulated by a leader of their mid-century abortive revolution, that "the fortune, credit, and confidence" of private copper capital be buttressed by the state; none would ever perform what Pedro Félix Vicuña Aguirre called, in 1861, this "most vital and greatest of services to the nation."[139] Only during that ephemeral historical moment under Balmaceda was the fruition imminent of this long-sought "vital service to the nation," of state protection and assistance to the copper industry. For in Balmaceda's regime, the leading mineowners now held what had escaped them in the past: the political power to shape state policy in their own interest. Thus the victory of the Balmacedistas in the civil war could well have provided the political impetus for Chile's relatively independent capitalist development.

For if they had won, the leading Balmacedistas surely would have sought to fulfill the hitherto frustrated political-economic objectives of the mining bourgeoisie; they were, in fact, the latter's political incarnation. A compact and cohesive group of men, the leading Balmacedistas came predominantly from the politically conscious and alert mining segment of the dominant class. Not only was the mining bourgeoisie bound by common "objective interests," but

[139] Vicuña Mackenna 1883, p. 600.

also it was aware of these interests, articulated them, occasionally with extraordinary prescience, and had organized and fought, even in armed combat, to fulfill them. Scarcely a generation earlier, the mining bourgeoisie had been defeated in two successive revolutionary insurrections, and now it had again engaged in a civil war; but this time, for once, it did so with its own representatives at the helm of state.

The historical connection between the two civil wars and the continuity in the aims of its leading protagonists—then fighting against the state; now, under Balmaceda, its leading helmsmen—was recognized even in the art and poetry mourning Balmaceda's death. For example, a poem by Juan Salazar published in late December 1891, shortly after Balmaceda's death, proclaimed that like Pedro León Gallo in 1858—"the champion of Loros"—Balmaceda also raised "the banner of the *zuavos*/the people's banner of Democracy/betrayed by the Aristocracy/as were so many courageous men at Cerro Grande." A Guillet lithograph in Jerónimo Peralta Flores' 1893 *Homage to the Defenders of Democracy* shows José Miguel Carrera, leader of the war of independence against Spain and Chile's first republican head of state (who was also, not incidentally, then the owner of major copper mines at Tamaya) distributing laurel wreaths to two groups of men: on one hand, to Francisco Bilbao, Benjamin Vicuña Mackenna, and Pedro León Gallo, two of the principal political theorists and the top military commander of the abortive 1850s revolution, and, on the other hand, to Manuel Arístides Zañartu and President Balmaceda.[140]

The fact is that not only were the leading Balmacedistas drawn overwhelmingly from the mining bourgeoisie, but there was also a contingent of men among them who had fought as young revolutionaries in the armed struggles of the 1850s. Of the 40 leading Balmacedistas in our sample, nearly a quarter had been active in that mid-century revolutionary movement, whose quintessential base was the mining bourgeoisie of the north; in particular, 8 of the 21 "prominent Balmacedistas," or roughly 40 percent of them (who, it will be remembered, were deeply involved public partisans of Balmaceda

---

[140] V. Figueroa 1897, pp. 26, 121; 1928, p. 364.

but not necessarily in his government), had fought to take state power, as radical democrats and bourgeois revolutionaries, over three decades earlier. They "belonged to that generation," in the words of a biographer, "that learned its lessons from . . . Francisco Bilbao and held advanced and even revolutionary ideas."[141] As the participants in that revolutionary generation, they had thronged to the same political clubs, issued manifestos, published pamphlets, edited newspapers, agitated at protest rallies, organized a constituent assembly to propose a new democratic constitution, and finally mounted an armed struggle and risked their lives on the same bloody hillsides in direct confrontation with the state.

The contrast between the representation of the 1850s activists among Balmacedistas and Congressionalists is sharp: whereas 8 of the 21 "prominent" Balmacedistas had been active as young men in the political struggles against the state, only 2 of the 15 "prominent" anti-Balmaceda rebels had been. Put differently, proportionally about three times as many prominent partisans of Balmaceda belonged to the revolutionary political generation of the 1850s as did his prominent enemies. (See Table 4.6.)

Table 4.6. Percentage of Leading Balmacedistas and Congressionalists in the 1850s Political Generation

Political Position	1850s Activists	(N)
"Prominent" Balmacedistas[a]	43	(21)
"Prominent" Congressionalists[b]	13	(15)
All leading Balmacedistas	22	(40)
All leading Congressionalists	9	(21)

[a] Prominent partisans of Balmaceda who were not necessarily members of his government or of congress, or later of the "rump" congress during the civil war itself.

[b] Prominent anti-Balmaceda "revolutionaries" who were not necessarily members of the "provisional government" during the civil war or of the immediate post-civil-war regime.

[141] V. Figueroa 1925–1931, I, p. 344.

Thus these Balmacedistas were not merely bourgeois politicians, inured to compromise, nor ordinary businessmen of calculating bent; they were men formed not only in the ruggedly individualistic milieu of mining but also, perhaps even more indelibly, in the revolutionary struggles of their youth. These common experiences had shaped them as young men and, since they found themselves suddenly and strangely together at the helm of state in still another civil war, now made them a close-knit and highly self-conscious body of political comrades. They held in their hands the coercive powers of the state with which to enforce their long-sought aim of protecting and advancing the interests of their own compact class segment. Bound simultaneously by common economic interests, mutual kinship ties, and the same formative generational experiences, there is every reason to suppose that had they retained state power, they would have finished the work begun by their political generation at mid-century.[142] They might have completed their revolution, however, with a historical twist that none of them could have anticipated. For these men, who had once fought and failed to put through a revolution from below, might now have found themselves trying to enforce a revolution from above.

Surely the Balmacedistas would have sought to impose on their class and nation the necessary political conditions of their own economic sovereignty, for this was in fact what they began to do while they held power—the promulgation of the state bank, as a centralized mechanism to foment industrialization and finance copper mining and to break the power of the "usurious bankers," having been merely their most emblematic political act. If they had won the civil war, it must be surmised that they would have pushed ahead with Balmaceda's program—and their own salvation—even more resolutely and with the determination to brook no further opposition. They would have continued and intensified the process already set in motion under Balmaceda before the outbreak of the civil war: to make huge state investments in railroad construction; to stimulate and subsidize heavy industry and, in particular, copper fabrication;

---

[142] Cf. Zeitlin 1967, chap. 9, for a very different time and a very different place— the mid-twentieth-century revolution in Cuba—in which political generations, formed by the varying historical exeriences of their youth, emerged as relatively independent bases of political alignment within the same class.

to expand communications; and to extend the network of roads and irrigation canals, coupled now perhaps with protection of the merchant marine and encouragement of a domestic shipbuilding industry. Under their resolute leadership, it may be supposed, Chile would have witnessed its own unique industrial revolution from above.

The mining bourgeoisie, despite its economic power, had long seen itself as, paradoxically, an exploited segment of its own class— reflected in the mineowners' old 1858 view that "Once we were exploited by the Spanish Court . . . now by the Court of Santiago" and in their recent 1883 declamation against the state's "accelerated and almost violent extraction" of tribute from them and the "unjust burdens" to which they were subject.[143]

The mineowners virtually saw themselves as a "universal class," whose own interests were the nation's interests and whose own economic emancipation was essential to Chile's advance; they believed, rightly, that the copper industry's "decadence," as Vicuña Mackenna wrote, "would drain the nation of its vitality." This sense of themselves was poignantly but sharply expressed in the National Mining Society's 1883 petition to the government for assistance:

> The copper industry in Chile . . . consumes a great part of the agricultural produce of the entire country. . . . It consumes most of the production of the coal mines of the south of Chile. It is also the principal consumer of the . . . foreign goods imported at . . . Valparaíso. At the same time, it consumes much of the lumber of our southern provinces and accounts for much of the country's trade. The increase or decrease in the production of the copper mines makes all the industries of the country grow or decay. In general, it is undeniable that the greatest part of the riches and prosperity of Chile comes from the copper and silver mining industry in the north—an industry whose exercise requires the highest personal sacrifice and intelligent devotion. . . . Yet despite its importance to Chile, the copper industry not only has never received the protection of the State, but has even been compelled to bear the weight of asphyxiating taxes.[144]

---

[143] Vitale 1971, III, p. 252; Vicuña Mackenna 1883, p. 590.
[144] Vicuña Mackenna 1883, pp. 246, 527–529.

Under Balmaceda, the mining magnates had the chance to reverse that historical pattern and to use the political power they held, not only to protect their own interests but also to "hasten, hot-house fashion," as Marx once remarked, the independent development of capitalism in Chile. Had they retained state power, Braden may well have found on his arrival in Chile in 1904 not dispirited mineowners and a decaying copper industry, and a government all but ready to barter the nation's patrimony at any price, but a fiercely independent, even arrogant and proud, mining bourgeoisie, presiding through the state over the resurgence of copper, the incessant growth of heavy industry, and rapid national development. This was a nation, it must be remembered, that surrendered its riches to foreign capital, not as the result of military conquest and occupation, as was the fate of so many elsewhere, but through the merest of business transactions, at a moment of national ennui, and in an ambience of drift and decline following civil war.

But it must also be said that, ironically, if the mineowners had won the civil war and had gone on successfully to promote rapid industrialization under state aegis, it might well have been at the cost of Chile's nascent democratic political institutions. For, as the political polarization under Balmaceda and the ensuing civil war showed, it was not only "against the will of the more backward members" of the landed aristocracy, as Barrington Moore observes of Germany and Japan, that the Balmacedistas would have been compelled to put through their industrial policies.[145] Rather, to assure their country's independent capitalist development, the Balmacedistas would probably have found it necessary to govern against the will of certain "advanced" but recalcitrant capitalists themselves.

This was also, as we know, already an era of monumental confrontations between capital and the emergent working class, in the cities and nitrate *pampas*, and that class would have required "disciplining" by any regime, especially one committed to rapid industrialization under state aegis. When the civil war ended, the class struggle intensified. Shortly after the fall of the Balmaceda regime, *El Ferrocarril* warned that "the scenes of vandalism in Iquique,

[145] Moore 1966, p. 253.

Antofogasta, and Pisagua are a clear expression of the appearance in Chile of the . . . plague of Communism—a plague that has so violently shaken the social order in other countries."[146] That the Balmacedistas, if they had won the civil war, would have found themselves confronting this "plague" and their own class simultaneously could scarcely have nurtured political freedoms in Chile. The quiescence of the peasantry might also have changed abruptly (as has happened elsewhere historically), sparked by the intensified exploitation and social dislocation and suffering accompanying the penetration of capitalism in the countryside. If repression of a restive and rebellious peasantry would have been combined with reforms to mollify it (and to increase agricultural productivity), thereby impinging adversely on powerful agrarian interests, this in turn would have heightened the hostility of their own class against the Balmacedistas.

Under such circumstances, it would have been necessary for the Balmacedistas, many once genuine radical democrats, to forge a regime equipped with a powerful repressive apparatus that could both assure domestic tranquility and enforce the nation's accelerated development. But it is not merely our retrospective knowledge of Chile's Prussian and Meiji contemporaries that suggests that this could have been the path taken in the aftermath of a Balmaceda victory. That path was already foreshadowed in the actual conduct and emergent organization of the Balmaceda regime during the civil war itself.

When the civil war broke out, the huge flow of public revenues from the nitrate boom had already equipped the Chilean state with what one historian, with some exaggeration, has called "a vast and ever-proliferating bureaucracy."[147] Governing fewer than 3,000,000 citizens, it was staffed by some 5,000 civil servants and 30,000 other public employees, and also indirectly employed—through the contracts it let for building the railroads, highways, bridges, and other public works projects—still another 40,000 workers involved in their construction.[148] Balmaceda's development projects were complemented by a concerted military program designed to expand and

---

[146] Ramírez Necochea 1956, p. 312.
[147] Bauer 1975, p. 75.
[148] Sears and Wells 1893, p. 45; Blakemore 1974, p. 174.

modernize Chile's army and navy. Warships, cruisers, and torpedo boats were ordered from abroad; military schools and a war academy were built and staffed and the latter put under the command of a former Prussian officer; combat-ready naval facilities and fortifications were built at the country's major ports; and the army was provided with the latest military equipment, including Krupp artillery and Winchester rifles. When the civil war began, Chile had an army of 5,000 but enough equipment to outfit 80,000; and the army grew by conscription to 39,000 within its first few months.[149] Here, certainly, was a formidable bureaucratic base and repressive apparatus with which to maintain order against a restive populace and to erect a centralized and powerful authoritarian capitalist state.

At the civil war's outset, Balmaceda had assumed "total public power," banned publication by 10 of the country's major newspapers, imposed martial law, and detained and purged many military men and public officials. Of course, these might have been no more than exigent—and temporary—defensive measures in civil war, and the same might also be said of the forced conscription of thousands of *inquilinos* and laborers; the compulsory levies and confiscation of horses, cattle, grain, and other equipment from the landed estates of known oppositionists; the intentional gutting and destruction of some estates, merchant houses, and other enterprises, as well as the intervention and closing down of the private banks; and the prohibition of land sales or transfers by the owners of 67 of the largest estates.

But the establishment of a sprawling secret police, charged with uprooting and suppressing the rebel committees and any opposition to the regime; the suspension of the civil courts and their replacement by military tribunals, which carried out summary trials and executions of dissident officers and soldiers; the search and seizure operations against the homes of citizens suspected of collaboration with the insurgents; the censorship and rifling of the public mails; and the beating and torture of many political prisoners (with whom, says one historian, "the jails overflowed"), represented the organization of an extensive and unprecedented apparatus of repression and the vir-

[149] Sears and Wells 1893, p. 7; Ramírez Necochea 1969, pp. 162–168; Galdames 1941, p. 343; Encina 1952, ii, p. 145.

tual abolition of preexisting civil liberties and personal rights. If the Balmacedistas had won, social tensions probably would have continued to sharpen under their reign, and that apparatus surely would have been extended and strengthened even further.

During the civil war, the highest military officers were given posts in the "civil administration" and seats in the constituent congress (three generals were named senators, five colonels became deputies). This, in Chile's history as a republic, constituted an unprecedented fusion of civil and military authority. The executive, legislative, judicial, and military apparatuses of the state became less and less distinguishable as the civil war intensified—to the point that, as the leading Balmacedista Juan Eduardo Mackenna wrote privately to the president (April 11, 1891), Chile was witnessing "the decomposition and corruption" of civil society. Balmaceda himself apparently felt that he had become the captive rather than the commander of the strengthened and expanded officers corps on which his regime now depended. He told another of his close partisans, Lauro Barros, that "the Army, having become enamored of its authority and inspired by the brilliant prospects opened up to it by the civil war . . . would surely revolt against a return to constitutional government."[150]

Material repression was also coupled with a propaganda campaign intended to mobilize the populace against Balmaceda's enemies and to convert the civil war into something akin to both a class war and a nationalist movement fighting against an "exploitative oligarchy" in league with "the foreign enemy." Balmaceda himself characterized the struggle against him as "an anti-democratic revolution, initiated by a small centralized social class . . . by a sawed-off [corta] ruling class." The official press declaimed, as one editorial did, against "the aristocracy without insignia or heraldry . . . industrialists who are loafers and layabouts [de combo y culero] . . . brokers . . . bank directors and stockowners. . . . The oligarchy is dead, the bankocracy will also die. When the vestiges of these calamities have disappeared, then Chile will be able to count itself among the true republics."[151] Here was the necessary rhetoric to legitimate the im-

---

[150] Encina 1952, II, pp. 176, 178; Heise González 1974, pp. 103–105; Galdames 1941, pp. 346–347.
[151] Heise González 1974, pp. 121–122; Encina 1952, II, pp. 129–130.

position of a revolution from above, designed to isolate socially and then break the power and tame the segments of the dominant class that opposed Chile's state-enforced development.

Balmaceda and his closest advisers also took steps to forge a permanent restructuring of the Chilean state. Seven months into the civil war, in mid-July 1891, Interior Minister Julio Bañados presented legislation to the constituent congress to reform the constitution in order to "place the independence of State Powers on a foundation of granite." In the draft constitution, the executive of the state arrogated to itself exclusive and autonomous powers not before accorded to it in the Chilean republic. There were fixed budgetary categories under the sole authority of the president, which included taxation to support a standing army and a regular secret police. The latter was to be under the "exclusive authority of the president," not only during an extraordinary "state of seige" but also as an inherent prerogative of presidential office.

The president was given the authority to dismiss public employees, "whatever their quality or category"; his ministers possessed all but nominal independence of congress; and congress itself was no longer empowered to call itself into special session. This, too, was to become the prerogative of the president, acting in his discretion, at the request of congress. With the consent of the senate, the president had the power to dismiss and replace supreme court justices as well as judges of the appeals and ordinary courts of law. Capping this extraordinary concentration of state power in the executive, the draft constitution also gave the president the exclusive authority to invest state funds, without the need for congressional approval, and independently to incur fiscal obligations and contract loans and to commit state credits.[152] Thus the revamped constitution, if passed, would have provided the legal framework for a centralized bureaucratic state, equipped with an expanded repressive apparatus and independent fiscal authority, enabling the men at its helm to marshal the nation's resources and impose their development policies on their own recalcitrant class and to ensure the forced march of industrialization.

[152] Yrarrázaval Larraín 1940, ii, pp. 268–272.

In the event, the constitutional project was approved by the rump chamber of deputies but had not yet passed the senate, where it met with contentious opposition, when the Balmaceda forces were decisively defeated in late August at Placilla. Several of the most prominent Balmacedistas, among them Juan Eduardo Mackenna, Alfredo Ovalle Vicuña, Adolfo Eastman, Manuel Arístides Zañartu, José Miguel Valdés Carrera, and Eusebio Lillo had, in fact, opposed passage of the new constitution. They and others resisted, as one of them put it, the regime's "abolutist tendencies" toward the creation of a "new imperial state." As the civil war wore on, these men had protested against the regime's severe repression and increasingly arbitrary acts, its use of torture against political prisoners, and its purge of the judiciary; when presented with the proposed constitutional "reform," they refused to ratify it. The new constitution would be, José Miguel Valdés Carrera proclaimed, "worse than conservative." In premonition of Chile's probable historical path under such a constitution, Valdés thundered: "I repudiate it as tremendously reactionary."[153]

Whether, if the Balmacedistas had won, Valdés Carrera and his radical democratic comrades would have held onto power or been replaced by others who, like Interior Minister Domingo Godoy, were partisans of "the iron fist"—whether, whatever their personal inclinations, the Balmacedistas would have gone on to put through a capitalist revolution from above, propelling Chile along its own unique variant of the "Prussian road"—we cannot know.[154] Their revolution from above was undone, thus assuring their nation not capitalist development but underdevelopment. But despite this, Chile was also to flower in the twentieth century into a vital parliamentary democracy. For, at a decisive historical moment, not absolutism but par-

---

[153] Yrarrázaval Larraín 1940, II, pp. 278, 268–281.

[154] Godoy, who as interior minister had organized the secret police and used it to terrorize Balmaceda's opposition, was unrepentant over a decade later, when he told a biographer: "I was a partisan of the iron fist. If the regime had done what I proposed, some heads would have rolled, but we would not have had a revolution, and the nation wouldn't be in the abyss in which it now finds itself" (V. Figueroa 1925–1931, III, p. 325). In the midst of the civil war he is also said to have remarked: "Yes, we are the revolutionists and the others [the Congressionalists] are mutineers." Quoted in Blakemore 1965, p. 395.

liamentary government, not authoritarianism but democracy, became the paradoxical means by which to safeguard the political hegemony and immediate economic interests of Chile's commanding landlords and capitalists. In our own day, however, when their descendants faced a new threat, this time from below, they chose to abandon democracy rather than abdicate their own class rule.

Chapter 5 ➤ REPRISE: CLASS RELATIONS, THE "WORLD SYSTEM," AND DEVELOPMENT

It was in and through the class and intraclass political struggles that erupted in civil war and in abortive bourgeois revolution, first from below and then from above, in the middle and late nineteenth century, and the class relations thus consolidated, that both the enduring pattern of capitalist development and the structure of the bourgeois state in Chile were produced historically. These class relations constituted, as Max Weber might have said, the "steel frame" that tended to impose limits on subsequent development. In Chile, as elsewhere, the historical shape of an entire epoch hinged "upon the outcome of specific processes of class formation, of class struggle."[1]

Chile's young mining and agrarian capitalists were neither tame nor timid in their attacks against the "old regime." They launched their own serious intellectual assaults on its bastions, probed them with an oppositional though inchoate theory aiming to transform both the state order and agrarian production relations and to protect the mining industry's growth in its competitive struggle with foreign capital, and fought the bloody 1850s clashes to make a democratic revolution.

These political struggles took place at a phase of capitalist development when the working class—as a class of wage laborers rather than artisans—was still incipient and thus posed no independent challenge to the reign of capital. The radical bourgeoisie fought sharply for its independent interests, mobilized subordinate classes on its behalf and as its armed allies, and identified its particular

[1] Brenner 1977, p. 91. Also see Brenner 1976 and 1982, and the references therein; this is an extraordinarily valuable debate on class relations and the origins of capitalist development. See also Kaplan 1977, especially pp. 37ff.

interest with the general expansion of individual freedoms and political rights. The violent class struggles between labor and capital
were decades beyond, scarcely discernible in these mid-century battles, in which mineowners, miners, artisans, grain-mill owners, small
holders, and yeomen farmers fought side by side under the banner
of democracy. As a result, on their armed revolution's defeat, the
mining bourgeoisie had neither the temptation nor the need to cement
a reactionary alliance with the landed estate owners and subordinate
itself to an authoritarian state able to contain and discipline the
working class.

On the contrary, supported by an expanding economic base, in
the following two decades, these radical democratic capitalists were
able gradually, through continuing political struggles, to dismantle
the old state—bourgeois in "structure" but no less an "instrument"
of landed property—and to construct a parliamentary democracy in
its place. But the defeat of their revolution also had an enduring
effect on the nation's development: without the dissolution of the
landed estate's dominion in the countryside, the growth of the domestic market was restricted and agricultural technique stagnated.
Without hegemony in their class and power in the state, the copper
capitalists would soon find themselves—when buffeted simultaneously in the 1880s by the cold winds of new international competition
and by the domestic diversion of transport, fuel, supplies, and labor
power to the burgeoning nitrate industry—unable to secure the necessary state protection and assistance to survive in these changing
conditions.

For an ephemeral historical moment, however, they themselves
held the helm of state, brought to power by a dissident aristocratic
president desperately seeking political allies. As Balmaceda sought
to modernize his country and to protect the national patrimony from
further foreign encroachment, he also unwittingly endangered the
interests and provoked the wrath of his own class, landlords and
capitalists alike. In particular, the copper-mine owners and nitrate
capitalists, each beset by separate but inseparable economic crises
and requiring opposing state policies for their resolution, were drawn
inexorably if unknowingly into internecine conflict and finally civil
war. Never again would the copper bourgeoisie have such a historic
opportunity to impose the state policies necessary to protect and

advance its interests: to provide massive public investment both to ensure the competitive productivity of Chilean mining in the international arena and to push its conversion into an integrated mining, smelting, and manufacturing industry, with the stimulus this would in turn give to domestic manufacturing in general and the heavy equipment industry in particular. With the defeat of the mineowners, moreover, not only they but also their victorious nitrate antagonists were to succumb to the denationalization of their industry. Whatever their intentions, the irony—and the tragedy—of the Congressionalists' successful overthrow of Balmaceda is that it assured not only the disintegration of the national copper mining industry and its eventual foreign penetration and control but also the swift foreign domination of nitrate production itself: their combined denationalization led, in turn, to the demise of Chile's infant capital goods industry, now bereft of these two main founts of domestic demand and of the state assistance and protection that Balmaceda's government had begun to provide. All this again tended to assure the further flow of capital into profitable but unproductive outlets—in real estate, land, finance, and commerce, often in association with foreign firms—rather than into productive investment and industrial growth.

The defeat of the Balmacedistas thus meant the suppressed historical alternative of independent capitalist development for Chile—of industrialization enforced "hot-house fashion" by the state, under the aegis of a peculiarly national segment of the dominant class itself. But had that class segment won the civil war, had the mining bourgeoisie successfully imposed its own political hegemony on its class and nation, it might well have done so only by putting through what amounted to Chile's own variant of a "revolution from above": the copper capitalists would likely have been compelled to impose their political hegemony, as their famous Prussian contemporary Otto von Bismarck declaimed, "not by speeches and majority votes, but . . . by blood and iron." For the Balmacedistas would have had to carry out their policies against the opposition of the bloodied but unbowed coalition of their fellow landlords and capitalists, liberals and conservatives alike, whom they had just defeated in civil war, while also trying to contain and discipline an already restive, and even insurgent, working class. Whether these radical democrats would thus have found themselves tragically forging a far more powerful repressive apparatus and authoritarian state than the one they had fought to abolish a generation earlier·is, of course, unanswerable. What in fact, happened, however, is clear: parliamentary democracy was consolidated rather than overthrown even as the economy tended to stagnate and to come increasingly under foreign control in subsequent decades. The defeat of the Balmacedistas was thus a decisive but contradictory watershed in Chile's history, for it both stymied capitalist development and buttressed bourgeois democracy.

POLITICAL STRUGGLES AND DEMOCRACY

The historically specific generalizations that emerge from the present analysis, then, are as follows: First, the political form of the bourgeois state, either democratic or authoritarian, is the relatively contingent historical product of concrete political struggles, not only between classes but also between rival segments of the dominant class itself. These struggles and their outcomes, given determinate historical circumstances, shape both the political form and the social content of the state, for they are crucial in determining which of the contending segments actually gains political hegemony within the dominant class and is able to impose its will as the general will, its particular interest as the universal interest of class and nation. Second, these specific class and intraclass relations and their concomitant state policies in turn structure a country's possibilities for capitalist development and underdevelopment and, as a result, its vulnerability to the penetration of foreign capital, thereby determining its relative location in and effect on global political-economic relationships.

Thus a critical theoretical question that this work's empirical analysis has implicitly addressed is what the now widely accepted generalization that nations, states, and classes "develop . . . within the context of the development of the world system" really means.[2] How that observation is translated into historically specific formulations and concrete hypotheses about the real connections between that so-called "world economy" and class relations, the nature of the state (and the sources and uses of political power), national identity, and

[2] Wallerstein 1974a, p. 67.

the pattern of development and underdevelopment is precisely the question. Surely, in every country that itself developed in the wake of the development of capitalism in England and Europe, especially in the aftermath of the former's industrial revolution, "class relations and the relation of the state apparatus to society bear in a specific manner the imprint of that country's position on the world market."[3] But, of course, the empirical question, and with it the theoretical content of that generalization, is what does the phrase "bears the imprint in a specific manner" mean? *What* that "imprint" is, and *how* it is stamped into the specific historical development of a particular society, is precisely what is at issue, both on a general theoretical level and in the explanation of specific empirical cases. Thus my analyses of the civil wars in Chile are not only substantive contributions to an explanation of Chile's own pattern of development and to the shaping of the characteristic uniqueness of Chilean society. They are meant also as contributions to the historical specification of how the prevailing global political-economic relationships themselves were produced historically, through the resolution of decisive class and intraclass struggles within particular countries and areas at crucial moments of transition in their own historical development.

For haunting much of the theoretical discussion of development and underdevelopment (not to speak of so-called "modernization" theory) is precisely the absence of historical specification. Instead, there is a pronounced tendency to conceive of present international relationships as if they were not themselves historical products. How the disparate areas of the globe and the class and class–state relations within them were related at the dawn of the capitalist era, how they became related under late nineteenth-century imperialist expansion, and how they are related in the present epoch may have quite different answers with quite different implications for our understanding of development and underdevelopment. Those answers can be discovered only through historically specific analysis of concrete causal relationships. Surely a critical theoretical question and social issue today is how the various nation-states fit into the workings of international capitalism and how they affect and are affected by the global political economy now dominated by multinational corporations based

[3] von Braunmuhl 1979, p. 171.

in a few of the advanced capitalist countries. These corporations now command labor, administer production, and accumulate capital throughout the world, as their singular theater of operations. The competitive struggle between them, conditioned by and conditioning their relations with labor nationally and internationally, and by the already existing class and class–state relations in the given countries and regions involved, are undoubtedly crucial in shaping today's realities. But even in the extraordinarily integrated "world economy" that now exists, not the so-called "world market context" or reified "world system" but the internationalization of class relations and class struggle should be the focus of our social analysis and political practice.

"WORLD SYSTEM THEORY"

The substantive analyses in this work thus also provide critical evidence against the theory that the world market, in Claudia von Braunmuhl's formulation, plays the *"dominant* role . . . in the determination of the particular form of development of the productive forces, of class relations and, last but not least, the specific configuration of the state apparatus, its function and its perception of its function as much as its position in the context of a class society."[4] It is to this theory *qua* theory that we now turn. In it, what is supposedly primary in the determination of the specific class relations and form and role of the state in a given country is the world market or world system itself. This world market or world system supposedly constitutes the "totality" of which specific states and national political economies are merely the "individual instances" or "integral components."[5] In some way, then, as Andre Gunder Frank puts it, a country's "participation in the world capitalist system" "imposes" and "maintains" its "domestic economic and political structure."[6]

Indeed, not only is the world system the primary cause of historical development or social change within particular societies but it also forms a veritable ontological principle in this theory. This world

[4] von Braunmuhl 1979, p. 167, italics added.
[5] von Braunmuhl 1979, p. 172.
[6] Frank 1967, p. 67.

system is the one and *only* reality: world systems, so it is said, "are the only real social systems."[7] The consequence of this rather strange contemporary melange of nominalism and idealism is that classes and their contradictory interrelations and real struggles in the specific social formations they constitute historically now become merely the phenomenal form of a self-unfolding world system. To name that world system is thereby to discover, without empirical investigation and specification of real causal relationships, the reality of all its constituents (or "instances").

By naming global relationships a "capitalist world system," all other coexisting productive forms and class relations are thereby transformed conceptually into merely variant forms of "capitalism": "The point is," says Immanuel Wallerstein, "that the 'relations of production' that define a system are the 'relations of production' of the whole system, and the system . . . is the . . . world-economy." Indeed, "the modern world-economy is, and can only be [!], a capitalist world-economy. It is for this reason," he continues, "that we have rejected the appellation of 'feudalism' for the various forms of *capitalist* agriculture *based on coerced labor* which grew up in a world-economy."[8]

Surely the various repressive adaptations of agrarian relations of production to the development of capitalism from at least the sixteenth century onward were not in any meaningful historical sense "feudal." I have many times emphasized this in my previous work.[9] The present substantive analysis of mid-to-late nineteenth-century Chile has also revealed that the development of capitalism itself led to the landowners' successful imposition of new forms of social domination, in the guise of "precapitalist" and "archaic" seignorial relations, and that agrarian resistance and revolt and an unsuccessful bourgeois revolution against these new forms of social domination were crucial in shaping Chile's subsequent pattern of development.

[7] Wallerstein 1974a, pp. 348, 351.
[8] Wallerstein 1974a, pp. 127, 350, italics added.
[9] See, for instance, Petras and Zeitlin, eds., 1968, and the articles by Stavenhagen (1968), Vitale (1968), and Quijano (1968), in which the myth of "feudalism" in Latin America is systematically criticized (a myth that until then was accepted by most liberal and Marxian theorists of development); the emphasis is placed on the significance of mercantile capitalism and the integration of Latin America into the world market in the origins of its specific class relations. Also see Zeitlin 1969, 1972.

But it is precisely the specific historical contradictions inherent in the development of "precapitalist" forms of exploitation (including even the construction of new slave civilizations in parts of the Americas and the United States) as the *result* of the development of capitalism that requires substantive analysis. To conceptualize them as "capitalist," despite the profoundly different class relations, internal dynamics, and state forms they involve in contrast to the relations between free wage labor and capital, results in the neglect of the most significant questions: How, in fact, do such class relations arise, or how are they resisted and free labor forms established? What class struggles between the agricultural producers and the landed proprietors, and between the latter and productive capitalists, occur? Under what conditions do they occur, and what are the long-term consequences for the development of the particular social formations produced by these struggles?[10]

These are precisely the kind of questions that I had to grapple with in trying to solve the conundrum of Chile's specific historical development; without an answer to such questions, the pattern of development of any particular "social formation" and indeed, as Robert Brenner has persuasively argued, the original emergence of capitalism in England and Europe, is incomprehensible.[11] By assum-

---

[10] There is no easy shorthand to distinguish the various types of "large landowners," which vary historically and contemporaneously in the productive relations, tenure systems, and market situations in which they are involved. As I stressed in my analysis of Chile's agrarian relations from the mid-nineteenth century on, the Central Valley landowners were thoroughly "integrated into the world market" as well as producing for the local and regional home market; but their relations to their estate tenants were quasi-seignorial, coercive, and debtor relations in contrast to the wage labor relations on which grain milling rested in the south-central zone. The sway of capital can, as it did here, thus vary considerably even within agriculture itself. Unless and until agriculture is not only subordinated to the "market" but also firmly premised on the employment of wage labor on a large scale and the terms and conditions of profitable investment in it are parallel to those in industry, landed property and capital (especially if the former also extracts "ground rent" from the latter) differ qualitatively in their locations in the social process of production and appropriation. This holds, moreover, even if land and capital have markedly coalesced within the dominant class. For the question remains as to how and to what extent the contradictory interests and social cleavages of landlords and capitalists coincide and with what social consequences, despite such coalescence. On this, aside from the concrete analyses in this book, see Zeitlin and Ratcliff 1975; Zeitlin, Neuman, and Ratcliff 1976; and Zeitlin and Ratcliff forthcoming.

[11] Brenner 1976, 1977.

ing the *prior* existence of capitalism, world system theory never has to address this central question: what explains the origins and consolidation of distinctively capitalist relations of production?

By an unwitting conceptual sleight of hand, which gives the same name to different realities, or sees them as merely "individual instances of the totality," world system theory's supposed attention to this totality makes the specific social realities that really *constitute it historically* disappear. The result is that an ostensibly historical theory is in practice unhistorical and even antihistorical. By its ontological assumption that only the world system itself is "real," and by its focus on market relations alone, the theory obscures rather than reveals the concrete internal social relations that underlie that so-called "capitalist world economy" and propel its contradictory historical development. *Within the theory*, there is no way to analyze how the potential for capitalist development is determined by the emergence of a specific ensemble of class relations, based on specific methods of production and appropriation of the surplus product, in a particular society.

Such critical questions as the following must go begging theoretically, for within the parameters of the metropolis-satellite or world system theory, they can neither be asked nor answered: How does the specific historical configuration of class relations in a given social formation affect its internal development? How did this class configuration originate historically, why did class relations take this determinate historical form, and what were its developmental consequences? What are the specific internal dynamics of accumulation peculiar to these class relations and how do they determine the impact of the world market on the society's development? What is the relative effect of the world market versus specific types of penetration and expansion by various units of capital, themselves affected by their internal relations with labor, on the pattern of development? What determines, on the one hand, the types of penetration and expansion of capital and, on the other, their consequences for a specific society?

Above all, the pattern of development of the world system, or world market, the source of the so-called core-periphery, metropolis-satellite structure, is simply taken as a given and left unexplained. Or, in place of explanation, tautologies appear: "the historical development of this world system [of this metropolis-satellite monopolist structure]," Frank informs us, "generated the development of the monopolizing metropolis and the underdevelopment of the monopolized satellites."[12] *Within the theory*, there is no way that the absolutely central and critical question can be posed: What are the effects on the world system itself of the actual class and intraclass struggles, state activities, and types of development in particular societies under specific historical circumstances? What are their transformative consequences for the nature and structure of global political-economic relations? How do class and intraclass struggles within nations and states, and national struggles within, between, and against states, by radically realigning or transforming these class, state, and national relations, thereby also profoundly alter the global reality itself?

Instead of conclusions that address these primary theoretical questions, we are offered such generalizations—bereft of historical content—as the following: "While the advantages of the core-states have not ceased to expand throughout the history of the modern world system, the ability of a particular state to remain in the core sector is not beyond challenge. The hounds are ever to the hares for the position of top dog. Indeed, it may well be that in this kind of system it is not structurally possible to avoid, over a long period of historical time, a *circulation of the elites* in the sense that the particular country that is dominant at a given time tends to be replaced in this role sooner or later by another country."[13] This usage of a crucial notion from elitist theory is no mere semantic lapse: for, despite its historical trappings, world system theory has no historical theory, no theory, that is, to explain the real historical development of the constituent *social relations* that actually structure the so-called world system. It is, in fact, not a theory of historical development, of the origins and transformations of social relations, but of moving equilibrium, of stasis, of altered appearances but unchanging realities, of a system within which states mysteriously slip in and out of an a priori categorical division between "core, semiperiphery and periphery." It is a system that, as Wallerstein (not accidentally borrowing from the

[12] Frank 1969, p. 240.
[13] Wallerstein 1974a, p. 350, italics added.

preeminent functionalist, Talcott Parsons) assures us, has "a strong trend toward self-maintenance."

What explains this division? How did the so-called "core, periphery, and semiperiphery" structure originate historically? The generic answer in world system theory is that "the capitalist world-economy was built on a worldwide division of labor in which various zones of this economy (that which we have termed the core, the semiperiphery, and the periphery) were *assigned* specific economic modes of labor control, and profited unequally from the workings of the system."[14]

But this is no answer at all. It does not even point toward an answer and cannot because it both reifies the so-called capitalist world economy and inverts the real historical process in which these global relations were created. The world economy itself, so it is said, appparently "assigned specific economic roles" within itself to its own "zones," and these "zones" then "used different modes of labor control" and so forth. What has happened here, unfortunately, is that the theory's atemporal categories have imperceptibly been given a life of their own and have imposed (whatever their author's intentions) on the social reality that was meant to be understood by them, so now the categories make that reality fit their own a priori selves.

Such a formulation, almost unnoticed, substitutes for historical explanation and thereby suppresses the central question: What explains the relative development of particular countries and areas and how they not only become located vis-à-vis each other within but actually *shape* the global political-economic relations in which they are involved?[15] Instead of disclosing how and why these global re-

---

[14] Wallerstein 1974a, pp. 350, 162, italics added.

[15] Extensive evidence appears in Wallerstein's book, the *theoretical* meaning of which he ignores, especially in the lengthy footnote quotations from various historical sources. His own account, together with these footnotes, of the emergent and changing roles of Spain, France, the Netherlands, and England in early capitalist development suggests strongly, contrary to his own "world system" theory, that it was the internal class and class–state relations in these countries—struggles between the mesta, the Catalan bourgeoisie and the crown in Spain, specific historical forms of agrarian production and tenure relations in England and France and their effect on the cohesion of the landed in their relation to the state, and the lengthy antifeudal struggles culminating in the Netherlands revolution—that explains their development and determined the nature and extent of their impact on and place within global political-

lationships eventuated as they did, an unwitting historical teleology assures us that this is what they had to become: "The world economy was based precisely on the assumption [whose?] that there were in fact these three zones and that they did in fact have different modes of labor control. *Were this not so*, it would not have been possible to assure the kind of *flow* of the surplus which *enabled the capitalist system to come into existence.*"[16] Just so: The world economy *originated* because of its *consequences*, because its inner purpose was realized in the birth of capitalism.

The reified categories and teleological propositions in the theory are inherent in its structure because it displaces classes and their interrelations—and therefore the specific productive relationships that require rising labor productivity and compel the continual reinvestment of labor's surplus product—from the center of the analysis of development and underdevelopment. Indeed, despite the many references to "classes" and "class formation" in the metropolis-satellite or core-periphery world system model, what appear instead are strata differentiated by their place in the world system's "hierarchy of occupational tasks," having differentiated values and receiving unequal "rewards" in accordance with their "productive tasks" or "levels of skill," à la functionalist stratification theory. "The division of a world-economy involves a hierarchy of occupational tasks, in which tasks requiring higher levels of skill and greater capitalization are reserved [how? by whom or what?] for higher ranking areas. Since a capitalist world-economy essentially rewards accumulated capital, including human capital, at a higher rate than 'raw' labor power, the geographical maldistribution of these occupational skills involves a strong trend toward self-maintenance. . . . The social system is built on having a multiplicity of value systems within it, reflecting the specific functions groups and areas play in the world division of labor."[17]

This stratification model conceals the real nature of class relations and mystifies their historical origins, and thereby also turns the real connection between the division of labor and class relations topsy-

---

economic relations. See Wallerstein 1974a, pp. 166–167, 181–184, 192–195, 227–235, and 301–311.

[16] Wallerstein 1974a, p. 87, italics added.
[17] Wallerstein 1974a, pp. 350, 356.

turvy. Within this abstract model, there are no relations of compulsion, coercion, and exploitation, no relationship between producers and appropriators, oppressors and oppressed, dominant and subordinate classes. Slaves, serfs, tenant farmers, yeomen, artisans, and workers become mere technical "occupational categories";[18] the real historical relations in which they are involved, the exploitation and domination to which they are subject by slaveowners, landlords, and capitalists, simply disappear from the model, replaced by "productive tasks" to which "rewards" are distributed by some invisible hand.

Absent from the model, the historical origins of specific class relations almost disappear from the substantive analysis. Despite the considerable (and correct) attention given to the discussion of slavery and other coercive forms of surplus appropriation that are erected anew as a consequence of the development of capitalism, even these real historical relations tend to appear only in a peculiarly disembodied form in the analysis itself. The impact of conquest, pillage, subjugation, and exploitation (and decimation) of populations in the Americas, India, and Africa by the armies of the various states of Europe and their merchants, slave traders, mineowners, and adventurers from the sixteenth century onward is certainly noted; but it appears, nonetheless, as if it were the result of some self-expanding world system.[19]

[18] Wallerstein 1974a, pp. 86–87.

[19] One difficulty in criticizing world system *theory*, as in this instance, is that it is the underpinning of a study in which, as just noted, there are a host of citations and lengthy footnote quotations of arguments and evidence from various historical studies, whose analytical relevance and theoretical meaning is not explicated; but, on examination, they are often inconsistent with world system theory. Limitations of space and the fact that this is not a review of Wallerstein's book but a critique of the *theory* in it precludes detailing them. One egregious example of Wallerstein's failure to confront the implications of his own footnotes might, however, be given. There are numerous references in the book, as there should be, to the works of such outstanding Marxian historians as Maurice Dobb and R. H. Hilton. The main evidence and theoretical reasoning of their own works on the development of capitalism directly contradict world system theory. But Wallerstein never grapples explicitly with their central thesis (enunciated sharply in their debate with Paul M. Sweezy and, by extension, with Henri Pirenne) concerning "the transition from feudalism to capitalism": that it was in the internal contradiction between petty production and coercive extraction of the direct producer's surplus product under feudalism, and not in trade originating "outside the feudal system" as Sweezy argues, that capitalist production relations emerged historically (Sweezy 1950, p. 139). As Hilton writes: "The eco-

Thus their real historical origins become obscured: "Why different modes of organizing labor—slavery, 'feudalism,' wage-labor, self-employment—at the same point in time within the world economy? Because each mode of labor control is best suited for particular types of production." Why are they "best suited"? Because, so it is said, of *the level of skill required*. For example, since slaves will do only what they are compelled to do, "once skill is involved, it is more economic [sic] to find alternative methods of labor control, since the low cost is otherwise matched by very low productivity." Thus "slavery was not used everywhere" (by whom?) primarily because certain types of production (grain, cattle-raising, and mining) "required a higher level of skill among the basic production workers.

---

nomic progress which was inseparable from the early rent struggle and the political stabilization of feudalism was characterized by an increase in the total social surplus of production over subsistence needs. This, *not* the so-called revival of *international trade* in silks and spices, was *the basis for the development of commodity production*" (Hilton 1953, p. 347, italics added). This quotation appears at the end of a lengthy footnote in which Wallerstein quotes other quite relevant passages from Pirenne and Sweezy, on the one side, and Dobb, on the other (1974a, n.90, pp. 41–42). But Wallerstein's only relevant comment on these quotes is to say that it was probably trade in staples rather than trade in luxuries that accounted for "the expansion of European commerce" (1974a, p. 41). So, the question is converted into what sort of trade leads to expanded trade, *and the production relations on which that trade rested and which made its expansion possible* disappears as a question, despite its appearance in a footnote. Even when it appears that this question is being obliquely addressed, the answer given is circularly contained by the theory. So the expansion of trade, it is argued, required the expansion of production, and this took place through "technological innovation . . . precisely where there was dense population and industrial growth . . . which were the very places where it became more profitable to turn the land use to commercial crops" (1974a, p. 42). But, of course, this ignores the basic question as to why in some places where it was "profitable to turn the land use to commercial crops" the result was not at all "technological innovation" or "industrial growth" but, on the contrary, the *reinforcement of coercive means of surplus labor extraction* and the *stagnation of technique*. The question is what relations of production, what relations between the peasantry and the landowners, made an absolute growth of production possible *not* on the basis of *existing* techniques in agriculture and heavier burdens on the peasantry but, on the contrary, through technical innovations and rising labor productivity by relatively independent cultivators. Brenner formulates it precisely: "To account for capitalist economic development is, therefore, at least to explain the basis for this conjunction between the requirements for surplus extraction and the needs of the developing productive forces" (1977, p. 68). This, in turn, means to discover the class relations produced historically, as an unintended consequence of class struggles in which the peasantry freed themselves from extra economic coercion by the landlords, that made accumulation through rising labor productivity possible.

. . . These workers therefore had to be compensated for ["re-warded"?] by a slightly less onerous form of labor control."[20] So, as in the functionalist stratification model, and even when confronted by historical realities entirely opposed to basic functionalist assumptions and presuppositions, we find that the various historical forms of exploitation dissolve themselves into "occupational categories" differentially rewarded (with a little bit of freedom) in accordance with their level of skill. So, slaves are slaves because what they produce makes them so, the objects produce their subjects, and the system provides its own rewards.[21]

Ignored both empirically and conceptually are the origins of the various coercive forms of appropriation and class domination in Africa, Asia, and the Americas as the unintended historical products of bloody struggles between colonial conquerors and native peoples, and the latter's capacity to resist their subjugation and exploitation, given their material conditions and the structure of their own society before it was attacked and penetrated. These real historical origins of specific types of social structures and political economies in the so-called periphery all but vanish analytically. The nature, origins, and consequences of their constitutive class relations are not integrated in any systematic fashion into the analysis of development and underdevelopment and of the origins of the historical division of the globe into its "metropolises" and "satellites."

Bereft of systematic analysis of the structural possibilities inherent in historically specific exploitative relations and the struggles to subvert or reinforce them, through which history is made (though not as anyone pleases), the historical process of development and underdevelopment is mystified. It takes on, instead, the appearance of a unilinear process of unexplained increasing social differentiation within the world system, of system expansion, or it becomes the result of "turbulence" in the value system, which disturbs the sys-

[20] Wallerstein 1974a, p. 90.
[21] Again, this explains the origins of class relations by their consequences and inverts the historical process. It may be true that slave labor was relatively less productive than free labor (i.e. that slavery impeded labor productivity). But it certainly was not low labor productivity that led to slavery. Apart from the theoretical issue, the fact is that many skilled craftsmen were slaves both in ancient Greece and Rome and in the American South, where their planter masters often rented them out for employment by others, even as factory workers.

tem's self-equilibration. What accounts for the development of the
world system? Attend to the answer: its "multilayered complexity
provided the possibility of multilayered identification and the constant
realignment of political forces, which provided at one and the same
time the underlying turbulence that permitted technological development."[22]

Attributing development to turbulence in the system is a logical
consequence of the theory's central focus on the "flow of surplus,"
on the system's distribution of "rewards," rather than on surplus
production and appropriation. Somehow, "the capitalist world-economy essentially rewards accumulated capital . . . at a higher rate
than 'raw' labor power," as a consequence of which comes its
systemic inequalities. The "system" itself, it will be remembered,
rewards its own components (e.g. "zones" and "occupational skills").
But whence cometh these "rewards"? What is their origin? How is
wealth produced? What is the source of the "surplus" that "flows"
within that world system? Is the social product, by the very way in
which it is produced socially, by the relations of production in which
it is produced, already divided between the immediate producers and
appropriators or must "extra-economic coercion" enter in, and why?
Within world system theory, as in functionalism and neoclassicism,
these questions cannot be posed let alone answered.

The social arrangements through which the dominant class(es)
extract and appropriate the surplus product of the direct producers,
and the struggles this involves and the way they are resolved account
for the development or underdevelopment of particular societies.
Once capitalism has arisen historically, the critical question becomes:
How are the various precapitalist formations fitted into the process
of capital accumulation, whether through conquest, colonialism, or
foreign investment and "incorporation into the world market"? What
will the consequences be for them and their own development and,
in turn, for the development of global political-economic relations?
It is impossible to understand how the so-called international division
of labor, in which particular societies (or global regions) are located,
was formed without a prior analysis that reveals how the latter's
specific class (and class–state) relations arose historically and how

[22] Wallerstein 1974a, p. 86.

these impel or impede the accumulation of capital. Otherwise, the only question that can be addressed, and then in only a very limited fashion, is one of "unequal exchange" within the so-called "world economy": that is, the issue remains only one of *distribution* of what is produced, as if the social product itself were preternaturally given. But any theory of *development* must ask how and why that product is *produced socially*. It is "slapping history in the face to want to *begin* with the division of labor in general," or with the market, as Marx once remarked, so as to *arrive* at the class relations that actually underlie and determine it.[23]

The *result* of "specialization of tasks" in the world division of labor, Wallerstein says, are "differing forms of labor control and different patterns of stratification." In short, "the different roles [in the division of labor] led to different class structures which led to different politics."[24] Or, as Frank says in an almost identical formulation: A country's "participation in the world capitalist system determine[s] . . . the underlying structure of its economy and society."[25] So the question as to why various countries "participate" as they do in the international division of labor—how, that is, their preexisting class structures led to "different roles" within it, thereby shaping that division of labor itself—is never asked. In this abstract, ahistorical model, the "capitalist world market" (or "international division of labor") thus appears upside down; it appears as the cause of class relations in particular societies rather than as, in reality, their refracted historical *product*.

There is no way, within world system theory, to ask how a specific constellation of historical circumstances, class relations, political struggles, and state activities in a particular society either allows its conversion into a so-called "satellite" and its condemnation to "peripheral raw material" production or, on the contrary, compels the growth of its productive forces and its internal development and therefore determines its place in, and its impact on, the shape of the international division of labor or world market.

Even using the satellite-metropolis and core-periphery imagery, however, already tends to obscure that central analytical question

23 Marx 1976, p. 183.
24 Wallerstein 1974a, p. 157.
25 Frank 1967, p. 33.

because, of course, these are mere metaphors. When hardened almost before our eyes into realities of their own, they detract our attention precisely from just such fundamental questions. Put simply, the central question is twofold: on the one hand, what determines the location and effect of a particular society in the so-called world market? On the other, what creates that world market? What determines its division of labor? What, for instance, determines the "specialization" between those countries or regions that produce mainly raw materials or agricultural commodities for export and those that produce both capital goods and consumption goods for domestic as well as foreign markets? The answer to both sides of the question is the same: it is only because specific types of productive social relations are established in a state or region (within determinate material conditions of production) in the first place, that "it"—that is, its dominant class(es)—can "specialize" in certain types of production. It is the reciprocal interaction between countries and regions, based on their internal class relations and material conditions and mediated through "world market" exchange, that creates the division of labor between them on a global level. *It is the class relations within nations that shape the global relations between them* and that determine how these global relations will affect their internal development.

But these conclusions, stated as general theoretical propositions, are already dangerously abstract (if not abstruse)—already too far removed from their requisite and only valid basis: in the concrete analysis of historically specific interrelations in particular societies. Only by such analysis, which I have attempted in my own study of the origins, course, and consequences of the civil wars in Chile, can the fruitfulness and validity of these general ideas about classes and historical development be assessed.

"Metropolis-satellite" or "world system" theory has borne the brunt of this critique as a way of further explicating the underlying method and theory of this work. But world system theory was not selected arbitrarily. It is, first of all, a theory whose basic assumptions and propositions are not borne out by my empirical analysis of a paradigmatic "test case," and it appears in particular as the underlying intellectual structure of recent influential (and voguish) self-consciously theoretical works. Yet, despite the scholarship and intelligence displayed in such works, they are grievously flawed by that theory—a theory that hobbles the analysis of the very historical-social realities their authors aim to understand. World system theory also bears the brunt of my critique because, despite the radical social vision of its authors, the theory itself is the latest influential variant of what has long been the dominant mode of thought under capitalism. It is regnant today in one form or another in every social science discipline in the United States, whatever the name attached to it (neoclassical synthesis, cliometrics, modernization theory, or structural functionalism). Indeed, this mode of thought has recently been put forth here and abroad as the essence of the latest form of "Marxism" (structuralism).

It is, however, an idealist mode of thought in which, as Marx himself long ago said, "fixed, immutable, eternal categories" masquerade as social reality. It is a mode of thought in which, in place of real men and women making the social relations that make them, the "social system" (world system) appears as a structure bereft of any subject (other than its own self-moving "market" or functional subsystems). Men and women make rare appearances only as evanescent systemic epiphenomena: as Parsonian "actors" or "concrete units" whose "interaction" is determined by the constituent "regulatory patterns" of the social system's "value system," in conformity with its own "goals" and "functional requirements" or, in its kindred Althusserian outlook, as "supports of functions" and above all as "*never anything more* than the occupants" or "agents" of "places and functions."[26] Society, as the ensemble of the real social relationships that men and women make and are made by and in which they are involved becomes instead a "social system [that] has the characteristics of an organism," and their history becomes merely a tale told of how, over that system's "life span . . . its characteristics change in some respects and remain stable in others . . . in terms of the internal logic of its functioning."[27]

In contrast to such notions, my own substantive analysis reveals, on the most general level of abstraction, how thoroughly "social structures" are partially contingent historical products, actively created and recreated by real men and women, involved in determinate

[26] Althusser 1970, pp. 112, 180, italics added.
[27] Wallerstein 1974a, p. 347.

social relations that were themselves produced historically, by prior human activity. Of these social relations it is the contradictory and exploitative relations in which men and women produce and transform their own conditions of existence, through which they thereby also reproduce and transform the ensemble of social relations among them that we call "society." Classes, and the societies they constitute, *form themselves* in the struggles not only between them but also within them, among their contending segments, shaping and being shaped by the already existing class and intraclass relations and their underlying forms of production.

Classes, indeed, are distinguished precisely by their inherent history-making potential. The social process of production in which classes make themselves sets objective limits to potential historical development and, as Adam Przeworski has put it well, simultaneously constitutes "a structure of choices given at a particular moment of history. Social relations are given to a subject, individual or collective, as *realms of possibilities* . . . a set of conditions that determine what course of action has what consequences for social transformations."[28] In this way, the consciousness of men and women— however inelegant, inchoate, or "false"—enters into social relations as an intrinsic and constitutive characteristic of these relations. The consciousness that men and women have of themselves is the consciousness expressed in their practical political activity, which in turn conditions and transforms their consciousness and consequently the very nature of the basic class relations in which they are involved. In this sense, political conflict and class formation are moments of the same historical process; neither follows as an "effect" or is necessarily prior. Rather, they reciprocally interact in the course of historical development. Classes, and the societies they constitute, are shaped by and in specific struggles and by the consequences (intended and unwitting) of these struggles, as well as by unique circumstances and events (including decisive defeats) that, as Max Weber once remarked, "load the historical dice." Classes and their internal segments are formed both by their objective location in a historically specific ensemble of production relations and by their own activity, through which men and women constitute and trans-

[28] Przeworski 1977, p. 377.

form these relations and their place within them. Thus in this sense, and to this extent, classes and class relations, and the societies they constitute, possess an inherent relatively contingent historicity. This conception was long ago summed up, of course, by another scholar who was committed not only to understanding history but to making it: "Men [and (he should have written) women] make their own history, but they do not make it just as they please; they do not make it under circumstances chosen by themselves, but under circumstances directly found, given and transmitted from the past."[29]

[29] Marx 1963, p. 15.

References ➤

Abrams, M.A.L.
  1931–1932 "The French copper syndicate, 1887–1889." *Journal of Economic and Business History* 4: 409–428.
Alessandri Palma, Arturo
  1950 *Revolución de 1891: Mi actuación*. Santiago: Editorial Nascimento.
Althusser, Louis, and Balibar, R. Etienne
  1970 *Reading Capital*. London: New Left Books.
Álvarez Andrews, Oscar
  1936 *Historia del desarrollo industrial de Chile*. Santiago: Imprenta y Litografía la Ilustración.
Amunategui Solar, Domingo
  1946 *La democracia en Chile: Teatro político (1810–1910)*. Santiago: Universidad de Chile.
Anderson, Perry
  1974 *Lineages of the Absolutist State*. London: New Left Books.
Andrews, Benjamin E.
  1889 "The late copper syndicate." *Quarterly Journal of Economics* 3 (July): 508–516.
Baran, Paul
  1957 *The Political Economy of Growth*. New York: Monthly Review Press.
Barros Borgoño, Luis
  1912 *La caja de crédito hipotecario*. 2 vols. Santiago: Imprenta Cervantes.
  1933 *Proemio para la obra de don Manuel Montt*. Santiago: Editorial Nascimento.
Bauer, Arnold J.
  1975 *Chilean Rural Society from the Spanish Conquest to 1930*. Cambridge, England: Cambridge University Press.
Bauer, Arnold J., and Johnson, Ann H.
  1977 "Land and labour in rural Chile, 1850–1935." In *Land and Labour in Latin America*, ed. Kenneth Duncan and

Ian Rutledge, pp. 83–102. Cambridge, England: Cambridge University Press.

Billinghurst, Guillermo
1889   *Los capitales salitreros de Tarapacá.* Santiago: Imprenta de "El Progreso."

Blakemore, Harold
1964   "Chilean revolutionary agents in Europe, 1891." *Pacific Historical Review* 33 (November): 425–446.
1965   "The Chilean revolution of 1891 and its historiography." *Hispanic American Historical Review* 45 (August): 393–421.
1974   *British Nitrates and Chilean Politics 1886–1896; Balmaceda and North.* London: University of London (Institute of Latin American Studies), Athlone Press.

Bohan, Merwin L., and Pomeranz, Morton
1960   *Investment in Chile: Basic Information for United States Businessmen.* Washington, D.C.: Department of Commerce. U.S. Government Printing Office.

Borde, Jean, and Góngora, Mario
1956   *Evolución de la propiedad rural en el Valle del Puangue.* 2 vols. Santiago: Editorial Universitaria.

Brenner, Robert
1976   "Agrarian class structure and economic development in pre-industrial Europe." *Past & Present* 70 (February): 30–75.
1977   "The origins of capitalist development: A critique of neo-Smithian Marxism." *New Left Review* 104 (July–August): 25–92.
1982   "The agrarian roots of European capitalism." *Past & Present* 97 (November): 16–113.

Brown, Joseph R.
1958   "The Chilean nitrate railways controversy." *Hispanic American Historical Review* 38 (November): 465–481.
1963   "Nitrate crises, combinations and the Chilean government in the nitrate age." *Hispanic American Historical Review* 43 (May): 230–246.

Bunster, Enrique
1965   *Chilenos en California: Miniaturas históricas.* 3rd ed. Santiago: Editorial del Pacifico.

Burr, Robert N.
1955 "The balance of power in nineteenth-century South America: An exploratory essay." *Hispanic American Historical Review* 35 (February): 37–60.
Cardoso, Fernando Henrique
1977 "The consumption of dependency theory in the United States." *Latin American Research Review* 12, no. 3: 7–25.
Cardoso, Fernando Henrique, and Faletto, Enzo
1973 *Dependencia e desenvolvimento na America Latina.* Rio de Janeiro: Zahar.
Centner, Charles William
1942 "Great Britain and Chilean mining, 1830–1914." *Economic History Review* 12, nos. 1 and 2: 76-82. First series.
Correa Vergara, Luis
1938 *Agricultura chilena.* 2 vols. Santiago: Imprenta Nascimento.
Dobb, Maurice
1947 *Studies in the Development of Capitalism.* New York: International Publishers.
Dobb, Maurice et al.
1954 *The Transition from Feudalism to Capitalism.* New York: Science & Society.
Donoso, Ricardo
1925 *Benjamín Vicuña Mackenna.* Santiago: Imprenta Universitaria.
Edwards Vives, Alberto
1932 *El gobierno de Manuel Montt, 1851–1861.* Santiago: Editorial Nascimento.
1945 *La fronda aristocrática, historia política de Chile.* Santiago: Editorial del Pacífico.
Elster, Jon
1978 *Logic and Society: Contradictions and Possible Worlds.* New York: Wiley.
Encina, Francisco Antonio
1949 *Historia de Chile: Desde la prehistoria hasta 1891.* Vol. 13. Santiago: Editorial Nascimento.

1952   *La Presidencia de Balmaceda.* 2 vols. Santiago: Editorial Nascimento.

1955   *Nuestra inferioridad económica: Sus causas, sus consequencias.* Nueva Edición. Santiago: Editorial Universitaria. (Originally published in 1911.)

1964   *Portales.* 2nd ed. Santiago: Editorial Nascimento.

Engels, Friedrich

1973a   "A critique of the draft social-democratic programme of 1891." In *Karl Marx and Frederick Engels: Selected Works in Three Volumes*, vol. 3, pp. 429–439. Moscow: Progress Publishers.

1973b   "Introduction to the class struggles in France, by Karl Marx." In *Karl Marx and Frederick Engels: Selected Works in Three Volumes*, vol. 3, pp. 186–204. Moscow: Progress Publishers.

1973c   "The role of force in history." In *Karl Marx and Frederick Engels: Selected Works in Three Volumes*, vol. 3, pp. 377–428. Moscow: Progress Publishers.

Escobar Cerda, Luis

1959   *El mercado de valores.* Santiago: Editorial del Pacífico.

Esping-Andersen, Gösta; Friedland, Roger; and Wright, Erik Olin

1976   "Modes of class struggle and the capitalist state." *Kapitalistate* 4–5: 186–220.

Fernández Canque, Manuel

1973   *Capitulos de la historia de Chile.* Santiago: Ranquil. Empresa Editorial Nacional Quimanto.

Figueroa, Pedro Pablo

1888   *Diccionario biográfico general de Chile (1550-1887).* 2nd ed. Santiago: Imprenta "Victoria" de H. Izquierdo y ca.

1889   *Diccionario biográfico general de Chile, 1550–1887.* Santiago: privately published.

1895   *Historia de la revolución constituyente, 1858–1859.* Santiago: Portera.

1897–1901   *Diccionario biográfico de Chile.* 3 vols. Santiago: Imprenta y encuadernación Barcelona.

1900   *Diccionario biográfico de extranjeros en Chile.* Santiago: privately published.

Figueroa (Talquino), Virgilio
1897 *Parnaso balmacedista: Recopilación completa de todas las poesías que se han escrito en homenaje a la memoria del Excmo. señor Balmaceda.* Santiago: Imprenta de "La Nueva Republica."
1925-1931 *Diccionario histórico biográfico y bibliográfico de Chile.* 4 vols. Santiago: Balcells and Co.

Frank, Andre Gunder
1967 *Capitalism and Underdevelopment in Latin America: Historical Studies of Chile and Brazil.* New York: Monthly Review Press.
1969 *Latin America: Underdevelopment or Revolution.* New York: Monthly Review Press.
1972 *Lumpenbourgeoisie: Lumpenproletariat. Dependence, Class and Politics in Latin America.* New York: Monthly Review Press.

Frías Valenzuela, Federíco
1965 *Manual de historia de Chile.* 6th ed. Santiago: Editorial Nascimento.

Fuentes, Jordi, and Cortés, Lía
1963 *Diccionario histórico de Chile.* Santiago: Editorial del Pacífico.
1967 *Diccionario político de Chile (1810–1966).* Santiago: Editorial Orbe.

Galdames, Luis
1941 *A History of Chile.* Translated by I. J. Cox. Chapel Hill: University of North Carolina Press. (Reprint by Russell and Russell, 1964.)

Gay, Claude
1865 *Historia física y política de Chile (según documentos adquiridos en ésta republica durante doce años de residencia en ella). Agricultura.* Tomo Primero. Paris: En Casa del Autor. Chile: En el Museo de Historia Natural de Santiago.

Genovese, Eugene D.
1965 *The Political Economy of Slavery: Studies in the Economy and Society of the Slave South.* New York: Pantheon.

1971   *In Red and Black: Marxian Explorations in Southern and Afro-American History*. New York: Pantheon.
Gil, Federíco G.
1962   *Los partidos políticos chilenos: Genesis y evolución*. Buenos Aires: Ediciones de Palma.
1966   *The Political System of Chile*. Boston: Houghton Mifflin.
Glade, William
1969   *The Latin American Economies*. New York: Van Nostrand-Reinhold.
Góngora, Mario
1960   *Origen de los 'inquilinos' de Chile central*. Santiago: Editorial Universitaria.
Hamilton, Nora
1982   *The Limits of State Autonomy: Post-Revolutionary Mexico*. Princeton, N.J.: Princeton University Press. .
Hancock, Anson U.
1893   *History of Chile*. Chicago: C. H. Sergel and Co.
Hardy, Osgood
1948   "British nitrates and the Balmaceda revolution." *Pacific Historical Review* 17 (May): 165–180.
Heise González, Julio
1974   *Historia de Chile. El período parlamentario, 1861–1925*. Vol 1: Fundamentos histórico-culturales del parlamentarismo chileno. Santiago: Editorial Andres Bello.
Hernández, Silva
1966   "Transformaciones tecnológicas en la agricultura de Chile central. Siglo XIX." *Cuadernos del centro de estudios socioeconómicos* (Santiago) 3: 1–31.
Hernández Cornejo, Roberto
1930   *El Salitre: Resumen histórico desde su descubrimiento y explotación*. Valparaiso: Imprenta Fisher Hermanos.
Hervey, Maurice H.
1891–1892   *Dark Days in Chile: An Account of the Revolution of 1891*. London: Edward Arnold.
Hilton, Rodney H.
1953   "The transition from feudalism to capitalism." *Science &*

Society 17 (Fall): 340–348. (Also reprinted in Dobb et al. 1954 and in Hilton et al. 1976.)

Hilton, Rodney H. et al.

1976   *The Transition from Feudalism to Capitalism.* London: New Left Books.

Holloway, John, and Picciotto, Sol, eds.

1979   *State and Capital: A Marxist Debate.* Austin: University of Texas Press.

Huntington, Samuel P.

1968   *Political Order in Changing Societies.* New Haven, Conn.: Yale University Press.

Hurtado, Carlos

1966   *Concentración de población y desarrollo económico: El caso chileno.* Santiago: Universidad de Chile (Instituto de Economía).

Jobet Burquez, Julio César

1955   *Ensayo crítico del desarrollo económico social de Chile.* Santiago: Editorial Universitaria.

1962   "El nacionalismo creador de José Manuel Balmaceda." *Combate* (Costa Rica), 23 (July–August): 57–67.

Kaplan, Temma

1977   *Anarchists of Andalusia, 1868–1903.* Princeton, N.J.: Princeton University Press.

Kay, Cristobal

1977   "The development of the Chilean hacienda system, 1850–1973." In *Land and Labour in Latin America*, ed. Kenneth Duncan and Ian Rutledge, pp. 103–139. Cambridge, England: Cambridge University Press.

Kiernan, V. G.

"Foreign investments in the war of the Pacific." *Hispanic American Historical Review* 35 (February): 14–36.

Kinsbruner, Jay

1967   *Diego Portales: Interpretive Essays on the Man and Times.* The Hague: Martinus Nijhoff.

1973   *Chile: An Historical Interpretation.* New York: Harper and Row.

Kirsch, Henry W.
1977 *Industrial Development in a Traditional Society: The Conflict of Entrepreneurship and Modernization in Chile.* Gainesville: The University Presses of Florida.

Lenin, Vladimir I.
1934 *Selected Works.* Vol. 3. Moscow and Leningrad: Cooperative Publishing Society of Foreign Workers in the U.S.S.R.
1954 *The Development of Capitalism in Russia.* Moscow: Progress Publishers. (Originally published in 1899.)
1967 *Selected Works in Three Volumes.* New York: International Publishers.

Macchiavello Varas, Santiago
1923 *El problema de la industria del cobre en Chile y sus proyecciónes económicas y sociales.* Santiago: Imprenta Fiscal de la Penitenciaria.
1931 *Política económica nacional.* 2 vols. Santiago: Balcells and Co.

Maitland, Francis J. G.
1914 *Chile: Its Land and Its People.* London: F. Griffiths.

Marx, Karl
1948 *The Class Struggles in France: 1848 to 1850.* Moscow: Foreign Languages Publishing House.
1952 *The Civil War in France.* Moscow: Foreign Languages Publishing House.
1963 *The Eighteenth Brumaire of Louis Bonaparte.* New York: International Publishers.
1965 *Der 18. Brumaire des Louis Bonaparte.* Berlin: Sammlung Insel 9, Insel-Verlag.
1973a "The class struggles in France: 1848–1850." In *Karl Marx and Frederick Engels: Selected Works in Three Volumes*, vol. 1, pp. 205–299. Moscow: Progress Publishers.
1973b "Die Burgerkrieg in Frankreich." In *Karl Marx. Friedrich Engels Werke*, vol. 17, pp. 313–365. Berlin: Dietz Verlag.
1973c "Die Klassenkampfe in Frankreich." In *Karl Marx.*

Friedrich Engels Werke, vol. 7, pp. 9–108. Berlin: Dietz Verlag.

1976   "The poverty of philosophy." In *Karl Marx and Frederick Engels. Collected Works*, vol. 6, pp. 105–212. New York: International Publishers.

Ministerio de Hacienda
1889   Delegación e inspección fiscal de salitreras. Santiago: Archivo Nacional.

Monteón, Michael
1982   *Chile in the Nitrate Era: The Evolution of Economic Dependence, 1880–1930*. Madison: University of Wisconsin Press.

Moore, Barrington, Jr.
1966   *Social Origins of Dictatorship and Democracy*. Boston: Beacon Press.

Moran, Theodore H.
1974   *Multinational Corporations and the Politics of Dependence: Copper in Chile*. Princeton, N.J.: Princeton University Press.

Muñoz, Oscar
1968   *Crecimiento industrial de Chile, 1914–1965*. Santiago: Universidad de Chile (Instituto de Economía y Planificación).

Nemo (Balmaceda, Rafael)
1893   *La revolución y la condenación del ministerio Vicuña*. Buenos Aires: Establecimiento Tipografía La Americana.

Neumann, Franz
1957   *The Democratic and the Authoritarian State*. Glencoe, Ill.: Free Press.

Norman, E. H.
1940   *Japan's Emergence as a Modern State*. New York: Institute of Pacific Relations.

O'Brien, Thomas Francis, Jr.
1976   "British Investors and the Decline of the Chilean Nitrate Entrepreneurs, 1870–1890." Ph.D. dissertation, University of Connecticut.

O'Brien, Thomas F. [Thomas Francis, Jr.]
1982 *The Nitrate Industry and Chile's Crucial Transition: 1870–1891*. New York and London: New York University Press.

Oppenheimer, Robert Ballen
1976 "Chilean Transportation Development: The Railroads and Socio-Economic Change in the Central Valley, 1840–1885." Ph.D. dissertation, University of California at Los Angeles.
1977 "The Financing of Chile's Central Valley Railroads in the Nineteenth Century." Unpublished paper, Department of History, University of California at Los Angeles.

Orrego Vicuña, Eugenio
1939 *Iconografía de Vicuña Mackenna. Obras completas de Vicuña Mackenna*. Primer Volumen Preliminar. Santiago: Universidad de Chile.

Ortuzar, Adolfo
1907 *Chile of Today: Its Commerce, Its Production and Its Resources*. New York: Tribune Association.

Pederson, Leland R.
1966 *The Mining Industry of the Norte Chico, Chile*. Evanston, Ill.: Northwestern University (Studies in Geography, No. 11).

Pérez Canto, Julio
1893 *La industria nacional: Estudios y descripciónes de algunas fábricas de Chile*. Santiago: Imprenta Nacional.
1912 *Chile: An Account of Its Wealth and Progress*. Chicago and New York: Rand McNally and Co.

Pérez Rosales, Vicente
1886 *Recuerdos del pasado, 1814–1860*. 3rd ed. Santiago: Imprenta Gutenberg.

Petras, James
1969 *Politics and Social Forces in Chilean Development*. Berkeley: University of California Press.

Petras, James, and Zeitlin, Maurice, eds.
1968 *Latin America: Reform or Revolution?* Greenwich, Conn.: Fawcett.

Pfeiffer, Jack B.
   1952   "Notes on the heavy equipment industry in Chile, 1880–
          1910." *Hispanic American Historical Review* 32 (Febru-
          ary): 139–144.
Pike, Frederick B.
   1963a   "Aspects of Class Relations in Chile, 1850–1960." *His-
           panic American Historical Review* 43 (February): 14–33.
   1963b   *Chile and the United States, 1880–1962.* Notre Dame,
           Ind.: University of Notre Dame Press.
Pinto Santa Cruz, Aníbal
   1959   *Chile: Un caso de desarrollo frustrado.* Santiago: Editorial
          Universitaria.
Poulantzas, Nicos
   1973a   "On social classes." *New Left Review* 78: 27–54.
   1973b   *Political Power and Social Classes.* London: New Left
           Books and Sheed and Ward.
Pregger Román, Charles G.
   1979   "Economic interest groups within the Chilean government,
          1851 to 1891: Continuity and discontinuity in economic
          and political evolution." *Science & Society* 43 (Summer):
          202–233.
Przeworski, Adam
   1977   "Proletariat into class: The process of class formation,
          from Karl Kautsky's the class struggle to recent contro-
          versies." *Politics & Society* 7: 343–401.
Przeworski, Joanne Fox
   1972   "The entrance of North American capital into the Chilean
          copper industry and the role of government, 1904–1916."
          Atti Del XL Congresso Internazionale Degli Americanisti
          (3–10 September): 391–415.
   1974   "The responses of Chilean entrepreneurs to changing cop-
          per prices, 1874–1887: A preliminary analysis." Paper
          presented at the 41st Congress of Americanists, Mexico,
          D.F. (September).
   1978   "The Decline of the Copper Industry in Chile and the
          Entrance of North American Capital, 1870–1916." Ph.D.
          dissertation, Washington University at St. Louis. (Pub-

lished with the same title and pagination, as a volume in the series, *Multinational Corporations*, ed. Stuart Bruchey. New York: Arno Press, 1980.)

Quijano Obregón, Aníbal
1968 "Tendencies in Peruvian development and class structure." In *Latin America: Reform or Revolution?* ed. James Petras and Maurice Zeitlin, pp. 289–328. New York: Fawcett.

Ramírez Necochea, Hernán
1956 *Historia del movimiento obrero. Siglo XIX.* Santiago: Empresa Editora Austral.
1958 *Balmaceda y la contrarevolución de 1891.* Santiago: Editorial Universitaria.
1960a *Balmaceda.* Santiago: Editorial Orbe.
1960b *Historia del imperialismo en Chile.* Santiago: Empresa Editora Austral.
1969 *Balmaceda y la contrarevolución de 1891.* 2nd ed. Santiago: Editorial Universitaria.

Reynolds, Clark
1965 "Development problems of an export economy: The case of Chile and copper." In *Essays on the Chilean Economy*, ed. Markos Mamalakis and Clark Reynolds, pp. 207–361. Homewood, Ill.: Richard D. Irwin.

Rippy, J. Fred
1948 "Economic enterprises of the 'nitrate king' and his associates in Chile." *Pacific Historical Review* 17 (November): 457–465.

Rippy, J. Fred, and Pfeiffer, Jack
1948 "Notes on the dawn of manufacturing in Chile." *Hispanic American Historical Review* 28 (May): 292–303.

Russell, William Howard
1890 *A Visit to Chile and the Nitrate Fields of Tarapacá.* London: J. S. Virtue and Co.

Schumpeter, Joseph
1955 "Social classes in an ethnically homogeneous environment." *Imperialism and Social Classes.* New York: Meridian Books. (Originally published in German in 1923.)

Sears, James H. (Lieutenant, USN), and Wells, B. W., Jr. (Ensign, USN)

1893   *The Chilean Revolution of 1891.* Washington, D.C.: U.S. Government Printing Office.

Segall, Marcelo

1953   *Desarrollo del capitalismo en Chile.* Santiago: privately published.

Sepulveda, Sergio

1959   *El trigo chileno en el mercado mundial.* Santiago: Editorial Universitaria.

Silva Vargas, Fernando

1974   *Pensamiento de Balmaceda.* Santiago: Editorial Gabriela Mistral.

Skocpol, Theda

1979   *States and Social Revolutions: A Comparative Analysis of France, Russia, and China.* Cambridge, England: Cambridge University Press.

Stavenhagen, Rodolfo

1968   "Seven fallacies about Latin America." In *Latin America: Reform or Revolution?* ed. James Petras and Maurice Zeitlin, pp. 13–31. New York: Fawcett.

Sternberg, Marvin J.

1962   "Chilean Land Tenure and Land Reform." Ph.D. dissertation, University of California, Berkeley.

Stinchcombe, Arthur L.

1978   *Theoretical Methods in Social History.* New York: Academic Press.

Subercaseaux, Guillermo

1920   *El sistema monetario i la organización bancaria de Chile.* Santiago: Soc. Imprenta Literaria Universo.

Sweezy, Paul M.

1950   "The transition from feudalism to capitalism." *Science & Society* 14 (Spring): 134–157. (Also reprinted in Dobb et al. 1954 and in Hilton et al. 1976.)

Takahashi, H. Kohachiro

1952   "The transition from feudalism to capitalism: A contribution to the Sweezy-Dobb controversy." *Science & So-*

ciety 16 (Fall): 313–345. (Also reprinted in Dobb et al. 1954 and in Hilton et al. 1976.)

Taylor, George V.

1964 "Types of capitalism in eighteenth-century France." *English Historical Review* 79 (July): 478–497.

1967 "Noncapitalist wealth and the origins of the French revolution." *American Historical Review* 72 (January): 469–496.

Thompson, E. P.

1978 *The Poverty of Theory and Other Essays.* New York: Monthly Review Press.

Tilly, Charles

1975 · "Revolutions and collective violence." In *Handbook of Political Science,* ed. Fred I. Greenstein and Nelson W. Polsby, vol. 3, pp. 483–555. Reading, Mass.: Addison-Wesley.

Tornero, Santos

1861 *Cuadro histórico de la administración Montt escrito segun sus propios documentos.* Valparaiso: Imprenta i Librería del Mercurio.

Trimberger, Ellen Kay

1977 "State power and modes of production: Implications of the Japanese transition to capitalism." *The Insurgent Sociologist* 7 (Spring): 85–98.

1978 *Revolution from Above: Military Bureaucrats, and Development in Japan, Turkey, Egypt and Peru.* New Brunswick, N.J.: Transaction Books.

Ure, Andrew

1835 *The Philosophy of Manufactures.* New York: Reprinted in facsimile by A. M. Kelley, 1967.

Valdés Carrera, José Miguel

1893 *La condenación del ministerio Vicuña. El ministro de hacienda y sus detractores.* Paris: Imprenta Universal.

Valdés Vergara, Francisco

1884 *La crisis salitrera i las medidas que se proponenen para remediarla.* Santiago: Imprenta de "La Época."

Valdés Vicuña, Samuel

1895 *La solución del gran problema del dia o manera pronta y*

*segura de llegar al mejoramiento del cambio y al enri-
quecimiento del país.* Santiago: (no publisher given).

Valencia Avaria, Luis
1951   *Anales de la Republica.* Vols. 1 and 2. Santiago: Imprenta
       Universitaria.

Vattier, Charles
1890   *L'avenir de la metallurgie du fer au Chili.* Paris: A. Roger
       et F. Chernoviz.

Vattier, Carlos [Charles]
1901   *Apuntes sobre la mineria i metalurjia de Chile. Sus ultimos
       progresos, sus mejoras posibles.* Santiago: Imprenta Li-
       tografía i Encuadernación Barcelona.

Vayssiere, Pierre
1973   "La division internationale du travail et la denationalisation
       du cuivre Chilien (1880–1920)." *Cahiers du Monde His-
       panique et Luso-Bresilien (Caravelle)* 20 (Numero con-
       sacre ou Chile): 7–51.

Véliz, Claudio
1961   *Historia de la marina mercante de Chile.* Santiago: Edi-
       ciones de la Universidad de Chile.
1963   "La mesa de tres patas." *Desarrollo Económico* 3 (April–
       September): 231–247.
1980   *The Centralist Tradition of Latin America.* Princeton, N.J.:
       Princeton University Press.

Vera Valenzuela, Mario
1961   *La política económica del cobre en Chile.* Santiago: Uni-
       versidad de Chile.

Vergara, Ximena J., and Barros, Luis L.
1972   "La guerra civil del 91 y la instauración del parlamenta-
       rismo." *Revista Latino Americana de Ciencias Sociales* 3
       (June): 71–94.

Vicuña Aguirre, Pedro Félix
1845   *Cartas sobre bancos. Recopiladas de las que ha insertado
       el Mercurio de Valparaíso.* Valparaiso: Imprenta del Mer-
       curio.
1858   *El porvenir del hombre, o relación íntima entre justa apre-
       ciación del trabajo y la democracia.* Valparaiso: Imprenta
       del comercio.

1862 *Apelación al credito publico por la creación de un banco nacional.* Articulos publicado en *el Mercurio.* Valparaiso: Imprenta y Librería del Mercurio de S. Tornero.

Vicuña Mackenna, Benjamín

1854 *Estudios sobre la agricultura.* Valparaiso: Imprenta y Librería del Mercurio de S. Tornero y ca.

1856 *La agricultura de Chile: Memoria presentada a la Sociedad de Agricultura en su sesión del 6 de septiembre de 1856 con el objeto de constituirla bajo nuevas bases.* Santiago: Imprenta Chilena.

1858 *La Asamblea Constituyente. Periódico político.* (No. 1, 20 October; No. 13, 11 December.) Santiago: (no publisher given).

1883 *El libro del cobre i del carbón de piedra en Chile.* Santiago: Imprenta Cervantes.

Vicuña y Vicuña, Félix

1887 "De la protección a la marina mercante nacional. *Revista Económica* no. 1 (4 June): 278–282 and no. 6 (15 July): 333–346.

Vilar, Pierre

1973 "Marxist history, a history in the making: Towards a dialogue with Althusser." *New Left Review* 80 (July–August): 65–106.

Villarino, Joaquin

1893 *Balmaceda, el ultimo de los presidentes constitucionales de Chile, desde septiembre 18 de 1866 hasta septiembre 18 de 1891.* 2nd ed. Barcelona: Tipografía de E. Domenech.

Vitale, Luis

1968 "Latin America: Feudal or capitalist?" In *Latin America: Reform or Revolution?* ed. James Petras and Maurice Zeitlin, pp. 32–43. New York: Fawcett.

1971 *Interpretación marxista de la historia de Chile.* Vol. 3. Santiago: Prensa Latina.

1975 *Interpretación marxista de la historia de Chile.* Vol. 4. Frankfurt: University of Frankfurt.

von Braunmuhl, Claudia

1979 "On the analysis of the bourgeois nation state within the

world market context: An attempt to develop a methodological and theoretical approach." In *State and Capital: A
Marxist Debate*, ed. John Holloway and Sol Picciotto, pp.
160–177. Austin: University of Texas Press.

Wallerstein, Immanuel
  1974a *The Modern World-System: Capitalist Agriculture and the
         Origins of the European World-Economy in the Sixteenth
         Century.* New York: Academic Press.
  1974b "The rise and future demise of the world capitalist system:
         Concepts for comparative analysis." *Comparative Studies
         in Society and History* 16 (January): 387–415.

Weber, Max
  1946 *From Max Weber: Essays in Sociology.* Edited by C. Wright
        Mills and Hans Gerth. New York: Oxford University Press.
  1949 *Max Weber on the Methodology of the Social Sciences.*
        Translated and edited by E. A. Shils and H. A. Finch.
        Glencoe, Ill.: Free Press.
  1961 *General Economic History.* Translated by F. H. Knight.
        New York: Collier.

Wiener, Jonathan M.
  1978 *Social Origins of the New South.* Baton Rouge: Louisiana
        State University Press.
  1979 "Class structure and economic development in the Amer-
        ican South, 1865–1955." *American Historical Review* 84
        (October): 970–1006.

Winter, Nevin O.
  1912 *Chile and Her People of Today.* Boston: L. C. Page and
        Co.

Yrarrázaval Larraín, José Miguel
  1940 *El presidente Balmaceda.* 2 vols. Santiago: Editorial Nas-
        cimento.
  1963 *La política económica del presidente Balmaceda.* Santiago:
        Academia Chilena de la Historia.

Zañartu Prieto, Enrique
  1940 *Manuel Arístides Zañartu, Z: O, historia y causas del
        pauperismo en Chile.* Santiago: Zig-Zag.

Zeitlin, Maurice
  1966 "Los determinantes sociales de la democracia política en

Chile.'' *Revista Latinoamericana de Sociología* 2 (July): 223–236.

1967 *Revolutionary Politics and the Cuban Working Class.* Princeton, N.J.: Princeton University Press.

1968 ''The social determinants of political democracy in Chile.'' In *Latin America: Reform or Revolution?* ed. James Petras and Maurice Zeitlin, pp. 220–234. New York: Fawcett.

1969 ''Cuba—Revolution without a blueprint.'' *Transaction* 6, no. 6 (April): 38–42, 61.

1972 ''Camilo's Colombia: The political, economic, and religious background to revolution'' In *Father Camilo Torres: Revolutionary Writings*, ed. Maurice Zeitlin, pp. 1–46. New York: Harper and Row.

Zeitlin, Maurice; Neuman, W. Lawrence; and Ratcliff, Richard E.

1976 ''Class segments: Agrarian property and political leadership in the capitalist class of Chile.'' *American Sociological Review* 41 (December): 1006–1029.

Zeitlin, Maurice, and Ratcliff, Richard E.

1975 ''Research methods for the analysis of the internal structure of dominant classes: The case of landlords and capitalists in Chile.'' *Latin American Research Review* 10: 5–61.

Landlords and Capitalists: The Dominant Class of Chile. Princeton, N.J.: Princeton University Press, forthcoming.

Index ➤

Library of Congress Cataloging in Publication Data

Zeitlin, Maurice, 1935-
    The civil wars in Chile, or, The bourgeois revolutions that never were.

    Bibliography: p.
    Includes index.
    1. Chile—History—Insurrection, 1851—Causes.
2. Chile—History—Insurrection, 1851—Influence.
3. Chile—History—Insurrection, 1859—Causes. 4. Chile—
History—Insurrection, 1859—Influence. 5. Chile—
History—Revolution, 1891—Causes. 6. Chile—History—
Revolution, 1891—Influence. 7. Middle classes—Chile—
Political activity—History—19th century. I. Title.
F3095.Z43 1984   983'.06   84-42551
ISBN 0-691-07665-0 (alk. paper)